Expected Returns on Major Asset Classes

RESEARCH FOUNDATION

OF CFA INSTITUTE

Statement of Purpose

The Research Foundation of CFA Institute is a not-for-profit organization established to promote the development and dissemination of relevant research for investment practitioners worldwide.

ISBN 978-1-934667-48-4

5 June 2012

Biography

Antti Ilmanen is a managing director at AQR Capital Management (Europe) Ltd. Since starting as a central bank portfolio manager in Finland in 1986, he has worn many hats to bridge academic finance and practitioner investing. After receiving his PhD, Dr. Ilmanen spent a decade at Salomon Brothers/Citigroup as a researcher, strategist, managing director, and proprietary trader. From 2004 to 2011, he was a senior portfolio manager at Brevan Howard, a macro hedge fund. Dr. Ilmanen has published extensively in finance and investment journals and received the Graham & Dodd Award of Excellence from the *Financial Analysts Journal* and the Bernstein Fabozzi/Jacobs Levy Award from Jacobs Levy Equity Management for his articles. His recent book *Expected Returns* (2011a) is a broad synthesis of the central issue in investing. Over the years, he has advised many institutional investors, such as Norway's Government Pension Fund Global and the Government of Singapore Investment Corporation. He has a PhD in finance from the Graduate School of Business at the University of Chicago.

Author's Note

Chapters 2–5 of this book have been adapted from chapters 8–11 of the author's book *Expected Returns* (Ilmanen 2011a), published by Wiley.

The views and opinions expressed herein are those of the author and do not necessarily reflect the views of AQR Capital Management LLC, the author's previous employers, their affiliates, or their employees.

Contents

Foreword vi

1. Introduction 1

2. Equity Risk Premium 7
   2.1. Introduction and Terminology 8
   2.2. Theories and the Equity Premium Puzzle 9
   2.3. Historical Equity Premium 11
   2.4. Forward-Looking (*Ex Ante* Objective) Long-Term
        Expected Return Measures 19
   2.5. Survey-Based Subjective Expectations 36
   2.6. Tactical Forecasting for Market Timing 40

3. Bond Risk Premium 47
   3.1. Introduction, Terminology, and Theories 48
   3.2. Historical Average Returns 51
   3.3. Alternative *Ex Ante* Measures of the BRP 55
   3.4. Yield Curve Steepness: Important Predictive Relations . . . 56
   3.5. Explaining the BRP Behavior: First Targets, Then
        Four Drivers 61
   3.6. Tactical Forecasting—Duration Timing 73

4. Credit Risk Premium 76
   4.1. Introduction, Terminology, and Theory 76
   4.2. Historical Average Excess Returns 80
   4.3. Focus on Front-End Trading—A Pocket of Attractive
        Reward to Risk 86
   4.4. Understanding Credit Spreads and Their Drivers 91
   4.5. Tactical Forecasting of Corporate Bond
        Outperformance 100
   4.6. Concluding Remarks 101

5. Alternative Asset Premia 102
   5.1. Introduction to Alternatives 102
   5.2. Real Estate 106
   5.3. Commodities 114
   5.4. Hedge Funds 123
   5.5. Private Equity Funds 141

Source Notes 147

References 151

 This publication qualifies for 5 CE credits under the guidelines of the CFA Institute Continuing Education Program.

Foreword

Can the art and science of investment management be reduced to a set of patterns that markets generally follow, in apparent violation of the efficient market hypothesis? Can investors reasonably expect to make money from the knowledge of these patterns, even after they have not only been identified but also widely exploited? Although one's first guess might be that the answers to these questions are no, in this volume, Antti Ilmanen presents powerful and voluminous evidence that, at least sometimes, the answer is yes. One reason is that, as Ilmanen demonstrates, asset class expected returns and risk premia are time varying and somewhat predictable.

Expected Returns on Major Asset Classes provides extracts, with some modification, from Dr. Ilmanen's masterwork, *Expected Returns* (2011a). It examines return expectations arising from three distinct kinds of risk exposures: (1) investing in asset classes, (2) engaging in specific trading strategies, such as momentum and value, and (3) exposing a portfolio to economic factors. Readers familiar with the existing literature on expected returns may find Ilmanen's emphasis on trading strategies and economic factors peculiar: Conventional finance theory has nothing to say about trading strategies, and in standard finance, only arbitrage pricing theory is concerned with economic factors. Almost all preexisting literature on expected returns, dating back even earlier than Ibbotson and Sinquefield (1976a, 1976b), focuses on asset classes.

Because of the familiarity of expected return analysis for major asset classes, we chose Dr. Ilmanen's chapters on that topic as the basis for this book. Readers interested in application of his methods to more exotic fields should consult *Expected Returns* (2011a), which we heartily endorse, not only because its writing was supported by the Research Foundation of CFA Institute but also because it is very good.

The history of research into asset class expected returns consists of three periods. During the preclassical period, before the discoveries of Markowitz, Sharpe, and their contemporaries in the 1950s and 1960s, expected returns on asset classes were naturally considered to be time varying. Analysts estimated the expected returns of each asset class from its own fundamentals. The dividend discount model (DDM) produced an estimate of the expected return of the stock market; the yield on a riskless bond was the expected return of that bond; and so forth.

The equity risk premium was not discussed much during this period, but one could calculate such a premium by subtracting the bond yield from the DDM-based expected return on stocks. According to this way of thinking, the equity risk premium is an artifact, a derived quantity that depends on the time and place for which it is being estimated. Other premia, or differences of asset class expected returns, have the same characteristic.

Ibbotson and Sinquefield's (1976a, 1976b) work exemplifies the next period, the classical period. They noted that expected returns on cash and bonds are, naturally, time varying because the expected returns for these asset classes are equal to the yield (minus an allowance for defaults in the case of corporate bonds). But they modeled the expected return on equities as being equal to the expected return on cash or bonds plus a *constant,* where the constant is the long-term equilibrium equity risk premium. Under a stringent set of assumptions (markets are fairly priced at all times; the amount of risk in the market is unvarying; there is no survival bias; and so forth), the expected equity premium is equal to the historical, realized equity premium. This stylized—but powerfully seductive—model of the market for asset classes persisted for about two decades.

The explorations that led to the postclassical, or modern, period began with the work of Campbell and Shiller (1988a, 1988b). Their work brought to prominence the notion of time-varying risk premia—that is, time-varying relationships between asset class expected returns. Subsequent work by Asness, Arnott, Fama, French, Cochrane, and others reinforced the notion of time variation to the extent that by the mid- to late 1990s, a time-varying risk premium had become more or less the standard model.[1] Typically, in the modern period, the expected return on equities is obtained through a DDM. This practice represents a counterrevolution or return to (some of) the principles that prevailed in the preclassical period. Ibbotson and Chen (2003) symbolizes the triumph of the DDM counterrevolution because co-author Ibbotson was one of the best-known proponents of the classical position that now was overturned.[2] Investors cannot reliably benefit from time-varying expected returns unless they have useful tools to predict them. (The classical model of random variation around a constant risk premium does not enable investors to benefit, other than by buying and holding for the long run if the risk premium is high enough.) If, however, expected returns have some predictability, then one has the hope of being able to make money through active management of asset class exposures.

---

[1] See Cochrane (2011) for a well-articulated, if somewhat overstated, summary of this position. Works by Asness, Arnott, Fama, French, and others are referenced in the main bibliography of this book.

[2] I confess to getting a chuckle out of the fact that way back in 1984, Diermeier, Ibbotson, and I wrote an article in the *Financial Analysts Journal* that prefigured the DDM counterrevolution, but it didn't get much attention.

Dr. Ilmanen's emphases in this book are on finding the predictable element of expected returns and on using this information to make money (beat a passive benchmark) in the market.[3] Of course, if alpha could be earned merely by following his instructions, everybody would do it, causing the money-making opportunity to evaporate. Active management necessitates much more; it involves both hard work and luck. But Ilmanen's meticulous research into the predictability of asset class returns is a wonderful start. We are extraordinarily pleased to present this book.

Laurence B. Siegel
Research Director
Research Foundation of CFA Institute

---

[3]In a separate work, Ilmanen (2011b) focuses on time variation in the equity risk premium, one of the principal themes of this book.

1. Introduction

Expected returns are arguably the most important input into investment decisions. Many investors determine their expectations for returns on investments in highly subjective ways, based on discretionary views. More objective predictions are anchored on historical experience, financial theories, and observation of prevailing market conditions. In *Expected Returns* (Ilmanen 2011a), I try to tackle this broad topic in a comprehensive manner. This book offers a more manageable reading experience by adapting four of the central chapters of *Expected Returns*, namely, those on asset class returns (stocks, government bonds, corporate bonds, and alternatives). Before we jump to these topics, let us put these key building blocks into a wider context.

The book calls for broadening the traditional paradigm of expected return estimation in two ways: (1) moving beyond the narrow perspective of asset class investing to focus additionally on expected returns for strategy styles (active management) and for underlying factors and (2) reducing the focus on historical performance and widening the set of inputs used.[4] Two key implications follow: better-diversified portfolios (avoiding exclusive reliance on the equity premium as the source of beta return) and more forward-looking analysis.

▮ Broadening away from equity concentration and the narrow asset class perspective

Even though many investors have improved portfolio diversification by shifting from home-biased holdings to truly global investments and by expanding their asset class opportunity set, they still largely rely on the equity premium for long-term returns. Both 60%/40% stock/bond portfolios and "endowment model" portfolios (which make significant investments in alternatives) have high stock market betas, and equity risk often accounts for 90% of the portfolio risk budgets in either type of portfolio.

This book covers in detail the building blocks of asset class diversification: the equity premium, term and credit premia in fixed income, and the performance of the principal alternative assets (real estate, commodities, hedge funds, and private equity). My 2011 book, to some degree in contrast to this one, argues that by looking *beyond* asset class allocation, investors can achieve more

---

[4]The idea that an active management strategy or trading strategy can have an *expected* return independent of the return of the market in which it is earned may be unfamiliar to those schooled in efficient market theory and the capital asset pricing model. Readers of my book are asked to bear with me.

effective portfolio diversification. The book uses a three-dimensional cube to add to the asset class perspective the complementary viewpoints of *strategy styles* and *risk factors*.

- *Strategy styles.* The strategy style perspective is important for understanding the profit potential of popular active trading approaches. The book drills into value, carry, momentum, and volatility styles, which are the styles that have most consistently outperformed buy-and-hold investments. Empirical research shows that the characteristics of cheap valuations, high starting yields, and recent success have provided long-run performance tailwinds in almost any investment context studied, often comparable in magnitude to the equity premium. The relation between volatility and future returns is tenuous, but there is a more consistent reward for asymmetric return patterns; selling insurance and "lottery tickets" in financial markets appears to create long-run profits.

- *Underlying factors.* Sophisticated investors are increasingly trying to look beyond asset classes and strategies in order to identify the underlying factors driving their portfolio returns. Each asset can be viewed as a bundle of characteristics or systematic factor exposures that largely determine its expected returns. For example, a corporate bond portfolio is subject to interest rate and default risks. Looking at even more fundamental drivers, it is exposed to fluctuations in inflation and real rates, to gyrations in global and firm-specific growth, and to liquidity and volatility developments (credits tend to underperform when liquidity conditions deteriorate or market volatility rises). A factor-based approach is also useful for thinking about the primary function of each asset class in a portfolio (stocks for harvesting growth-related premia, certain alternative assets for collecting illiquidity premia, Treasuries for deflation hedging, and so on) as well as for diversifying across economic scenarios. Among many potential underlying risk factors, I opt to focus in my book on growth, inflation, illiquidity, and tail risks.

In summary, investment returns can be viewed from many angles—which asset classes earn them, what active strategy types deliver them, what underlying factors explain them. **Exhibit 1.1** shows how four asset classes (front) and four dynamic strategies (top) can be viewed in concert with the four underlying return drivers (side). In Ilmanen (2011a), I present all three complementary angles, drilling into the 12 return sources displayed in the cube. This book focuses exclusively on the familiar asset class perspective, the front of the cube.

First key investment implication: Harvest market rewards from multiple sources to achieve more effective portfolio diversification and superior risk-adjusted returns.

Exhibit 1.1. The Cube: Asset Class (front), Strategy Style (top), and Risk Factor (side) Perspectives on Investments

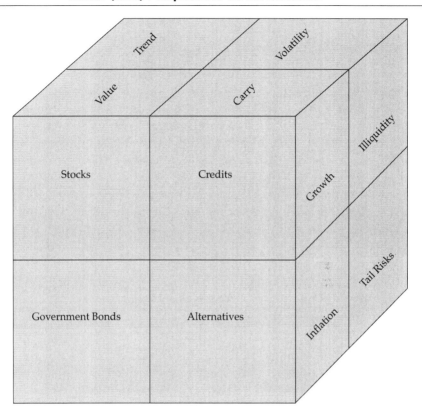

■ *Better-balanced inputs: less historical extrapolation, more forward-looking analysis*

Perhaps the most common investor mistake is chasing returns by overweighting stocks, sectors, asset classes, or strategies that have been successful in recent years. In fact, extrapolating past performance *from recent months* can be moderately profitable, as the record of trend-followers shows; sadly, most investors appear to extrapolate *over multi-year windows* when reversal tendencies have taken over.

Judgments about the expected returns of any investment are based on different mixtures of the following four inputs: (1) historical average returns; (2) financial and behavioral theories; (3) forward-looking market indicators (such as yields and valuation ratios); and (4) discretionary views. The challenge is to refine the art of investment decision making in a way that exploits all of our knowledge about each of the four inputs without being overly dependent on any one of these.

Historical Performance

Historical average returns are a common starting point for judging expected returns. The idea is that if expected returns are constant over time, the long-run average realized return (of an asset or of the difference in returns between two assets) is a good estimate of expected future return. However, any sample period may be biased, perhaps including one-off windfall gains from falling bond yields or improving market valuations. In principle, longer historical windows reduce sample specificity and enable more accurate estimates of average returns, but historical data from the distant past may be irrelevant due to structural changes and involve much lower data quality. Even worse, any cyclical variation in expected returns over time makes extrapolation of multi-year performance particularly dangerous. Periods of high realized returns and rising asset valuations—think stock markets in the 1990s—are often associated with falling forward-looking returns. Finally, various selection biases can overstate published returns.

These concerns notwithstanding, we should learn from history, while being wary of excessive extrapolation and hindsight biases. Thus, this book presents extensive evidence on long-run realized returns, when possible covering 50–100 year histories.

Theory

The state of finance theory has changed dramatically over the past 30 years, away from the restrictive theories of the single-factor capital asset pricing model (CAPM), efficient markets, and constant expected returns (see Cochrane 2011). Current academic views are more diverse, less tidy, and more realistic. Expected returns are now commonly seen as driven by multiple factors. Some determinants are rational (risk and liquidity premia); others, irrational (psychological biases, such as extrapolation and overconfidence). The expected return on any investment or factor may vary over time, again for rational or irrational reasons.

A central insight from finance theories that start with the assumption of investor rationality is that required investment returns have little to do with an investment's standalone volatility and more to do with the co-variation of its losses with "bad times." Investors should require high risk premia for assets that tend to fare poorly in bad times (think of recessions, equity bear markets, and financial crises—or their combination in 2008). In contrast, safe-haven assets (such as government bonds since at least the late 1990s) can justify low or even negative risk premia. Strategies that resemble selling financial catastrophe insurance (such as index volatility selling or carry-seeking strategies characterized by steady small gains punctuated by infrequent but large losses) warrant especially high risk premia because their losses are so highly concentrated in the worst times.

Forward-Looking Analysis

Forward-looking indicators, such as valuation ratios, have a better track record in forecasting asset class returns than do rearview-mirror measures. The practice of using the historical average return as the best estimate of future return—as is often done with the 85-year history of the equity premium—relies on the idea of constant expected returns.[5] The boom–bust cycles of the 2000s have helped to cause both academic and practitioner views to shift toward accepting the idea of time-varying expected returns. As a result, institutional investors no longer embrace static asset class weights, nor do they reject market timing out of hand.

While I endorse some amount of market timing based on tactical market forecasts, it is important to stress humility. Hindsight bias makes us forget how difficult forecasting is, especially in highly competitive financial markets. Expected returns are unobservable, and our understanding of them is limited. Even the best experts' forecasts are noisy estimates of prospective returns. Moreover, market-timing trades lack breadth,[6] and being "right but early" involves substantial career risk. Finally, systematic contrarian trading signals often disagree starkly with discretionary timing views that are predicated on structural changes (valuation signals point to buying into weakness while the view that a structural change has occurred often points to selling into weakness). Given all these challenges, tactical tilts should constitute a minority of the risk budget for most institutional investors—but not zero.

Second key investment implication: Humbly attempt to exploit time-varying expected returns.

---

[5] When we refer to constant expected returns or risk premia, the constancy is assumed only for assets or portfolios with certain relatively stable characteristics. Many asset characteristics change gradually over time and occasionally experience sudden jumps. Bond durations shorten; credit ratings change; firms mature from volatile, startup, growth stocks to stable income-producing value stocks; and liquid assets turn into illiquid ones through a buyout. Assets' required returns (discount rates) evolve over time in line with these changing characteristics—even if the underlying factor risk premia are stable over time. The fact that asset characteristics evolve over time blurs the boundary between *static holdings* and *dynamic strategies*. Buy-and-hold strategies are static (passive) in terms of assets, but they allow changing characteristics over time. Conversely, to maintain a portfolio with stable characteristics, whether it is the S&P 500 Index, a small-cap value stock portfolio, or a constant-duration Treasury portfolio, a certain amount of portfolio rebalancing or trading is required.

Whether we study asset classes, strategy styles, or risk factors, then, the assumption of constant premia may be inappropriate. Even many characteristics or factor exposures exhibit time-varying *ex ante* rewards.

[6] Breadth is the ability to diversify the impact of a given beat-the-market insight across multiple bets (say, by buying a wide variety of stocks believed to be cheap). See Grinold and Kahn (2000).

Takeaways for Investors

This book focuses on the building blocks of investing but says little about how to use these building blocks to construct well-designed portfolios. The last chapters of Ilmanen (2011a) have more to say about those topics. Here, I just summarize my key takeaways for investors:

- There are many ways to improve investment practices to enhance long-run returns. The most important is to collect risk premia from diverse sources. Equity and illiquidity premia are good return sources but should not dominate the portfolio, especially at times when their *ex ante* rewards are slim. Entry and exit valuations matter.

- Investors can try to boost returns by exploiting value, carry, and momentum tilts; valuation-based timing of any return source; and view-based alpha-seeking. Because some of these return sources produce only modest amounts of return when unleveraged, the prudent use of leverage enables effective diversification and helps investors avoid often-overpriced high-volatility assets.

- The next generation of best practice for enhancing returns involves pursuing several of these paths in parallel, instead of embracing one idea. It is up to every institution to decide—based on its objectives, constraints, natural edges, and inclinations—what its priorities are. Diversity in approaches helps investors avoid overcrowded positions and reduces the danger that too homogeneous approaches across investors will lead to systemic problems.

2. Equity Risk Premium

- Historical annual excess returns of U.S. stocks over government bonds average 3% to 5% over long data windows, a further 1% over short-dated bills, and about another 2% higher if arithmetic means are used. Global excess returns of stocks over bonds are somewhat lower.

- Forward-looking measures of the equity–bond premium—based on a yield ratio or Gordon model (dividend discount model, or DDM)—exhibit significant time variation, probably for both rational and irrational reasons. Extreme values range between zero (or even negative) and 10%.

- The Gordon model states that long-run real equity returns equal the sum of the dividend yield and the real dividend growth rate (assuming no valuation changes). Both inputs can be debated, but estimates in the 2000s point to modest real returns (say, 2% + 1% = 3%) and an even thinner premium over Treasuries. Any higher expected return estimates must be justified by broader yield measures, more optimistic growth inputs, or expanding valuation multiples.

- Real long-run growth in dividends and earnings *per share* has clearly lagged the GDP growth rate. Aggregate earnings growth also includes net new equity issuance, which does not benefit existing shareholders.

- Equity market valuations have been especially high amidst stable mild inflation and low macro-volatility, which is not a promising sign for future multiple expansion.

- Standard economic models suggest that the equity premium should be negligible (<1%). A cottage industry of academic papers offers diverse explanations for the puzzle of stocks' much stronger historical outperformance.

- Survey forecasts of equity premia vary across sources and over time. Retail investor expectations appear extrapolative and procyclical; professional investor views, less so. The latter tend to predict a long-run equity premium of 3% to 4%—below the historical average but above some estimates from valuation models. Academics' estimates average near 6%, the higher value apparently reflecting the benign 20th century experience and/or the widespread use in academia of the future-equals-past model for the equity premium.

- Valuation, cyclical, and sentiment indicators can be useful for market timing, but all such relations are fragile.

2.1. Introduction and Terminology

The equity premium or equity risk premium (ERP) refers to the (expected or realized) return of a broad equity index in excess over some nonequity alternative. Different alternatives have been used: a short-term "riskless" asset (Treasury bill or other money market asset), a long-term Treasury bond (which is a better horizon match for a long-term equity investment), a corporate bond, or even a hypothetical asset returning the rate of inflation. I will use the term ERPC for the premium over short-dated assets ("cash") and ERPB for the premium over long-dated Treasuries ("bonds"). I will discuss both measures, ERPC and ERPB, in the context of both nominal and real (inflation-adjusted) returns. This entire analysis focuses on pretax returns.[7]

The other important distinction among equity premium concepts is between the *ex post* equity premium (historical realized excess return) and the *ex ante* equity premium (forward-looking excess return, or the excess return that one expects). Furthermore:

- either can be measured either as an arithmetic average or a geometric average;

- the latter may be based on objectively feasible future returns (rational expectations) or subjective return expectations (that are possibly irrational). Thus, the label "ERP," signifying that the premium is for risk, can be misleading if nonrisk considerations cause equities' *ex ante* return advantage.

---

[7]One simple way to view expected returns is to ask what returns investors require for major asset classes. Short-term Treasury bills earn expected inflation plus the expected near-riskless real rate. Long-term Treasuries earn the short-term bill rate plus a bond risk premium (BRP). Long-term corporate bonds earn the Treasury bond rate and a credit risk premium (CRP) minus an allowance for losses from defaults. Equities earn a further premium for being equities rather than debt—the residual or junior claimants to firm assets. The equity risk premium (ERP) can be narrowly defined as this last term, but it is more common to compute the ERP as the excess return over short-dated or long-dated Treasuries. This "demand-based" decomposition of returns into their elemental parts (after Ibbotson and Sinquefield 1976a, 1976b, *et seq.*) is simplified, and it does not get into the fundamental drivers of each premium. This chapter discusses later other (more useful) decompositions of equity returns. Moreover, it is problematic to view the broad equity premium (ERPC) as the *sum* of the BRP, CRP and ERP over corporate bonds. Equities share some long-term real risk with long-dated Treasuries, but they have different exposures to inflation risk, different effective durations, and very different safe-haven characteristics; it follows that many drivers of the BRP have no impact on equities' expected returns. Thus, certain declines in the BRP will directly be offset by widening the ERPB. Equities also contain a different type of exposure to issuer risk than corporate bonds; in particular, volatility tends to hurt the firm's debtholder and benefit the equityholder, as the former has effectively written a call option on the firm's assets to the latter.

The equity premium is ideally computed for stock market indices that are market-capitalization weighted. Early research also analyzed equally weighted stock indices that effectively overweight small-cap stocks and require frequent turnover to maintain equal weights. Newer research focuses on fundamental-value-weighted indices and (inversely) volatility-weighted indices, given the historical tendency of both kinds of indices to outperform market-cap indices.

The rest of this chapter covers the equity premium from different angles: theoretical determinants, historical experience, forward-looking value measures, survey forecasts, and tactical forecasting models.

2.2. Theories and the Equity Premium Puzzle

On the normative question of how high the equity risk premium should be, the academic literature provides limited guidance. The CAPM implies a cross-sectional relation—that each asset's expected excess return is the product of its market beta and the market risk premium—but it does not specify how large the market risk premium should be. The required market risk premium should reflect the *price* of risk and the *amount* of risk. While the CAPM is a static model, a more realistic approach might reflect the view that market risk aversion varies with recent market moves and economic conditions and that the amount of risk in the market varies with stock market volatility and asset correlations.

For many academics, equilibrium asset pricing models have been a more important path of inquiry. Recall the general idea that required risk premia reflect the way that asset returns covary with the marginal utility of an extra dollar of investor wealth. Consumption-based asset pricing models say that an additional dollar is worth more (has higher marginal utility) when consumption growth is slow or negative. In such a model, the single factor that drives risk premia is consumption growth rather than equity index performance. While it is satisfying to derive asset pricing theories from economic fundamentals like consumption, such theories have found it hard to explain why equities have historically outperformed bonds by several percentage points.

The *equity premium puzzle* refers to the difficulty of explaining the magnitude of the observed (historical) equity risk premium (4% to 8%) in the context of a standard macroeconomic model and rational expectations equilibrium. Mehra and Prescott (1985) use a standard neoclassical finance model (for those familiar with the jargon: an exchange economy, a serially uncorrelated consumption growth rate, and a representative agent with a utility function that exhibits constant relative risk aversion). The model predicts a very low equity risk premium (well below 1%) due to the low observed volatility of consumption growth and the low observed correlation between consumption growth and asset returns unless an extremely high risk aversion coefficient is used. A huge

9

academic literature has tried to reconcile this puzzle using market frictions (borrowing constraints, limited market participation, incomplete markets, and idiosyncratic risk), nonstandard utility functions (habit formation, recursive utility), modified consumption data (durable goods, luxury goods, long-term consumption risk), and biased sample explanations (survivorship bias among countries studied, absence of negative rare events in the sample, unexpected repricing of equities or bonds) as rational explanations for the high observed equity outperformance—but there is little consensus to date.

The following explanations advanced in some recent studies ring particularly true to me:

- *Rare-disaster risk*: Investors may have historically assumed that rare catastrophic events would occur at a higher frequency than actually materialized during the sample period. This idea—closely related to peso problems and fat tails—can justify a higher historical premium.

- *Structural uncertainty*: In contrast to assumptions in standard economic models, investors do not fully know the structure of the economic system, so they must gradually learn about the unknown structural parameters. The premium for such uncertainty can be an order of magnitude larger than the premium in a well-understood economic model. A topical example of structural uncertainty is political risk. The ongoing changing of the "rules of the game" by policymakers, regulators, and politicians in the post-2008 world is understandable. Yet, the related (significant if unquantifiable) uncertainty presumably raises the risk premia that investors demand—especially for assets most exposed to such political risk.

- *Long-run risk*: Short-term volatility in consumption and output is easily measured (albeit with noise), but for investors, the bigger concern is the uncertainty about long-run growth rates. Academics have developed theoretical models on this theme, while some empiricists argue that the secular decline in dividend yields and other equity premium proxies has been matched by a secular decline in macroeconomic volatility.

Straddling the above explanations, the legacy of the Great Depression may have sustained for decades a widespread morbid expectation or fear of another serious slump. Learning about rare events requires many observations, so Depression-induced pessimism dissipated extremely slowly, ending only in the 1960s. New research confirms that investors' risk attitudes depend on their lifetime experiences and memories, in the spirit of conservative "depression babies." These stories are especially relevant now that two major bear markets during the past decade may cast a long shadow on investor behavior and cause another period of pessimism.

The two main behavioral explanations for the large size of the historical equity risk premium both require combining loss aversion with another behavioral feature—in one case, a short time horizon (myopia) and in the other case, the house money effect.

- *Myopic loss aversion.* The myopic loss aversion model of Benartzi and Thaler (1995) relies on a variant of mental accounting related to the investment time horizon (evaluation period). A given expected return advantage will attract investors more, the longer their investment horizon is. If investors evaluate their portfolios very frequently, the odds of risky assets outperforming riskless ones are close to 50/50 and loss aversion kicks in. Over longer horizons, the odds steadily improve. A typical degree of loss aversion applied to *annual* changes in financial wealth can justify an equity premium of 6.5%, suggesting that an annual portfolio evaluation period is plausible for the overall market.

- *House money effect.* Barberis and Huang (2001) develop an equilibrium model in which investors derive utility both from consumption and from annual changes in wealth. They too assume a typical degree of loss aversion (just above 2) but find that a model with constant loss aversion cannot fully explain the equity premium puzzle. However, they can resolve the puzzle if they include in their model the "house money effect"—the idea that the degree of loss aversion varies dynamically with prior gains and losses. Specifically, investors are less averse to losing money that they have recently "won" in markets because they perceive it to be "house money" or free money. The model thus implies that investors' risk attitudes become more conservative in down markets.

The next section shows that estimates of the equity premium have edged lower since the 1990s. During the Great Moderation years, it was popular to argue that lower macro-volatility and investor learning about equities' long-run return advantage could justify a sustained fall in the required equity premium. Such arguments ring hollow after the 2008 experience. Yet, it remains plausible that the fair premium has declined somewhat due to lower trading costs and better global diversification opportunities and, in particular, the wide availability of low-cost index funds.

2.3. Historical Equity Premium

Exhibits 2.1 and 2.2 recap the U.S. experience since the 19th century, documenting compound (geometric) nominal and real returns as well as equity premia over cash (mainly one-month Treasury bills) and over bonds (mainly 10-year Treasury bonds). The variation in average nominal equity returns across very long (at least 50-year) samples may partly reflect different inflation

Exhibit 2.1. Compound Average U.S. Equity Returns and Equity Premia over 200+ Years

	Nominal Equity Market Return	Real Equity Market Return	Equity Premium vs. Cash (ERPC)	Equity Premium vs. Bond (ERPB)
1802–2009	7.90%	6.33%	na	2.68%
1802–1899	6.00	6.21	na	0.50
1900–1999	10.75	7.47	6.37	5.93
2000–2009	−0.95	−3.38	−3.65	−7.21
1926–2009	9.94	6.70	5.99	4.54
1960–2009	9.52	5.22	3.90	2.38

na = not available.

Sources: Arnott and Bernstein (2002), Bloomberg.

levels over time—near zero inflation in the 19th century versus 3% in the 20th century. Real equity market returns have been more stable over time, with a 6.3% annual average. The geometric equity premium was 2.68% (arithmetic 4.17%) between 1802 and 2009 but clearly higher in the 1900s and lower in the 1800s and the early 2000s.

Exhibit 2.2. Cumulative Real Return to Equity Investing Has Been Surprisingly Stable, but a Large Premium over Bonds Is Mainly a 20th Century Phenomenon

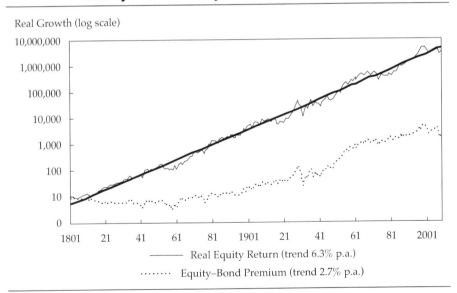

Real Growth (log scale)

——— Real Equity Return (trend 6.3% p.a.)

········· Equity–Bond Premium (trend 2.7% p.a.)

Note: "p.a." stands for per annum.

Sources: Arnott and Bernstein (2002), Bloomberg.

It is dangerous to extrapolate the 6% real growth trend for equities, partly because some of it reflects one-off valuation gains from expansion of the P/E multiple. Moreover, 20-year real returns varied between 1% and 13%. The highest 20-year real returns took place *after* calamities such as the Civil War, World War II, and the Great Inflation. It is also important to remember that, in reality, most investors could not have achieved 6% real returns even if they had regularly reinvested their dividends and had managed to avoid poor market timing. Trading costs, investment management fees, and taxes would have eaten into the performance for even such unusually disciplined investors.

The equity premium over bonds was especially high from the 1950s to the 1970s as the persistent rise in inflation hurt bonds. This premium was only one-half of 1% during the 19th century but 10 times higher in the 20th century.[8] Since the Civil War (1861–1865), U.S. equities have almost never underperformed bonds over a 20-year window. This consistency of long-horizon outperformance was made famous by Jeremy Siegel (2002) in *Stocks for the Long Run,* first published in 1994. However, the Dimson, Marsh, and Staunton (2002) data remind us that in other countries, there have been many examples of negative 20-year equity premia—most recently, of course, in Japan. During the early 2009 trough, U.S. equities had underperformed bonds over 20 years. If stocks are compared with 20-year Treasuries (rather than the 10-year bonds used in **Exhibit 2.3**), they had even underperformed over a time span in excess of 40 years (November 30, 1968, to March 31, 2009), by far the longest such period window since the Civil War.

Lower equity premium estimates by studying global evidence

Many observers attribute the high equity premium to the particular success of the U.S. economy. Even multi-country studies involve various biases that suggest that realized market returns exceed the returns that were anticipated.

- Survivorship bias raises the odds that we examine countries that have had good or at least continuous capital market performance (say, the G5 as opposed to Russia, Austria-Hungary, India, Turkey, or Argentina).

---

[8]However, markets were evolving and data quality was lower in the earlier periods. Equity returns are disputed for the period before the 1870s, especially due to uncertainty about dividend yield levels. Government debt was hardly considered default free and sometimes was proxied by high-quality nongovernment debt, so the meaning of the equity–bond premium was different at the time. Also, while cash returns are not shown in Exhibit 2.1, they are relevant to the general ERP question, and it should be noted that short-dated commercial paper, used as the cash return in some studies of the 19th century, promised equitylike real returns (of 4% to 10%) in that century, albeit with significant default risk.

Exhibit 2.3.   Rolling Average 20-Year Returns and Premia of U.S. Equities

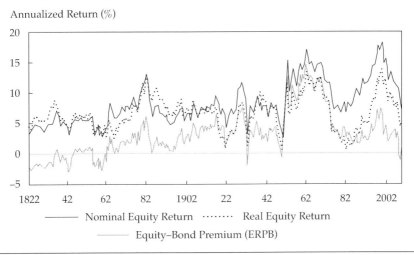

Sources: Arnott and Bernstein (2002), Bloomberg.

- "Easy data" bias makes it likely that we start samples after unusual events (war, hyperinflation, market closure), which often means that assets are cheap at the start of the period and that no comparable turmoil reoccurs during the period.

- The literature on the "peso problem" recognizes that past U.S. market pricing was influenced by rare disasters that could have happened but did not. Hindsight tells us that the United States and its market economy survived two world wars, the Cold War, and the Great Depression and did not suffer the hyperinflation, invasion, or other calamities experienced by many other countries. This was never a foregone conclusion, so it is little wonder that realized equity returns were boosted by the absence of catastrophes and then by a repricing effect by the end of the 20th century, when the perceived likelihood of catastrophe had fallen.

The comprehensive global studies by Dimson *et al.* (2002, 2010) address these questions by analyzing the performance of equity markets in 19 countries since 1900. **Exhibit 2.4** shows that the (market-cap- or GDP-weighted) global equity premium is about 0.5% to 0.8% lower than the U.S. premium for 1900–2009—consistent with mild selection bias. The authors argue that the use of their worldwide premium captures the bulk of any survivorship or selection bias, given that the 19 countries in their database may have accounted for 90% of

Exhibit 2.4. Compound Annual (Geometric) Equity Returns and Premia, 1900–2009

	Real Equity Return	ERP vs. Cash (ERPC)	ERP vs. Bonds (ERPB)
U.S.	6.2%	5.2%	4.2%
World ex U.S. (in $)	5.0	4.0	3.8
World (in $)	5.4	4.4	3.7
Range among 19 markets	2.1–7.5	2.5–6.8	1.8–6.0

Source: Dimson, Marsh, and Staunton (2010).

world equity market capitalization at the start of the 20th century.[9] Equity returns are a tad lower outside the U.S., but the broad patterns are similar.

▨ *Lower premium if realized returns are adjusted for unexpected windfall gains*

Despite concerns about survivorship bias, peso problems, and time-varying expected returns, many investment textbooks still use historical excess returns as a proxy for the *ex ante* risk premium. Historical average returns equal expected returns, however, only if expected returns are constant and unexpected returns from persistent growth surprises and valuation changes do not distort the within-sample results. Such valuation changes can materially impact average realized returns even over long sample periods—and, indeed, they have done so in the 20th century. Starting from the early or mid-20th century, equity market dividend-to-price (D/P) and earnings-to-price (E/P) ratios have fallen, while bond yields have returned to their previous low levels, having visited double digits around 1980. Thus, the realized equity–bond excess return in the 20th century almost surely exaggerates the premium investors actually expected and required (in the past, let alone now, after required returns have arguably declined).

A key theme in this book is the crucial distinction between realized (*ex post*) average excess returns and expected (*ex ante*) risk premia. If required returns vary over time, past average returns may be poor predictors of future returns—and they can even be poor proxies of past *expected* returns, returns that were expected or demanded by investors at the time. If markets undergo significant valuation changes, realized average returns are strongly influenced by unexpected capital gains and losses even over long sample periods.

---

[9] An aside: counterintuitively, the world ERPB has a lower geometric mean than either of its components. This fact seems to reflect time-varying weights in the capitalization-weighted "World" index—that is, poor apparent market timing in having maximum weights in Japan in 1990 and in the U.S. in 1999–2000. Studying data since the 1980s, I find that the relative weight of the U.S. versus the rest of the world has a −0.4 correlation with next year's relative performance. Rebalancing U.S. and non-U.S. weights to 50/50 each year would have clearly improved portfolio performance.

We can try to recover past average expected returns by adjusting realized returns for the estimated impact of repricing (unexpected capital gains or losses). Several studies take this approach, notably, Dimson *et al.* (2002), Fama and French (2002), and Ibbotson and Chen (2003). Each study uses a slightly different method of removing the impact of unexpected windfall gains to recover the equity risk premium that was expected over some past sample period. All three studies find an (adjusted) expected equity–bond risk premium near 4% in the United States, averaged over long histories.

▨ *Lower expected premium if current equity market valuations are especially high*

The estimates we have been reviewing are still based on *past average* expectations and are not necessarily relevant for the *current* environment if current market valuations differ materially from historical averages. I will soon discuss forward-looking expected returns in detail, but I first review the Ibbotson and Chen (2003) building-block approach.

Exhibit 2.5 decomposes the realized 110-year (1900–2009) compound annual stock market return of 9.6% into its elemental parts, using separate decompositions for the "demand" and "supply" of returns. The total return is split into either:

- The sum of required (demanded) returns—on the assumption that sample averages capture required returns well (4.7% nominal Treasury bond return + 4.7% *ex post* equity risk premium + small interaction/reinvestment terms) or

- The sum of supplied returns (3.0% average inflation + 4.3% average dividend yield + 1.3% average real earnings-per-share growth rate + 0.5% repricing effect, that is, the annualized impact of the expansion of the P/E ratio by 75% from 12.5 to 21.9 during the sample period + small interaction/ reinvestment terms).

Following Ibbotson and Chen (2003), I regard the 0.5% repricing gain as an unexpected windfall and subtract it from the supplied returns (third bar). I could use the real dividend growth rate (averaging 1.2%) and the repricing effect based on dividend yield changes (having a slightly higher annualized impact, 0.7%) instead of earnings data, with broadly the same results.

The third bar suggests, then, that investors required an *ex ante* nominal geometric equity market return of 9.1% between 1900 and 2009, on average. This inference carries over to the return that is expected now or in the future only if we assume that expected returns are constant. If expected returns vary over time and current values differ from the average levels over the sample, this analysis can be misleading. Given that long-term Treasury yields are below 4%, few observers would extrapolate the realized average return of 4.7% on these

Exhibit 2.5. Decomposing Historical Equity Market Returns, 1900–2009

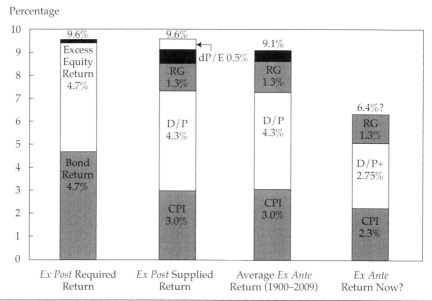

Note: RG = real earnings growth; D/P = dividend yield; CPI = inflation; dP/E = repricing gains.
Sources: Arnott and Bernstein (2002), Bloomberg, Robert Shiller's website (www.econ.yale.edu/~shiller).

bonds into the future. Similar considerations suggest that we might reduce the U.S. Consumer Price Index (CPI) and D/P components for equities. The fourth column shows that using 2.3% CPI (consensus forecast for long-term inflation) and 2.0% D/P, a forward-looking measure, predicts only 5.6% nominal equity returns for the long term. Admittedly, the D/P value can be raised if we use a broader carry measure including net share buybacks, so I add 0.75% to the estimate. Even more bullish return forecasts than 6.4% would have to rely on growth optimism (beyond the historical 1.3% rate of real earnings-per-share growth) or expected further P/E expansion in the coming decades (my analysis assumes none). More generally, these building blocks give us a useful framework for debating key components of future equity returns.

> **Box 1. The Cross-Sectional Relation (or the Lack of It) between Equity Betas and Return**
>
> This chapter focuses on the equity premium computed as the difference between the return on an equity market index and the return on default-free Treasury debt. The CAPM predicts a positive risk–reward relation (given a beta of 1.00 for the equity market and a near-zero beta for fixed income). The CAPM also predicts a cross-sectional relation across equities: expected returns rise as a linear function of equities'

betas. However, in postwar data, the empirically observed relation (security market line) has been too flat relative to what the CAPM predicts, or even inverted. High-beta stocks have not outperformed low-beta stocks. In **Exhibit 2.6**, I show six Fama–French size- and value-sorted portfolios as well as three beta-sorted portfolios (courtesy Eric Falkenstein). In contrast to the clearly positive long-run equity premium over bonds, there is no evidence for a positive beta premium across equities.

The surprisingly good performance of low-beta stocks may reflect their tendency to have large loadings on other priced factors or characteristics. To me, the most compelling explanation is that many volatile high-beta stocks are bought as lottery tickets and as proxies for high-leverage investments, whereas low-beta stocks tend to be stable and dull stocks with a value bias. While high-beta stocks outperformed low-beta stocks between 1926 and 1963, perhaps because value stocks had higher betas than growth stocks in these decades, Fama and French (2006) stress that any variation in betas unrelated to size and value was unrewarded both before and after 1963.

Another plausible explanation stresses the distinction between "good" betas and "bad" betas—that is, sensitivities to discount rate changes as opposed to cash flow changes, respectively. Value stocks and low-beta stocks are more exposed to bad beta, which has a more permanent price impact. Thus, they warrant higher premia.

Exhibit 2.6. Positive Beta Pricing Relation between Stocks and Bonds but *Not* across Stocks, 1962–2009

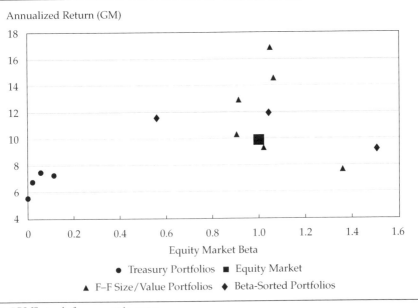

Note: "GM" stands for geometric mean.

Sources: Kenneth R. French's website (http://mba.tuck.dartmouth.edu/pages/faculty/ken.french), Bank of America Merrill Lynch, Center for Research in Security Prices, Eric Falkenstein.

MSCI Barra (2010) recently estimated a similar decomposition for their global equity index between 1975 and 2009, but they used book values rather than earnings as the measure of fundamental value. The annual gross compound (i.e., geometric) return of 11.1% consisted of 4.2% inflation, 2.9% dividend income, 2.1% real book value growth, 1.5% valuation multiple expansion, and 0.4% residual interaction terms. The past decade (the 2000s) saw the fastest real book value growth (3.8%), but this was more than offset by valuation multiple contraction (−8.3%).

2.4. Forward-Looking (*Ex Ante* Objective) Long-Term Expected Return Measures

Among forward-looking measures of equity market carry or value, dividend yield was the early leader. However, broader payout yield measures that include (at least) share buybacks have replaced dividend yield as the preferred carry measure, while earnings yield and the Gordon model (DDM) equity premium have become the preferred valuation measures.

2.4.1. Carry (Narrow Dividend Yield vs. Broader Total Payout Yield)

Here, we use the word "carry" to designate an asset's income return or yield. Dividend yield (D/P) is the classic proxy for equity carry and was seen as a useful predictor of future equity returns until it failed in the 1990s. Having ranged between 3% and 6% for 40 years, the D/P of the S&P 500 fell for the first time ever below 3% in 1993 and then below 2% in 1997, remaining there for the next decade. Thus, D/P gave a bearish signal through the whole 1990s equity rally, denting its record as a market-timing signal. The trend decline in D/P in the 1980s and 1990s partly reflected a structural change: many firms replaced dividends with repurchases (i.e., stock buybacks), which were more tax efficient and more flexible and which had a more positive impact on share price. If top executives are compensated based on share price, they naturally prefer buybacks over dividend payments as a means of distributing cash to investors.

The obvious improvement for measuring equity market carry is to include share buybacks, which became much more prevalent starting in the early 1980s. One reason was the 1982 change in SEC rules that provides a safe harbor from price manipulation charges for firms conducting share buybacks. The buyback yield never exceeded 1% before 1985 but did in most years thereafter. Even though the buyback yield has in some years even exceeded the dividend yield, the former arguably should not get as high a weight as the latter in any long-run carry measure because it is not as persistent. It is much easier for a management to reduce repurchase activities than to cut dividends.

Only adding share buybacks but not deducting share issuance, as is sometimes done, would overstate the effective carry. Firms may repurchase shares or pay dividends when they have excess cash, while they issue "seasoned" equity (additional equity in an existing company) when they need more capital from investors. The net-buyback-adjusted yield, net payout yield, and the change in Treasury stock use somewhat different data to adjust dividend yields, but the intent of all of them is the same—to estimate total cash flow from the company to the investor. Some argue that cash-financed merger and acquisition (M&A) deals are a further component of cash flows to the investor that should be included in a carry or yield measure. This component is less frequently included—and its predictive ability is worse because high M&A volumes tend to coincide with bull markets. **Exhibit 2.7** plots some of these time series.

Exhibit 2.8 shows that the net-buyback-adjusted dividend yield (the sum of dividend yields and buybacks less issuance) has the highest correlation with next-quarter equity market returns (0.27). The same is true when predicting annual equity returns (0.42). Moreover, this carry measure is less persistent than others; the autocorrelation between its values 12 months apart is lowest. Dividend yield was by far the most persistent carry component, as expected. The data confirm that including the M&A yield would reduce the predictive ability of a broad carry composite. These data start only in 1985, but academic

Exhibit 2.7. *Ex Ante* Equity Carry Measures, 1984–2009

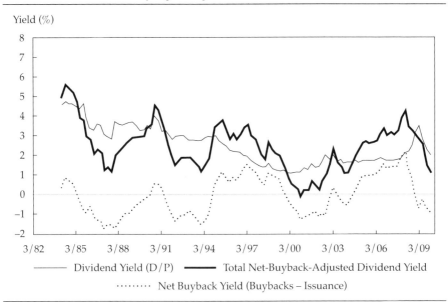

Sources: Haver Analytics, Michael Afreh (Nomura).

Exhibit 2.8. Predictive Market-Timing Correlations of Narrow and Broad Carry Measures, 1985–2009

	Dividend Yield (1)	Net Buyback Yield (2)	M&A Yield (3)	Sum 1 + 2	Sum 1 + 2 + 3	Next-Quarter Equity Return
Correlation with next-quarter equity market return	0.22	0.08	0.04	**0.27**	0.15	1.00
12-month autocorrelation	0.88	0.61	0.69	0.54	0.67	0.07

Sources: Haver Analytics, Michael Afreh (Nomura).

studies document good market-timing ability using total payout yield and net buyback yield since the 1920s. The strong results may partly reflect corporate managers successfully market-timing their equity issuance to coincide with expensive market levels.

2.4.2. Value Measures: Earnings Yield and the Fed Model

▨ *Absolute valuation*

A stock market's price-to-earnings ratio and its inverse, the earnings yield (E/P), are the most popular equity market valuation indicators. The spread (arithmetic difference) or, alternatively, the ratio of the government bond yield (Y) over the earnings yield (E/P) is the most popular measure of relative valuation between the two major asset classes—and thus shorthand for the equity–bond premium.

Several choices need to be made in determining which earnings series to use in E/P measures.

* *Nature of earnings*: Trailing versus forward looking (based on a consensus of analyst estimates) and operating versus reported. Trailing reported earnings are available for almost a century for the S&P 500 and its predecessor index, the S&P 90, while the latter (operating versus reported) only became available in the 1980s. Analysts typically forecast operating earnings, which ignore nonrecurring items, such as writeoffs, that may distort the picture of "normal" earnings. However, forecasts of operating earnings are almost invariably higher than trailing reported earnings— partly due to analysts' overoptimism, partly to the management bias toward viewing good news as recurring but bad news as nonrecurring, and partly due to the normal uptrend in earnings (so that next-year earnings are, on average, higher than trailing earnings, all other things being equal).

• *Window length.* Trailing reported earnings are traditionally shown for the past year. Annual earnings are so volatile, however, that E1/P can fall during a bear market (1932, 2002, 2009). Longer windows with smoothed earnings may thus be preferred, and Robert Shiller has popularized the use of a real version of Benjamin Graham's nominal E10/P series.[10]

• *Adjustments to earnings* to make E/P a more realistic measure of expected real return. For example, Wilcox (2007) shows that because reported earnings are not real but based on current-period prices, it makes sense to make an accounting adjustment for depreciation expenses and a debt adjustment for creditor claims. Wilcox shows that the earnings yield thus inflation adjusted is empirically a better predictor than an unadjusted earnings yield. The correlation of the former measure with next year's real equity market return is 0.28 (over 1970–2006), more than twice that of the latter.

See **Exhibit 2.9**.

Exhibit 2.9. Variants of Earnings Yields, 1982–2009

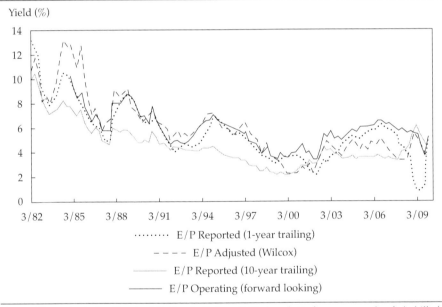

Sources: Haver Analytics, Standard & Poor's, Robert Shiller's website (www.econ.yale.edu/~shiller), Stephen Wilcox's website (www.business.mnsu.edu/wilcox/).

---

[10] See Campbell–Shiller (1998) and Shiller (2000).

Relative valuation: Lower bond yields explain lower earnings yields

Note that E/P is an "absolute value indicator"—relating an asset's price to its earnings and judging whether the current E/P level is high or low compared with its *own* history. Of course E/P and other value measures (book to price, dividend yield, Tobin's *q*) can be compared *across* individual equities or equity market sectors and countries, thus making them "relative value indicators." The most popular relative value indicator across major asset classes is the spread or ratio between the equity market E/P and the 10-year Treasury yield. **Exhibit 2.10** shows the history of the earnings yield and the 10-year government bond yield for over a century. Unless otherwise stated, our earnings yield refers to the trailing one-year operating earnings per share of the S&P 500 and its predecessors.

The broad picture is that the earnings yield has ranged between 2% and 18% but has been near historical lows since the 1990s. Bond yields traded systematically below earnings yields for most of the century but traded above them between 1980 and 2002. While earnings yields and bond yields were almost uncorrelated until 1960, since then, they have shared common uptrends and downtrends.

Exhibit 2.10. Trailing and Forward Earnings Yield and Treasury Yield, 1900–2009

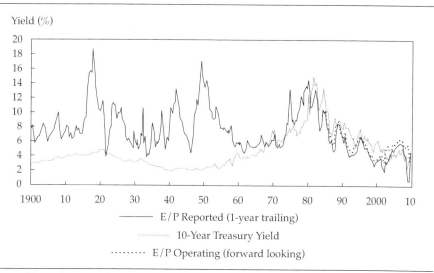

Yield (%)

———— E/P Reported (1-year trailing)

———— 10-Year Treasury Yield

········· E/P Operating (forward looking)

Sources: Haver Analytics, Standard & Poor's, Robert Shiller's website (www.econ.yale.edu/~shiller), Federal Reserve Board, Homer and Sylla (1991).

'ots the ratio of the Treasury yield to the earnings yield. This ·ocks are expensive versus bonds. For nearly half a century, ...er neatly mean reverting, providing good relative value signals .. allocation trades between stock and bond markets. Over this period, we can say that lower bond yields explain lower earnings yields. This is not surprising, because bonds are the main asset class competing with equities for investor capital and the bond yield constitutes the riskless part of equities' discount rate. It is more surprising that the nominal bond yield (or even the inflation rate) gives a better fit to E/Ps than the real bond yield, even though the equity earnings yield is a real, not nominal, concept.

Whatever the fundamental reason for the close relation between equity and bond yields, investors have tried to exploit it. The yield ratio became a popular relative value indicator labeled "the Fed Model" after Federal Reserve Board Chairman Alan Greenspan referred to this indicator in Congressional testimony in 1997. Asness (2003) stresses that while the Fed Model is poorly constructed, in that it mixes real and nominal quantities, it may describe well how investors choose to set the stock market P/E. In other words, if investors set the P/E in relation to the nominal bond yield, whether rationally or irrationally, over the short term the Fed Model may be a moderately useful trading tool. Over the long run, Asness argues, the Fed Model gives poor timing signals.

Exhibit 2.11. **Yield Ratio (E/P Divided by Treasury Yield) Tracks the Return Volatility Ratio between Stocks and Bonds**

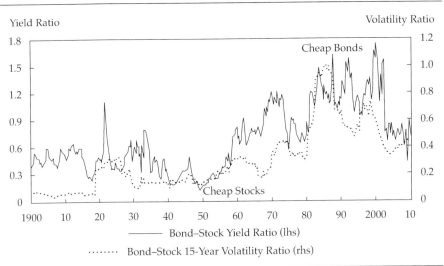

Sources: Haver Analytics, Standard & Poor's, Robert Shiller's website (www.econ.yale.edu/~shiller), Federal Reserve Board, Homer and Sylla (1991), author's calculations.

What are we to make of the long-run trends in the yield ratio? The series was relatively trendless in the first half of the 20th century but clearly upward-trending in the postwar decades, signaling relative richening of stocks versus bonds. One appealing explanation for this upward trend is that the relative risk of bonds versus stocks grew over time. The thin line in Exhibit 2.11 shows the relative return volatility of 10-year government bonds and of the stock market index, measured by 15-year moving standard deviations. In the first half of the century, stock market returns were about seven times as volatile as bond returns. By the 1980s, relative volatilities were virtually equal—although subsequent disinflation reduced bond volatility to less than half of stock market volatility. The trend increase in the volatility ratio reflects an increase in bond volatility, particularly in the 1970s and 1980s, and a decline in stock volatility from the 1930s until recently. In addition to time variation in volatilities, the changing recession-hedging ability of bonds contributed to changing asset class valuations. In the 1930s, 1950s, and 2000s, Treasuries were perceived to be good recession hedges—and were thus negatively correlated with equities. In contrast, Treasuries did not have such safe-haven characteristics and actually lost money during the 1970–1982 stagflationary recessions.

Shifts in the relative risk of asset classes are a structural change that undermines the usefulness of valuation signals like the yield ratio. This ratio serves well as a mean-reverting signal within any one regime, but it typically gives a wrong value signal when a structural or regime change occurs. How should one watch out for those structural changes? One guidepost is a secular change in long-run inflation expectations or in long-run economic growth rates or in their volatilities. Both of these variables are fundamental drivers of the relative prospects and risks of bond and stock asset classes.

Puzzlingly close relation between earnings yield and inflation

Since stock prices reflect the expected values of discounted future cash flows, it is a mathematical identity that low earnings yields (high P/E ratios) reflect some combination of low discount rates and/or high expected earnings growth rates. Yet, various growth indicators are only loosely related to earnings yield fluctuations and the market P/E ratio has only a modest ability to predict subsequent earnings growth. The discount rate may affect the riskless yield component or the required equity–bond risk premium. Historical analysis suggests that earnings yields have been more closely related to inflation than to nominal or real bond yields or any growth metrics.

Exhibit 2.12 depicts the relation between U.S. earnings yields and realized inflation rates. A comparable relationship exists in many other countries, in either *ex post* or *ex ante* inflation data. A high correlation between earnings yields

Exhibit 2.12.   Over 1900–2009, Trailing Earnings Yield Tracked Inflation Surprisingly Closely for the First Half of the Period, Then Less Closely

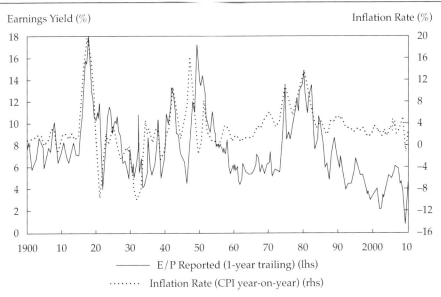

Source: Robert Shiller's website (www.econ.yale.edu/~shiller).

and inflation rates may be surprising, because the E/P is supposed to be a real variable. The textbook view is that stocks are real assets. Since higher inflation should be fully compensated by higher nominal earnings growth rates, changing inflation rates should have little impact on stock prices or valuation ratios. However, this principle does not hold up in practice. Many empirical studies have documented a negative relation between (expected or unexpected) inflation and stock returns, but the slow-moving relation between inflation and equity market valuation ratios is even stronger.

What explains this apparently anomalous relation? Here are the main candidates, all of which may contribute:

- Inflation may impact real earnings growth prospects; high inflation is detrimental to growth.

- Required real equity returns may be correlated with expected inflation (rational inflation-related risk premium).

- Inflation may raise prospective real returns because the irrational money illusion, discussed below, makes equity markets undervalued (overvalued) when inflation is high (low).

- Distortions due to accounting rules and taxation. Accounting rules include inflationary gains in reported earnings. Higher inflation boosts reported earnings due to inventory gains and insufficient depreciation expenses. The interaction of depreciation, corporate taxes, and inflation also influences reported net profits.

The last candidate could explain why the correlation is strongest between past-year inflation and past-year trailing earnings. It turns out that Wilcox's adjusted earnings yield has a lower correlation with the inflation rate than the simple earnings yield.

The third candidate, irrational money illusion, has attracted the most attention. Modigliani and Cohn (1979) argue that when inflation is high, investors and analysts incorrectly discount real dividend streams using nominal discount rates, resulting in a price that is below fundamental value. Another variant of the money illusion hypothesis says that investors and analysts actually discount nominal cash flows using nominal discount rates but make an insufficient inflation adjustment to their nominal growth forecasts so that here, too, high inflation implies underpriced stocks. While academics often argue that confusing nominal and real values is too basic an error for investors to make, it seems plausible that the money illusion is common at low to moderate inflation levels. Even the commentaries of professional market practitioners frequently reveal such confusion, as does the use of the Fed Model. The money illusion story explains both the apparent cheapness of equities in the 1970s and their richness in the 1990s—but not the equity market cheapness in the 1930s or in 2008–2009 (or cheapness in Japan in the 1990s and 2000s).

Bekaert and Engstrom (2010) argue that the second explanation—a rational inflation-related premium on equities—can explain much of the observed covariation between equity yields and bond yields in the U.S. They start by assuming that two variables cause equity premia to be time varying—real economic uncertainty (in survey data on the consensus probability of recession and on cross-sectional disagreement about next-year GDP growth) and time-varying risk aversion (based on the habit formation model and consumption data)—and then document that high expected inflation coincides with high rationally required equity yields. Intuitively, if inflationary episodes tend to occur during recessions (stagflation), both equity and bond risk premia tend to be high at the same time. The authors also show a clear positive *cross-country relation* consistent with their hypothesis: countries with a higher inflation–recession correlation tend to also have a higher correlation between stock and bond yields.

The first candidate, high inflation being detrimental to real growth, has its merits too, but it needs to be qualified. It is true that high inflation tends to hurt equity markets, but so does deflation. Steady, low-but-positive inflation appears to be the optimal environment for real growth and asset valuations. **Exhibit 2.13** shows a sombrero-shaped relation between equity market valuation levels (P/E10) and inflation levels over the past 110 years. The sweet spot of peak valuations occurs with inflation in the 1% to 4% range. The graph also hints at a mechanism behind this nonlinear relation. Economic uncertainty—here measured by inflation volatility and equity market volatility—tends to be higher amidst deflation and high inflation. Thus, inflation may not directly influence equity market valuations but affects it through its impact on economic growth and uncertainty. Whatever the reason, the pattern is bad news for market valuations because the likelihood of both deflation and high inflation for the coming decade has substantially increased after two decades at the sweet spot.

Exhibit 2.13. Sweet Spot for U.S. Equity Market Valuations Is Low Positive Inflation: U.S. Experience, 1900–2009

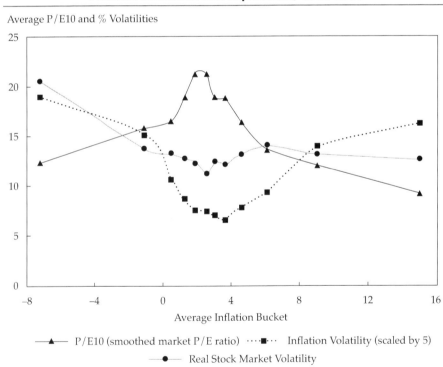

Note: The graph was created by sorting each month into one of 12 buckets based on the level of inflation during the month and then computing the average level for inflation (on the *x*-axis) and for the P/E10 valuation ratio and the two volatility series (on the *y*-axis) in these 12 subsets of the history.

Sources: Haver Analytics, Robert Shiller's website (www.econ.yale.edu/~shiller), author's calculations.

What E/P drivers are there besides inflation?—volatility, profit cycle, demographics

The inflation level is highly correlated with the earnings yield, but the absolute deviation of inflation from the sample average fares even better (0.69), consistent with the "sombrero" graph. Other useful explanatory variables include output volatility (e.g., rolling GDP volatility in recent years), profit/GDP ratio, and a demographic pattern discussed below.

One broad story is that a secular decline in macroeconomic volatility can justify secular richening in equity market valuations. However, some argue that the fall in macroeconomic volatility after World War II merely reflects better-quality data or a change in the output mix (industrial versus services).

Even though P/E ratios are conceptually a forecast of future growth, they have had a limited correlation with subsequent actual growth. Still, it is empirically clear that P/E levels—both across firms and over time for the market aggregate—are linked to analysts' consensus forecasts of long-term earnings growth. Disappointments following excessive growth optimism may be a key reason for the success of contrarian stock-selection and market-timing strategies.

The share of prime-age savers in the population peaked in Japan in the late 1980s and in the U.S. around 2000, consistent with broad patterns in market valuations. Some observers call the 1990s "the baby boomer rally" in the U.S. and predict market declines when the retiring boomers begin to dissave. The story rings true, but demographic developments are at best only one influence on asset prices. Moreover, there is some evidence of retirees continuing to save rather than dissave and the story ignores the entry of savers from younger, emerging-market countries.

2.4.3. *Ex Ante* Equity Premia Based on the DDM

While the yield ratio is useful shorthand for the equity–bond premium, the dividend discount model (DDM) gives us directly what we want to see: a numerical estimate of the difference between stocks' and bonds' expected long-run returns.

In the basic version of the DDM (Gordon's 1962 growth model), equity cash flows (dividends) are assumed to grow at a constant annual rate G. A feasible long-run return on equities is then the sum of the cash flow yield (D/P) and the trend cash flow growth rate G.

Now, the required return on equities, or the discount rate, can be viewed as the sum of the riskless long-term government yield (Y) and the required equity–bond risk premium (ERPB). Intuitively, markets are in a steady state when the equity market return that investors require (Y + ERPB) equals the return that markets are able to provide (D/P + G). These expressions can be reshuffled to state the *ex ante* equity–bond premium in terms of three building blocks:

$$ERP = D/P + G - Y. \qquad (1)$$

The DDM can be expressed in nominal terms (with G_{nom} and Y_{nom}) or in real terms (with G_{real} and Y_{real}) if we adjust both expected cash flow growth and the bond yield for expected inflation. The model can also be expressed as an Earnings Discount Model if we assume a constant dividend payout rate $k \equiv$ D/E. With a constant payout rate, the growth rates of dividends and earnings are equal. Moreover, if we assume that retained earnings are reinvested at the expected return level, it can be shown that E/P equals the real expected return.

It is easy to extend the DDM to include different short-term and long-term growth rates, but the use of the DDM to analyze time-varying equity premia is only informal, given that it is a steady-state model that assumes constant expected returns and valuation ratios. In a dynamic variant of the DDM, one that allows time-varying expected returns, D/P is a combination of the market's expectations of future (required) stock returns and dividend growth.[11]

The DDM framework is simple and flexible, but there is wide disagreement about what inputs to use in calculating the equity premium. Even the observable inputs—dividend yield and bond yield—are ambiguous. It may be debated whether to include share repurchases in addition to the dividend yield and whether to use inflation-linked bonds or nominal bonds adjusted for expected inflation. One must also decide which maturity of bonds to use. The main source of contention, though, is the assumed trend profit growth rate G. Instead of assuming a constant profit growth rate, we may allow G_{real} to vary over time according to survey forecasts or statistical estimates.

For illustration, I use a D/P proxy based on smoothed earnings, a constant payout ratio (60%), and a G_{real} proxy that is based on an average of a survey forecasts of future output growth and several realized real growth rates (of GDP, corporate profits, and earnings per share over the past decade). The sum of these two terms (D/P proxy + G_{real}) gives a proxy of the real *ex ante* equity market return. I subtract from it the expected real bond yield (the 10-year Treasury yield minus an estimate of expected long-term inflation that is based on surveys for the past 30 years and on statistical estimates by central bank economists for earlier dates) to estimate ERPB (the *ex ante* equity premium over bonds). As **Exhibit 2.14** shows, the ERPB estimate peaked during the 1970s and troughed in the 1980s when bond risk premia were particularly high. The *ex ante* ERPB fell below 1% at the turn of the millennium when the tech boom peaked and rose above 4% in 2003 and even higher in late 2008.

---

[11]Campbell and Shiller (1988a) developed an approximate dynamic version of the DDM identity. With only a few additional assumptions, they show that a high price-to-dividend ratio reflects some combination of a high expected dividend growth rate and low expected future stock returns (i.e., low discount rates). Similarly, unexpected stock returns in a given period can be decomposed into changing expectations of future dividend growth ("cash flow news") and changing required returns on equities ("discount rate news"). Such exercises can help us interpret expected and realized asset returns without fully developed theoretical models.

Exhibit 2.14. One Estimate of the Equity Market's Forward-Looking Returns, 1958–2009

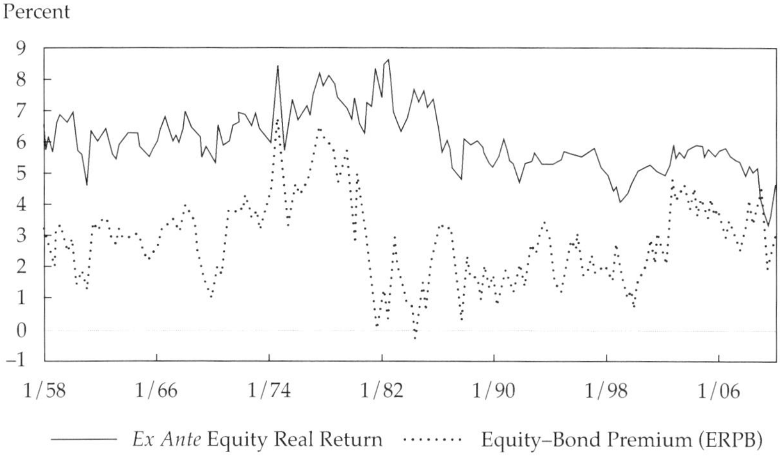

Sources: Haver Analytics, Robert Shiller's website (www.econ.yale.edu/~shiller), author's calculations.

Forward-looking analyses of the ERP became more popular after the tech bubble, partly because they sent a good warning signal about low future returns (albeit prematurely) and because they highlighted the shortcomings of basing equity premium estimates on historical average returns. The best-known study in this genre is Arnott and Bernstein (2002), who constructed *ex ante* real long-term stock and bond return series since 1802, given information available at the time. Despite similar contours, their estimates for the common period are lower than mine, mainly because they use the historical average real dividend growth rate to proxy for G_{real}, and this series averages about 1%, which is lower than my proxy above. (I use yet another data set in my 2003 *Journal of Portfolio Management* article, Ilmanen 2003a, which discusses these issues in much more detail.)

Debates on growth rate G in dividend discount models

There will never be full agreement about the equity–bond premium because there is a wide range of views about DDM inputs. The main debate is about the *long-run growth rate (G),* the least-anchored DDM input.

Earnings or dividend data? In historical analyses, some authors use earnings data, others, dividend data, and yet others, gross domestic product data to proxy for cash flows. While earnings data have their own shortcomings, I use them. Historical dividend growth is understated by the declining trend in dividend payout rate since the late 1970s, which is partly related to firms' substituting share repurchases for dividend payments.

31

Relation to GDP growth? Historical evidence on the gap between earnings (or dividends) and GDP growth is discouraging. Several recent studies show that per share earnings and dividends growth have, over long histories, lagged the pace of GDP growth and sometimes even per capita GDP growth (see **Exhibit 2.15**). **Exhibit 2.16** shows that between 1950 and 2009, earnings and dividends per share (EPS, DPS) growth rates almost matched the 1.9% real growth rate of GDP per capita but clearly lagged real GDP growth (3.1%).

- Taking longer histories or studying the global evidence does not help. The last row shows that the first half of the 20th century looked even worse for earnings and dividend growth. Dimson *et al.* (2002) show that, between

Exhibit 2.15. Cumulative Real Growth of U.S. Output and per Share Earnings and Dividends, 1900–2009

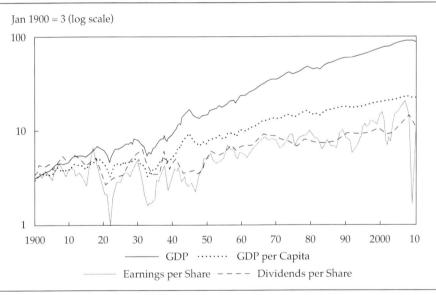

Jan 1900 = 3 (log scale)

——— GDP ········ GDP per Capita
——— Earnings per Share – – – – Dividends per Share

Sources: Arnott and Bernstein (2002), Haver Analytics.

Exhibit 2.16. Average Real Long-Term Growth Rates (Geometric Means) since 1900

	Real GDP	Real GDP per Capita	Real Earnings per Share	Real Dividends per Share
1950–2009	3.1%	1.9%	1.5%	1.3%
1900–1949	3.2%	1.8%	1.0%	1.0%

Sources: Arnott and Bernstein (2002), Haver Analytics.

1900 and 2000, real dividend growth lagged real GDP per capita growth in 15 of the 16 countries they examine. Across countries, real dividend growth averaged near zero and lagged real GDP per capita growth by 2.4 percentage points. U.S. dividend growth was somewhat better but still lagged real GDP per capita growth by 1.4 percentage points.

- Taking shorter histories did give a prettier picture, for a while. Between 1988 and 2007, U.S. real earnings per share growth averaged 3.7% per annum, clearly faster than the real GDP growth rate (2.4%). However, this was an exceptionally benign period for capital markets; for example, the corporate profits share of GDP rose from 8% to 11%. After 2008, the trailing 20-year real EPS growth rate was negative; after the 2009 recovery, it was still only 1.3%.

While many practitioners think that the GDP growth rate is a floor for earnings and dividend growth, historically it has been a ceiling that has been broken only during benign decades. In the long run, GDP and profits should have similar trend growth rates or else the corporate sector would eventually dominate the economy. Admittedly this argument is only relevant over extremely long periods. Nonetheless, it seems puzzling that earnings per share growth has lagged GDP and corporate profits growth by as much as it has. (The further gap between dividend and earnings growth rates is less puzzling because it may reflect declining payout rates—that is, the shift toward share buybacks.)

What explains these disappointing results? Arnott and Bernstein (2002) attribute them to the dynamic nature of entrepreneurial capitalism. New entrepreneurs and labor (including top management) capture a large share of economic growth at the expense of shareholders of existing companies. Stock market indices (made up of listed stocks) do not participate in all growth and, indeed, may miss the dynamic growth of yet unlisted start-up ventures, other small businesses, and sole proprietorships—all of which count toward total business profits.

- Aggregate earnings growth of the corporate sector (listed *and* unlisted firms) should better keep pace with aggregate GDP growth. Indeed, aggregate earnings and corporate profits have kept pace with GDP since the late 1940s—with real annual growth a little over 3% for all series. EPS growth lags because it does not include new enterprise creation.

- Total corporate profit growth is thus effectively diluted by net equity issuance. Bernstein and Arnott (2003) and Cornell (2010) show that the annual dilution rate (mainly through new business creation but also through net stock issuance of existing firms) since the 1920s is 2% and reasonably stable over time.

- Despite several studies confirming the underlying logic of the proposition, it is not widely appreciated that investors in existing listed stocks only capture part of aggregate profit growth because a portion of this growth is financed with newly issued equity. Cornell (2010) concludes that subtracting the 2% dilution effect from 3% real aggregate earnings growth makes 1% real EPS growth a realistic long-run prospect. Adding the dividend yield to this 1% gives a modest prospective real return for equities, though some claim that expected returns are better measured by arithmetic means, which exceed the geometric means (compound growth rates) used above. Arguing that the structural increase in repurchase rates is not fully included in these estimates is another way to increase the estimate of the expected return.[12]

Can we do better than using historical averages? Empirical studies find limited predictability in long-term aggregate dividend or earnings growth rates. Unpredictability means that the historical sample average may be the best estimate of future earnings growth. How long a sample? Exhibit 2.16 shows that very long windows point to lower estimates, while the Great Moderation period boosted this number. Here are some other ideas:

- Payout rates appear to have some ability to predict future growth, but the empirical relation is surprising to many. On theoretical grounds, low dividend payout rates should signal high future growth rates (because companies should hoard money, instead of paying it out in dividends, only if they have promising internal investment prospects), but the empirical experience has been exactly opposite.

- While dividend yields don't forecast dividend growth, the ratio of dividends to slow-moving macro variables like consumption or labor income does have predictive ability. That is, dividend growth predictability may be concealed by correlated variation between expected growth and expected returns. For example, in a recession, dividends may be temporarily depressed and expected to grow faster in the future, but this effect may be offset by a higher required risk premium. The former effect reduces the

---

[12]The debate on whether and how to include buybacks and dilution will not end soon. If the growing use of share repurchases is deemed to be a persistent structural change, we should ignore data starting in the 1920s and focus on evidence after the 1980s. Adding 0.5% to 1%, for buybacks net of dilution, to dividend yields, then adding the long-run DPS or EPS growth rate seems to me a reasonable approach to estimating prospective long-run real equity returns. Almost equivalently, we could use the current dividend yield together with a growth rate between EPS (real 1%) and aggregate earnings (real 3%). This latter alternative would count the net change in amount of shares in the growth term instead of the yield term, arguing that the net dilution from aggregate earnings growth is less than 2% in recent decades because large buybacks now offset more of the share issuance.

dividend yield, while the latter raises it. Using a control variable such as the consumption/wealth or consumption/dividends ratio in a regression, in addition to dividend yield, can uncover such cyclical predictability.

- The long-run rate of productivity growth is important because it deter-mines the potential earnings growth rate and because persistent changes in productivity growth should influence stock prices much more than cyclical changes. Economists can identify some time variation in the trend rate of productivity growth, but this is incredibly hard to measure in real time. We only understood in hindsight the 1970s decline in productivity, and there was later much debate about a renewed productivity increase in the 1990s, perhaps due to information technology and the Internet as well as the growth of the financial sector.

- Time variation in the profits/GDP ratio might be more predictable, given its apparent mean-reversion tendency. A high profit share—as in 2007, for example—may suggest that future profits growth will be slower. If this signal is used, it is worth recalling that corporate profits in national accounts and S&P earnings series are only imperfectly correlated; for example, the former peaked in 1997 and the latter in 2000.

- There are some signs that real earnings growth is higher when the inflation rate is low (but positive; deflation hurts earnings so much that even real earnings tend to be poor in a deflation) and when earnings volatility is low. **Exhibit 2.17** (column 3) reminds us, as we are often told in Wall Street research, that the arithmetic annual average of (nominal) earnings growth rates has been a relatively stable 7% over long periods. However, the compound average real growth rate is much lower, only 1% to 2%, due to volatility and inflation drags. The table also shows that the inflation drain has been larger since 1950 while the volatility drain was larger before 1950. Lower drains from inflation and volatility boosted real earnings after the mid-1980s, but this pattern has not been sustained.

Exhibit 2.17. Compound (Geometric Mean) and Simple Average (Arithmetic Mean) Growth Rates of Earnings per Share in the U.S.

	1	2	3	4 = 3 − 2	5 = 2 − 1
	Real Earnings (geometric mean)	Nominal Earnings (geometric mean)	Nominal Earnings (arithmetic mean)	Volatility Drain	Inflation Drain
1950–2009	1.5%	5.3%	6.7%	1.4%	3.8%
1900–1949	1.0%	3.2%	7.1%	3.9%	2.2%

Sources: Arnott and Bernstein (2002), Haver Analytics.

2.5. Survey-Based Subjective Expectations

Subjective *ex ante* equity returns may be based on direct return forecasts or on estimates of future growth (G); the latter may be combined with carry to arrive at estimates of the expected return. I first discuss investors' return forecasts, then academic views on the equity premium, and finally, economists' GDP forecasts and analysts' earnings growth predictions.

While there are many surveys of investors' equity market views, the questions are often qualitative—say, asking whether investors expect the market to go up or down. The main surveys that poll investors' numeric equity return forecasts are Duke University's quarterly CFO survey since 2000, the University of Michigan's consumer survey over 2000–2006, and the UBS/Gallup poll taken of individual investors over 1998–2003. The time horizons in these surveys differ, but a plot in **Exhibit 2.18** suggests that return optimism peaked in 1999–2000 and declined during the subsequent bear market. Short-horizon forecasts by retail investors appear to be particularly extrapolative, but even the CFOs' long-horizon forecasts reached double digits in 2000. This pattern stands in stark contrast to more objective, and inherently contrarian, *ex ante* measures that were quite low at the time given the high market valuations.

Retail investors: The Michigan survey's medium-term (two- to three-year) forecasts are higher following strong realized returns and during perceived good economic times. Moreover, when investors *expect* improving macroeconomic conditions, they tend to expect higher equity returns and lower volatility; this result provides direct evidence of procyclical expected Sharpe ratios. Amromin

Exhibit 2.18. Survey-Based Expected Equity Market Returns, 1998–2009

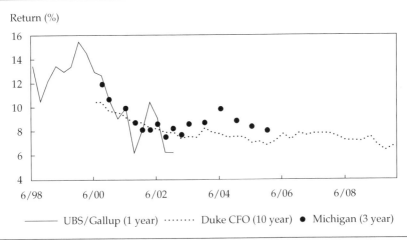

Sources: Vissing-Jorgensen (2003), Graham and Harvey (2010), Amromin and Sharpe (2009).

and Sharpe (2009) argue that these results lend support to behavioral explanations related to representativeness: optimism regarding the macroeconomy translates (too) directly into optimism about stock market prospects. Conversely, during recessions, retail investors have an unduly pessimistic view of the macroeconomy and equity markets; their selling drives down equity prices and causes equity expected returns to rise. In this way, low subjective return expectations "cause" high objective expected returns.

The UBS/Gallup poll focuses on even shorter-term expected returns—the next 12 months' equity market return—and finds extreme extrapolative tendencies. The correlation between this series and trailing 12-month equity returns is over 0.9. The predicted 10-year returns in this poll are more stable and high, hovering around 14% between 1998 and 2002. Most survey questions stress the near-term outlook, however.

Another survey (polling individual investors on what they consider respectable rates of return on their investments) documents even more extreme exuberance during the end of the tech boom: The Securities Industry Association's annual survey reports that between 1999 and 2003, median, year-by-year "respectable" stock returns were 30%, 33%, 19%, 13%, and 10%.

Professional investors: Portfolio managers and CFOs may be more cool headed than retail investors and have more countercyclical views when making long-run forecasts. Institutional investors in Bank of America Merrill Lynch's global fund manager survey are polled on the equity risk premium they use to assess equity valuations. The ERP started at 3.6% in July 2006, edged lower and troughed near the global market peak in late 2007 at 3.4%, then rose to a peak of 4.0% in late 2008 before edging back to 3.8% in 2009. Graham and Harvey (2010), who conduct the Duke CFO surveys, provide an even longer series of views on the equity–bond premium. They report that the expected ERP started above 4% in 2000, troughed at 2.4% in 2005, then rose again and peaked at 4.7% in early 2009 amidst the financial crisis. They also document a strong positive relation with market volatility (a high survey premium when the VIX is high, as **Exhibit 2.19** shows; the correlation was 0.61) but little extrapolation bias or correlation with market valuation levels.

These survey measures suggest that the relative sentiment of retail investors compared with institutional investors may be a useful contrarian indicator for aggregate market timing. Edelen, Marcus, and Tehranian (2010) survey the literature. They focus on a more direct measure of relative sentiment and show that when the share of retail investable wealth held in equity relative to the share of total investable wealth held in equity is high (low), subsequent stock market returns tend to be low (high).

37

Exhibit 2.19. Expected Long-Term Equity–Bond Premium and Equity Market Volatility, 2000–2009

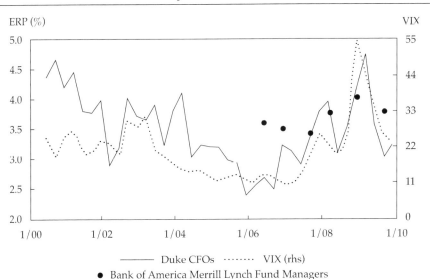

Sources: Bank of America Merrill Lynch, Graham and Harvey (2010), Bloomberg.

Academics: Even academic views on the equity premium have evolved during the past decade—perhaps reflecting a shift from basing equity premium estimates on historical average returns to basing them on forward-looking analysis like the DDM. Ivo Welch has polled hundreds of finance professors about their view on the equity premium on four occasions: 1997–1998, August 2001, December 2007, and January 2009. His main survey question focuses on the (arithmetic) 30-year equity premium (over short-dated Treasury bills, so the premium is slightly higher than the equity–bond premium). The mean premium fell from the first survey's 7% to 5.5% in 2001, then edged up to 5.7% in 2007 and 6.0% in 2009. Academics' forecasts of one-year equity–bill outperformance fell sharply from 6% to 7% in the first survey to 3% in 2001 before recovering to 4.9% in 2007 and 6.2% in 2009. Interestingly, near-term forecasts were reduced after a large market selloff in 2000–2001, while the opposite happened after the 2008 selloff. Fernandez (2009) surveyed an even broader set of finance professors, finding an average expected premium of 6.3% among U.S. academics and 5.3% among European academics. He also finds a 7% mean premium among academics who cite classic textbooks and sources of historical average premia (Ibbotson yearbooks) as references but a mean of only 5% among those who cite newer references, highlighting the influence of personal history (specifically, where, when, and how a given person learned about the ERP) on current thinking. In a subsequent survey, he finds an average required market risk premium near 5% among analysts and 5.5% among corporate executives.

Economists' GDP forecasts: Expected long-term growth estimates may be based on economists' real GDP forecasts or analysts' (nominal) earnings growth forecasts. Consensus long-term real GDP forecasts have been relatively stable, fluctuating between 2.3% and 3.5% for the past 25 years. Earnings and dividend growth forecasts are often mechanically tied to the GDP growth forecasts, at least beyond the first 5 to 10 years.

Analysts' earnings forecasts: More commonly, studies use analysts' long-term earnings forecasts even if these have been historically upward biased, presumably due to behavioral biases and analyst incentives. Moreover, **Exhibit 2.20** is indicative of time-varying analyst sentiment. Analyst forecasts are almost as procyclical as retail investors' return forecasts. Both in the U.S. and in Europe, analysts' consensus forecasts peaked above 16% in 2000—more than 10 percentage points above nominal GDP forecasts at the time—and fell significantly during the 2000–2003 bear market and again in 2008–2009. The thin line shows one natural benchmark—economists' consensus forecast of long-term output growth, which have been pretty sensible. Note that equity premium estimates that rely on analyst forecasts will inherit their overoptimism.

Exhibit 2.20. Analyst Forecasts of Long-Term Earnings Growth Are Overoptimistic (but Less Than in 2000)

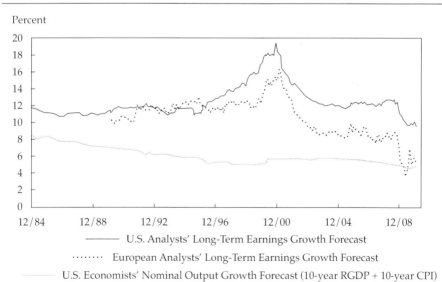

Sources: Citigroup, Credit Suisse, *Blue Chip Economic Indicators.*

Surveys provide direct estimates of changing return expectations, but they may reflect wishful thinking rather than required returns. We can contrast *objectively feasible* return prospects and less rational *subjective* expectations. Are survey-based risk-premium estimates useful proxies for the equity risk premium that the market requires? One can always question how representative any survey is of market views. More importantly, because of behavioral biases, survey-based expected returns may tell us more about hoped-for returns than about required returns—and these hopes tend to rise in bull markets, despite rising valuations. Retail investors' short-term forecasts appear more prone to extrapolation and procyclicality than those of finance professionals, leaving open the question of what impact such biases have on aggregate market pricing.

As a light-hearted exercise I create a proxy of investors' subjective return expectations by combining three irrational factors: extrapolation of past market returns, long-term earnings growth forecasts by analysts, and money illusion. The composite series troughed in 1981, exactly when a successful market timer should have bought, and peaked in 2000, when the timer should have sold. The composite series is, not very surprisingly, in line with market valuation ratios and gives almost perfectly wrong forecasts. All three proxies contributed to the increase in return expectations in the 1980s and 1990s. My composite series lines up reasonably well with the limited data we have on the equity returns that investors say they expected and has a correlation of −0.9 with the "objective" market earnings yield and the "objective" equity premium proxy. If we take these estimates seriously, it appears that subjective and objective expected returns are very much inversely related.

2.6. Tactical Forecasting for Market Timing

Both professional and amateur investors have tried to "time" equity markets as long as markets have existed. Some do fundamental analysis on economic/profit prospects or the monetary policy outlook ("don't fight the Fed"), others focus on technical indicators and price momentum ("don't fight the tape"), while others rely on slow-moving valuation indicators ("buy low P/Es, sell high") as discussed above. However, tactical market timing gradually earned a bad name as a mug's game because very few investors were consistently successful doing it. It is not easy, and its bets are highly concentrated; at least security selection strategies can benefit from wide diversification. Finally, if the long-run equity premium is large, it requires considerable market timing ability to offset the disadvantage of being in cash part of the time and forfeiting the ERP at those times.

By the 1980s, academic research on "anomalies" had hinted that market timing might add value. Rising inflation and interest rates appeared to predict poor equity market returns, average returns were seasonally high in January and cyclically high after business cycle troughs, and volatility seemed excessive given a model of rational investors and constant expected returns. Academic studies reporting long-horizon return predictability using dividend yields, term spreads, and default spreads attracted much attention but were challenged on econometric grounds.

The 1990s mantra of buy-and-hold investing gave way to renewed interest in market timing after the repeated boom–bust cycles of the 2000s. The tech stock bubble and the later credit/housing bubble indicated that absolute market valuations can deviate from fundamental values by large amounts and for extended periods. Yet, they also made it clear that exploiting such misvaluations was difficult, because few investors had the patience to stay with a bearish stance through a lengthy bull market. **Exhibit 2.21** highlights the best-known relation—the ability of market valuation ratios to predict future equity market returns—which has been popularized by Robert Shiller.

Exhibit 2.21 shows that buying stocks when market valuations are cheap tends to produce much better returns than buying when valuations are rich. Of course, such contrarian market timing takes nerve and sometimes fails; that is why the relation is there. (To be fair, the strength of the timing ability is

Exhibit 2.21. Future Equity Returns Are Higher When the Market's Starting Valuations Are Cheap, 1900–2009

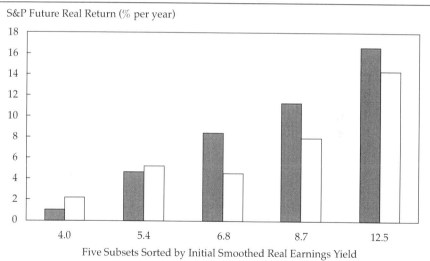

S&P Future Real Return (% per year)

Five Subsets Sorted by Initial Smoothed Real Earnings Yield

■ 1 Year Ahead   □ 5 Years Ahead

Note: The graph is created by sorting each month into one of five buckets based on the level of real E10/P at the beginning of the month and then computing average level for E10/P (*x*-axis labels) and subsequent 1-year and 5-year real stock market returns (*y*-axis values) in these five subsets of the history.

Sources: Robert Shiller's website (www.econ.yale.edu/~shiller), Haver Analytics.

overstated in the graph because I use hindsight, specifically in-sample knowledge of the range of E/P outcomes. Investors in 1921 and 1932 did not know in real time that the E/Ps prevailing in those years would be the highest of the whole period between 1900 and 2009.) The reason for predictability has long been debated: rational time-varying risk premia and irrational investor sentiment have been the main alternatives. Worse, while practitioners and academics kept coming up with new market-timing indicators—many of them listed below—few performed well "out of sample." For example, low dividend yields emitted a bearish timing signal as early as the early 1990s, and naïve market timers following such signals would have missed the massive equity rally of 1995–1999. This poor out-of-sample performance raised the possibility that any appearance of predictability was due to data mining. Thus, it is understandable that many observers remain skeptical about the usefulness of market timing.

▓ *Short- and long-horizon predictive ability*

As a basic measure of an indicator's market-timing ability, **Exhibit 2.22** shows the simple correlation between a host of predictors and the subsequent (next quarter, one year, and five year) excess return of the S&P 500 equity index over Treasury bills between 1962 and 2009. This is an in-sample measure and

Exhibit 2.22. Correlations with Future Excess Return of S&P 500, 1962–2009

	Horizon		
	Next Quarter	Next Year	Next 5 Years
Dividend yield (D/P)	0.11	0.23	0.35
Real smoothed earnings yield (E10/P)	0.10	0.19	0.34
GDP/stock market capitalization	0.15	0.24	0.42
Yield curve	0.12	0.20	0.37
Short-rate momentum	−0.10	−0.10	−0.12
Long-rate momentum	−0.15	−0.15	−0.11
Consumption–wealth ratio (CAY)	0.21	0.40	0.69
Broker-dealer leverage growth	−0.20	−0.10	0.08
ISM business confidence	−0.21	−0.20	−0.32
Unemployment rate	0.15	0.21	0.53
Real GDP growth rate (10-year average)	−0.15	−0.23	−0.51
Stock market volatility (60-day)	0.05	0.07	0.03

Sources: Haver Analytics, Robert Shiller's website (www.econ.yale.edu/~shiller), Amit Goyal's website (www.hec.unil.ch/agoyal/docs/PredictorData2010.xls), author's calculations.

can be misleading if the correlations are not stable over time. Note, though, that most academic studies rely on such in-sample relations; econometricians simply *assume* that any observed statistical relation between predictors and subsequent market returns was known to rational investors already in real time. Practitioners who find this assumption unrealistic try to avoid the in-sample bias by selecting and/or estimating statistical models repeatedly using only data that were available at each point in time so as to assess predictability in a quasi-out-of-sample sense, but never completely succeeding in doing so.

Valuations: Various valuation ratios have predictive correlations between 10% and 20% for the next quarter.[13] Perhaps more importantly, their correlation with long-horizon returns is much higher, but these results are especially plagued with econometric problems. Dividend yields adjusted for net buybacks have the best timing ability, but data for this variable are only available since the 1980s. Different variants of earnings yields (raw or smoothed trailing, forward-looking, adjusted) and of the Fed Model (the earnings yield versus the Treasury yield) also have reasonably consistent positive correlations, as have ratios of GDP and corporate profits to equity market capitalization.

Money and credit: Monetary policy indicators have quite mild predictive correlations. The old adage "Follow the Fed" reflects the idea that easy monetary policy—falling or low real short rates and a steep yield curve—is bullish for equities. However, the Fed's increasing transparency and predictability may have reduced any such delayed effects, and these patterns are not evident in data after the mid-1980s. The impact of inflation has also become weak over time (not shown).

Secular credit and leverage developments appear to be important drivers of asset markets. Positive feedback effects can be important in credit creation and contraction, and in related asset valuation changes over the business cycle, but these patterns also operate at lower frequencies. Empirically, the growth of broker-dealer balance sheet leverage has been a strong predictor of aggregate market returns. In Exhibit 2.22 the quarter-ahead correlation is −0.20 but the

---

[13] Some indicators (D/P, the Fed Model) have much higher correlations for two subsamples than for the full sample, but this may reflect one insidious aspect of hindsight in in-sample correlations. Both predictors experienced a large mean shift between the two subsamples; for example, the mean D/P halved from near 4% to near 2%. Correlation measures the covariation of D/P's deviation from the sample mean with that of the subsequent return's deviation from the sample mean. "Knowing" with foresight that the sample mean fell sharply after the mid-1980s would have improved the econometrician's forecasting ability, just as it would have improved the trading success of anyone buying (selling) equities when the D/P was above (below) the sample mean. An econometrician who only knew the full-sample mean D/P (near 3%) or a market timer who incorrectly sold equities when D/P fell below 3% in the early 1990s would have underperformed his more hindsighted counterpart.

43

number is –0.35 since the mid-1980s (approximately the pivot point of the transformation in the U.S. from bank-based intermediation to a market-based financial system). Adrian, Moench, and Shin (2010) show that aggressive levering by financial intermediaries is a sign of strong risk appetites and low prospective returns, while deleveraging episodes signal high risk aversion and bode well for subsequent returns. On the other hand, Chava, Park, and Gallmeyer (2010) show that tightening credit conditions, measured by the Fed's survey of senior loan officers, predicts lower near-term stock market returns. Thus, both excessively loose credit conditions and recent tightening in these conditions are bearish market-timing signals. These patterns may seem mutually inconsistent, but in fact, they echo the long-term reversal (due to overreaction) and short-term momentum (due to underreaction) patterns observed in many asset return series.

Real activity: Business cycle indicators are classic equity market predictors. While equities have some ability to predict future growth developments, the opposite relation is more controversial. The consumption-to-wealth ratio (CAY) is the strongest predictor—with a 21% correlation with next-quarter equity returns and a much higher correlation over long windows. Yet, CAY is based on in-sample fit, so its values would not have been available to investors in real time. Cooper and Priestley (2009) find that an output gap measure has an in-sample correlation of –0.22 and an out-of-sample correlation of –0.14 with next-quarter equity returns. Thus, near-term expected equity returns are predictably high in recessionary environments and low in boom times. In the same vein, the unemployment rate has a 0.15 correlation with next-quarter equity returns; manufacturing confidence (Institute for Supply Management, or ISM), –0.21; and consumer confidence (Conference Board), –0.14. Both the past year's and past decade's average real GDP growth and economists' consensus forecast of future GDP growth have correlations around –0.11 to –0.13 with next-quarter equity returns.

- Such cyclical indicators may have worked especially well in the second half of the 20th century when business cycles were driven by countercyclical Fed policy actions but work less well when recessions are caused by financial de-risking and de-leveraging. Broader indices of financial conditions may serve better now (and are likewise countercyclical; favorable financial conditions augur low future returns).

- Over a longer horizon, persistent strong economic growth and a low unemployment rate predict low stock market returns.

- One rational interpretation is that the cyclical asset return predictability reflects the high required equity risk premium during bad times when investors' risk aversion is especially high. Many studies document counter-cyclical *ex ante* Sharpe ratios based on valuation ratios or yield curve steepness and then assume that such predictability reflects investors' rational risk assessments and preferences. While I firmly believe that wealth-dependent risk aversion (implying countercyclical required returns) is an important real-world phenomenon, I also believe that psychological factors exacerbate boom–bust cycles. At least retail investors' subjective return expectations exhibit procyclical expected Sharpe ratios in a manner consistent with behavioral sentiment stories.

Risk: Looking at various risk indicators, the relation between equity market volatility and subsequent market returns is famously fragile. The *contemporaneous* correlation between volatility news and equity returns is strongly negative, but the *predictive* relation is weak—see the single-digit correlations in the table. Here, I just note the Pollet and Wilson (2010) finding that the weak empirical relation reflects two offsetting effects. Equity market volatility reflects both the average volatility of individual equities and the average correlation among equities. The latter part is more important: high intra-equity-market correlation—typical during market crises—predicts high future market returns (with a correlation of 0.20). In contrast, high average time-series variance of individual equities mildly predicts low future market returns and thus conceals a systematic relation between risk and returns. It also appears that the gap between implied and realized volatilities has some timing ability.

Sentiment and technicals: Besides the long-run valuation indicators, a host of contrarian sentiment indicators have attracted attention. Baker and Wurgler (2006) identify several sentiment indicators—for example, the share of equities in new corporate issuance, market turnover, as well as IPO market activity and pricing—and create a composite indicator with a predictive correlation of −0.11. Among practitioner work, the Crowd Sentiment Poll of Ned Davis Research combines timing signals from stock market newsletters, individual investors, commodity advisers, and put–call ratios. Other potentially useful momentum-style technical indicators include net volume, breadth, fund flow momentum, and lead–lag relations (say, from core markets to peripheral ones or from large caps to small caps). However, short-term contrarian trading is difficult in markets that exhibit any momentum bias. Equity market momentum is mild, but trend-following models have had some success in market timing. Retail flows have the best ability to serve as contrarian indicators; see Trim Tabs (2010) for short-term flows and Edelen *et al* (2010) for long-term flows.

Seasonals: The best-known seasonal regularities are January and Halloween effects (respectively: higher average returns in January, especially for small-cap stocks; and higher returns in November–April than in May–October). Research also documents higher average returns around major holidays, the turn of month, and days of scheduled macroeconomic news announcements. Few of these seasonal patterns can be profitably exploited due to high turnover and trading costs, but they are a puzzle for risk-based explanations and especially for models with constant relative risk aversion. Repeated data mining of the same history must have contributed to some of these findings.

Market timing is not easy; it requires judicious choices to leave risky assets *and* later re-enter the market at lower levels, if such levels are reached. It involves a high tolerance of regret and of being "wrong and alone" for a long time. Still, the last decade's experience has, rightly, made many investors reconsider the wisdom of static market exposures. Even if expected returns vary over time, it may not be advisable for a typical investor to change the optimal risky-asset mix. But large, long-horizon investors arguably have a natural edge in contrarian market timing, because in bad times, their risk aversion does not rise as much as that of most investors. At a minimum, disciplined rebalancing to constant weights implies a mild contrarian bias that tends to add value in the long run.

3. Bond Risk Premium

- The bond risk premium (BRP) or term premium is the expected return advantage of long-duration government bonds over short-term (one-period) bonds.

- The yield curve reflects both the BRP and the market's interest rate expectations. Yield curve steepness is a noisy measure of either part. Better BRP proxies try to isolate out the unobservable rate expectations from the curve.

- Historical average returns increase with duration, especially at short durations. The realized average excess return is about 1% but is higher during periods when falling yields give unexpected windfall gains.

- Empirically the yield curve has been a better predictor of near-term excess bond returns than of future yield changes. Survey data hint that much of the predictability in the bond market may reflect expectational errors rather than rational BRPs.

- The yield curve is not able to predict multi-year excess bond returns. It may be a poor BRP proxy because mean-reverting rate expectations dominate curve steepness when short-term rates are exceptionally high or low. High inflation and yield levels are associated with falling rate expectations but with elevated bond risk premia. These forces tend to push the curve shape in opposite directions and offset each other. The clearest example of this tension occurred in 1980–1982 when the curve was inverted but the required *ex ante* BRP was high—as were subsequent realized bond returns in the 1980s.

- Since rate expectations taint the information about the BRP in the yield curve, a natural solution is to estimate the rate expectations—for example, with the help of survey data—and subtract them from bond yields.

- The survey-based BRP has been primarily driven by a level-dependent inflation premium—rising in the 1960s and 1970s from near zero to 3% to 4% and falling back in the 1980s and 1990s. Other key drivers of the BRP are safe-haven, supply/demand, and cyclical factors. Since the late 1990s, the safe-haven role of Treasuries (negative stock market beta) has contributed to a negative BRP. Overall, the *ex ante* BRP has been near zero through the 2000s but could well rise in the 2010s.

- Duration timing models predict near-term bond returns. A steep yield curve, weak economic growth, or weak equity markets, as well as positive bond market momentum, have historically been bullish indicators.

3.1. Introduction, Terminology, and Theories

The bond risk premium is the *ex ante* excess return of a default-free long-term bond over holding a sequence of short-term bonds, or loosely speaking, the required reward for duration extension. A one-period variant of the BRP is the next-period expected excess return of a long-term bond over the one-period riskless bond. The BRP is also called the term premium, horizon premium, maturity premium, or duration premium. The terminology used in the literature varies, but I distinguish the BRP (the expected term premium) from the realized average excess bond return and from yield curve steepness (term spread). The BRP needs to be estimated, but the latter two are directly observable.

Analysis of the BRP is typically done using government bond data because the BRP compensates for the uncertainty in default-free yields (uncertain discount rates). Other bonds' yields also reflect issuers' uncertain creditworthiness or otherwise uncertain cash flows as well as possible illiquidity premia.

After a section on terminology and theories, I present evidence on historical average returns. In the case of bonds, such rearview-mirror evidence is obviously less important because *market yields provide relatively transparent information on prospective or expected nominal returns.* Even this picture can be surprisingly murky, so *a key focus in this chapter is to identify useful ways to extract information about bond risk premia from the yield curve.*

Approximate Identities

I first describe some identities (which are less ambiguous) and then discuss theories and evidence (which are more open to debate).[14] For illustration, I use a 10-year maturity to represent the long bond and a 1-year maturity for the short-term rate. The choice of a one-year horizon lets me ignore annualization terms in the exposition.

Realized and expected (excess) bond return

The realized bond return (H) over a year has two components: the yield income earned over time and the capital gain or loss due to yield changes:

$$H_{10} \approx Y_{10} - \text{Duration}_{10} \times \Delta Y_{10}. \tag{2}$$

---

[14]The identities are actually approximations because I ignore small compounding effects, convexity effects, coupons, and bond aging/rolldown effects. The analysis would be more accurate if I used continuously compounded zero-coupon rates. However, the basic ideas work as good approximations and, because I do not restrict my analysis to zero-coupon issues, apply to popular traded assets. Both on-the-run bonds and interest rate swaps closely resemble coupon-bearing par bonds (bonds whose coupon rate equals the market yield), and there are straightforward mathematical mappings between par, zero-coupon (spot), and forward rate curves.

We can subtract the return of the short-term asset (Y_1) and take expectations to get a variant of the bond risk premium related to near-term *returns*:

$$\text{BRP}_H \equiv E(\text{excess bond return over the riskless rate for next year})$$
$$\approx (Y_{10} - Y_1) - \text{Duration}_{10} \times E(\Delta Y_{10}). \tag{3}$$

Bond yield

Here is a brief explanation of how bond yields reflect the market's rate expectations and required risk premia. Break-even (forward) rates are, by construction, a sequence of future short rates such that an investor rolling over short-term securities at those rates would earn exactly the same return as the long bond. If investors are risk neutral, these break-even rates equal the market's expectations and the long yield equals the expected average of future short rates. If investors are, instead, risk averse, the long yield also contains a risk-premium term. This observation merely states a consistency requirement for expectations: if the market long-term yield is currently high while future short-term yields are expected to be low, and if yields are equal to expected returns, then the long-term bond yield includes a positive premium. Assuming investor rationality, that premium, or higher expected return, is what investors require as compensation for some perceived risk, so we call it a risk premium:

10-year yield ≈ Expected average 1-year rate over the next decade

+ Bond risk premium

or

$$Y_{10} \approx E(\text{avgY}_1) + \text{BRP}_Y. \tag{4}$$

This BRP_Y is the average expected return of the bond *over its life* in excess of a sequence of riskless one-year investments. The two BRP variants, BRP_Y and BRP_H, are closely related: BRP_Y is an average of the bond's expected future BRP_H each year (a 10-year bond's BRP_H for the coming year, 9 year bond's BRP_H for the following year, etc.). I will not make a distinction between these two variants outside this subsection.

We can further slice nominal rate expectations into inflation and real rate expectations, averaged over the next decade:

Expected average 1-year rate = Expected average inflation

+ Expected average *real* 1-year rate

or

$$E(\text{avgY}_1) = E(\text{avgInf}) + E(\text{avgR}_1). \tag{5}$$

49

Combining the two equations above, we get our three-way decomposition of 10-year yield:

$$Y_{10} \approx E(avgInf) + E(avgR_1) + BRP_Y. \tag{6}$$

Curve steepness

The decomposition of yield curve steepness follows easily:

$$
\begin{aligned}
YC &\equiv Y_{10} - Y_1 \\
&\approx \left[E(avgY_1) - Y_1 \right] + BRP_Y \\
&= E(\Delta avgY_1) + BRP_Y.
\end{aligned} \tag{7}
$$

Alternatively, we can rearrange the BRP_H Equation 3 to get:

$$YC \approx Duration_{10} \times E(\Delta Y_{10}) + BRP_H. \tag{8}$$

A steep curve reflects either market expectations of rising yields or high required bond risk premia—or, more likely, some combination of the two. The rate-expectation component can be expressed either in terms of expected multi-year changes in the 1-year yield over the next decade or, alternatively, the expected next-year change in the 10-year yield, scaled by its (end-of-horizon) duration. The first yield curve equation focuses on gradual changes in short rates and the yield-based BRP_Y, while the second equation focuses on near-term changes in long yields and the return-based BRP_H.

▨ *Alternative theories*

Which of the two components has a larger influence on the yield curve shape? To interpret the yield curve, one can usefully contrast the classic pure expectations hypothesis (PEH) with the random walk hypothesis. The PEH makes the extreme assumption that risk premia are zero and is consistent with the idea of investor risk neutrality. One can then virtually read the market's rate expectations off the yield curve (specifically, off the forward rate curve). Suppose a particularly steep yield curve indicates that, according to the PEH, the market expects short rates to rise quickly over time (to exactly offset longer bonds' initial yield advantage; thus, all bond investments have the same expected return). The random walk hypothesis makes the *opposite* extreme assumption, that an upward-sloping yield curve only reflects required compensation for bearing duration risk and does not contain any information at all about the market's rate expectations. Since both the market's rate expectations and required risk premia are *unobservable*, economists have long debated the relative importance of the two components.

Both hypotheses have had their days in the sun. For decades, investors and central bankers seemed to take the PEH as a given, as they equated forward rates with the market's rate expectations, despite accumulating contrary evidence. Yet, when empirical studies in the 1980s ran direct horse races between the two hypotheses, they clearly supported the random walk hypothesis: an upward-sloping yield curve predicts empirically high future excess bond returns rather than rising yields. It is ironic that just as risk premia became smaller in the past decade, gradually making the PEH a more realistic approximation of yield curve behavior, consensus shifted away from the PEH and toward time-varying risk premia. The pendulum shifted too far; I will argue that mean-reverting rate expectations have a greater role in yield curve behavior than the current academic consensus appreciates.

A few words on modern term structure models. So-called arbitrage models of term structure are, by design, silent on the determinants of bond risk premia in that they focus on relative pricing and take current market prices of risk as a given. So-called equilibrium models at least link the premia to interest rate volatility, and the idea of covariance with bad times always lurks in the background. Such models can be mathematically complex, but still most "only" imply constant risk premia. For understanding the determinants of expected returns, I find empirically oriented models, such as that of Campbell, Sunderam, and Viceira (2009), more relevant than either pure term structure models or so-called macro-finance models.

3.2. Historical Average Returns

Exhibits 3.1 and 3.2 present the longest available history of monthly returns for a broad set of maturity-subsector portfolios of U.S. Treasury bills and bonds—from 1952 to 2009. Importantly, this is also a reasonably neutral period, in that bond yields ended the period at roughly the level where they started. Thus, average return differences largely reflect *ex ante* yield spreads rather than unexpected yield changes. The starting point is also guided by data availability for multiple maturities and by the end (in 1952 with the Treasury–Fed accord) of a decade-long period of regulated (capped) Treasury yields.

Clearly, the risk–reward relation is positive, but the more interesting pattern is that the relation is quite nonlinear.[15] In my earlier research, I claimed that the long-run risk–reward relation in the Treasury market looks like a hockey stick: very steep up to two years and flat thereafter. Also, for the longer sample used

---

[15] One can display average returns as geometric or arithmetic means and relate either to the volatility of total returns or of excess returns over the one-month bill. Exhibit 3.1 shows that arithmetic means and the volatility of excess returns make the reward–risk relation more linear. The 1952–2009 period is also not quite neutral because short rates fell and long rates rose, on net, during the sample period; that is, the curve steepened. Adjusting for the sample-specific yield changes would boost the longest portfolio's return and make the average return curve flat after the five-year maturity (geometric mean near 6.5%).

51

Exhibit 3.1. **Long-Run Reward for Bearing the Risk of Longer-Maturity Treasuries, 1952–2009**

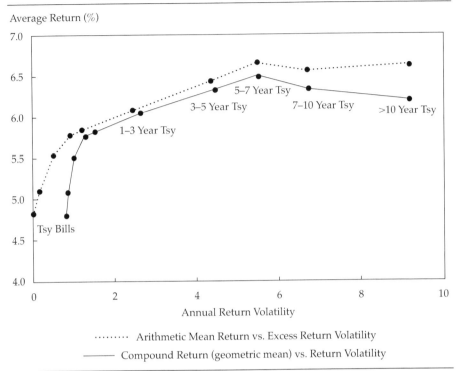

.... Arithmetic Mean Return vs. Excess Return Volatility

————— Compound Return (geometric mean) vs. Return Volatility

Note: Tsy = Treasury.
Sources: Bank of America Merrill Lynch, Center for Research in Security Prices, Ibbotson Associates (Morningstar).

here, the reward for extending duration is highest at short maturities and decays at longer maturities. Indeed, the Sharpe ratios at short maturities exceed 1 (if the one-month Treasury bill is used as the riskless rate) and decline monotonically from the shortest to the longest portfolios. The hockey-stick shape is more attenuated in subperiods of the sample during which longer-duration bonds benefited from falling yields and where the richness of the shortest Treasury bills was less extreme.

What about yield data? Looking at average yield curve shapes—e.g., the Fed's fitted Treasury curves since 1961—tells a similar story. Average yields rise monotonically between one-year and seven-year durations (corresponding roughly to 1-year and 10-year maturities) and are 0.8 percentage points higher

Exhibit 3.2. Exhibit 3.1 in Numbers

	1 Mo	0–3 Mo	3–6 Mo	6–9 Mo	9–12 Mo	1–3 Yr	3–5 Yr	5–7 Yr	7–10 Yr	10 Yr+
Arithmetic mean	4.81	5.09	5.52	5.76	5.83	6.07	6.42	6.63	6.55	6.61
Geometric mean	4.80	5.08	5.51	5.75	5.81	6.04	6.31	6.47	6.32	6.17
Return volatility	0.82	0.88	1.05	1.31	1.54	2.66	4.45	5.52	6.75	9.16
Mean excess return	0.00	0.28	0.71	0.96	1.02	1.27	1.61	1.82	1.75	1.81
Excess return volatility	0.00	0.18	0.55	0.94	1.24	2.50	4.36	5.45	6.69	9.13
Sharpe ratio	NA	1.55	1.30	1.02	0.82	0.51	0.37	0.33	0.26	0.20
Mean duration (approx.)	0.1	0.1	0.4	0.6	0.8	1.6	3.5	4.8	6.0	10.0

Sources: Bank of America Merrill Lynch, Center for Research in Security Prices, Ibbotson Associates (Morningstar).

for the long duration than the short duration (6.7% vs. 5.9%). These yield curve histories miss the curvatures that appear below 1 year and beyond 10 years.[16]

Large changes in the overall yield level can cause capital losses or gains that overwhelm *ex ante* expected returns even over relatively long horizons.[17] Whenever we study historical bond data, the results are dominated by the persistent yield increases until 1981 and decline thereafter. **Exhibit 3.3** contrasts the return–volatility scatterplots for the first and second halves of the 58-year sample. The reward–risk relation was steeply upward sloping in recent decades but downward sloping (beyond money market or very short maturities) in the earlier period. Bond return volatility was also higher during the second sub-period (visually, the average return curve extends further to the right).

---

[16] Arithmetic average bond returns at intermediate maturities are 0.3–0.5 percentage points higher than average yields because they benefit from the *rolldown effect*. For example, a five-year duration bond has, on average, a 0.1% higher yield than the four-year bond; as a bond ages and becomes a 4-year bond, its yield falls even if the yield curve stays unchanged (the bond is "rolling down the yield curve"), resulting in a roughly 0.4% capital gain (rolldown return ≈ duration times rolldown yield decline). Rolldown returns tend to be largest at intermediate maturities because at the front end, curve steepness creates a smaller rolldown effect due to short duration, whereas at the back end, a long duration can even hurt because there, the yield curve is often mildly inverted.

[17] The *ex ante* expected return reflects initial yield spreads and rolldown returns, perhaps adjusted for expected yield changes. I will ignore here the value of convexity, that is, the expected economic value of the nonlinearity in a bond's price–yield relation. The effect is quite small unless yield volatility is extremely high and/or bond duration is very long.

Exhibit 3.3.   Treasury Market Reward and Risk during Two Subperiods

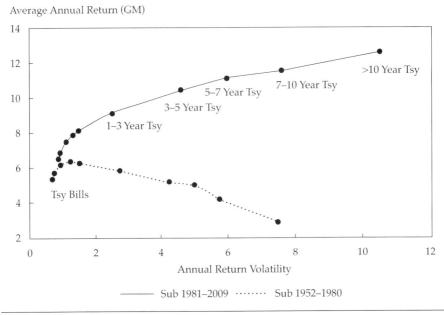

Average Annual Return (GM)

Sub 1981–2009 ········ Sub 1952–1980

Note: Tsy = Treasury.

Sources: Bank of America Merrill Lynch, Center for Research in Security Prices, Ibbotson Associates (Morningstar).

Box 2. Front-End Treasury Richness

Average Sharpe ratios are especially high at short maturities, and the reward–risk curve is very steep at the front end (with longer maturities providing higher returns) even in the bond-bearish subsample. Private-issuer curves in the money market tend to be much flatter. Duration extension from one-month Treasury bills looks like a no-brainer.

• Why did the opportunity arise in the first place? (The past tense seems appropriate because this opportunity has declined steadily since the mid-1980s, except in 2007–2008.) The main reason was the limited desire of natural holders of short-dated Treasury bills to maximize return. Foreign central banks and other buyers—who parked their money into short Treasury bills due to regulatory reasons, liquidity needs, or sheer laziness—have, over recent decades, learned to put more emphasis on asset returns instead of safety and liquidity goals. The opportunity cost of only seeking safety at the expense of return conservatism became increasingly apparent as flight-to-quality spikes in money market spreads were seldom seen—until 2007 and 2008.

- Why did arbitrageurs not remove this opportunity? Investors other than short-term Treasury bill holders (and the U.S. Treasury as the debt issuer) were unable to exploit this opportunity because they could not sell short 1-month Treasury bills to buy 6- to 12-month bills. These arbitrageurs faced a financing rate that was much higher than the one-month Treasury bill rate; markets were effectively segmented. The main way to eliminate this opportunity was for conservative investors to become less conservative; as a group, they could influence the relative price of different money market assets. This happened gradually between the mid-1980s and the mid-2000s, so it took some time for conservative investors to become sufficiently conscious of the opportunity costs they were incurring. And perhaps they went too far, given the reappearance of extreme safe-haven premia during the 2007–2008 systemic financial crisis.

Enough on historical bond returns. Forward-looking or expectational measures of bond returns can tell us more about whether the reward for duration extension is currently high or low. I turn next to such measures, covering various longer-term *ex ante* proxies for the bond risk premium and ending with more-tactical forecasting models.

3.3. Alternative *Ex Ante* Measures of the BRP

I discuss four *ex ante* measures: curve steepness and three smarter measures of the bond risk premium (BRP):

▧ *Yield curve steepness (YC)*

Yield curve steepness is the simplest and most popular proxy for the *ex ante* BRP, but it has its flaws. Since the shape of the yield curve reflects the market's expectations of future rate changes as well as the required BRP, it is desirable to separate rate change expectations from the BRP. Some alternative measures below try to isolate the BRP component by purging the rate-expectation component from the YC.

▧ *Empirical BRP estimates predicted by the forward rate curve (C–P BRP)*

Cochrane and Piazzesi (2005) find an even better predictor of future bond returns than the YC, loosely related to yield curve curvature. They regress subsequent realized bond returns on five one-year-forward rates (the marginal discount rates for the first, second, third, fourth and fifth years in the term structure) and find that across maturities, all bonds' returns seem to be predicted by the same single forecasting factor. I label this factor the "C–P BRP." The slope coefficients on the five forward rates have a neatly symmetric tent-shape (−2.1, +0.8, +3.0, +0.8, −2.1), peaking at the forward rate between two and three years. The forward rate between four and five years has a negative coefficient, suggesting that yield curve curvature rather than steepness predicts returns. The more curved (humped) the forward rate curve is, the higher the expected excess return of all long bonds. The authors later find that this expected return factor, C–P BRP, is a reward for the first empirical factor that drives the yield curve (changes in the level of the curve). This factor is most likely related to persistent changes in inflation expectations and productivity that influence all yields roughly equally across maturities. Other empirical factors do not appear to be rewarded.

■ *BRP measures extracted from term structure models (example: K–W BRP)*

The most common academic approach for disentangling rate-expectation and risk-premium components is to posit a term structure model and extract rate expectations from its assumed dynamics and from the cross-sectional restrictions implied by the no-arbitrage condition (the assumption that bonds are priced consistently with each other). Pure term structure models may only use yield data, while macro-finance models also include macroeconomic factors. I use the Kim and Wright (2005), or K–W, model because it incorporates survey data and because its realistic-looking curve histories are regularly updated in the Fed website.

■ *BRP measures based on survey data (SBRP)*

Using survey data (consensus forecasts of future interest rates) is the most direct way to assess the market's rate expectations. Fortunately, academics' aversion to using survey data is gradually receding because such data are important in a world of time-varying expected returns. The most useful data series is the long-term consensus forecast of average future short-term rates (only available in the United States and even there, only on a semiannual basis starting in 1983). Simply subtracting this measure from the current long-term yield gives an estimate of the BRP. In March 2010, for example, both the 10-year Treasury yield and the survey forecast of the 2010–2020 average Treasury bill rate were near 3.5%, indicating an SBRP around zero. Apparently, the very steep YC at the time reflected only market expectations of steeply rising short rates, and no BRP was built into the curve.

3.4. Yield Curve Steepness: Important Predictive Relations

Exhibit 3.4 assesses the YC's predictive ability by estimating the correlation of the 10-year vs. 3-month yield spread (that is, the "gross" slope of the yield curve) with the next quarter's and next year's excess returns for 7-year to 10-year bonds, 10-year bond yield changes, and 3-month bill rate changes. This is a crude

Exhibit 3.4. Predictive Power of Yield Curve Steepness: Correlations with Future Returns and Yield Changes, 1962–2009

	Excess Bond Return	Change in 10-Year Yield	Change in 3-Month Rate
Next quarter	0.21	−0.14	0.13
Next year	0.34	−0.25	0.23

Sources: Bloomberg, Federal Reserve Board, Center for Research in Security Prices, Bank of America Merrill Lynch.

approach, but it gives results similar to those of more careful studies by Fama and Bliss (1987) and Campbell and Shiller (1991). The yield curve predicts future excess bond returns rather than future yield changes: see the positive correlations in the first column and negative correlations in the second column. Admittedly the empirical relation has become weaker over time.

The last column shows that while the yield curve is a poor forecaster of near-term changes in long-dated yields (wrong sign!), it is better at forecasting changes in short-dated yields, especially over medium horizons. In the next pages, I link the latter predictive ability to mean-reverting short-rate expectations.

Having put the YC up on a pedestal as a good forecaster of bonds' *near-term* expected return, I now take it down a notch by noting that *the YC is quite a poor proxy for the long-term BRP.* I will argue that the main story about the *ex ante* BRP's postwar behavior is the mountain shape: a secular rise and fall apparently related to level-dependent inflation uncertainty and the related inflation premium. This shape is evident in the (limited) data we have on *ex ante* real yields and bond risk premia. In contrast, curve steepness has not exhibited any secular uptrend or downtrend. It has been range bound between +400 and −400 bps for most of the past half century (and longer). Worse, it was steeply inverted when inflation expectations peaked in 1980–1981. The early 1980s episode highlights YC's inability to predict the high long-run bond returns that followed in the 1980s, in contrast to the survey-based BRP's good forecast (see **Exhibit 3.5**).

Let us compare the empirical ability of these measures to predict excess bond returns over short (one-quarter) and long (five-year) horizons. I already noted that the YC is an excellent predictor over the quarterly horizon with a correlation of 0.21. The *ex ante* real bond yield is even better at 0.28 as is the Cochrane–Piazzesi BRP measure at 0.24. (The survey-based BRP series that begins only in 1983 has a predictive correlation of 0.19.) The five-year predictive correlation is 0.69 for the *ex ante* real yield and 0.67 for the survey-based BRP—compared with just 0.06 for the YC (that is, no predictive ability). The Cochrane–Piazzesi measure fares better, with a 0.32 correlation.

Exhibit 3.5. (A) YC Does Not Exhibit the Secular Trends Implied by a Level-Dependent Inflation Risk Premium

A. YC Measures

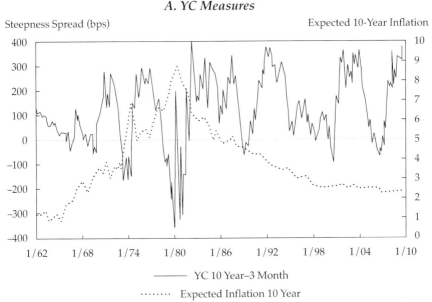

Steepness Spread (bps)   Expected 10-Year Inflation

——— YC 10 Year–3 Month

········ Expected Inflation 10 Year

(continued)

▦ *Why does the YC fare so poorly as a secular predictor?*

The best explanation for this puzzle appears to be mean-reverting rate expectations. To repeat, curve steepness reflects both rate expectations and required risk premia. Unless we can identify those rate expectations (as we will try to do with the help of survey data as well as term structure models), curve steepness gives us a very noisy measure of the BRP.

When short rates are exceptionally low or exceptionally high, yield curves clearly contain mean-reverting rate expectations: the market expects increases from record-low rate levels (thus the steep curve in 2003) and declines from record-high levels (thus the inverted curve in 1981). Even simple one-factor term structure models capture the idea of mean reversion, but such models assume that the longest rates are constant. **Exhibit 3.6** suggests that the long-end anchor has not been constant over time but fell significantly between 1981 and 2003, presumably due to lower long-term inflation expectations. Thus, formal term structure models often include at least two factors. Informal yield curve commentary suggests that central bank policy determines the front end of the curve while the market's inflation expectations determine the back-end levels. This is, of course, a too simplistic statement, but it does capture the essential drivers of the curve.

Exhibit 3.5.   (B) Survey-Based Measures Exhibit the Secular Trends Implied by a Level-Dependent Inflation Risk Premium

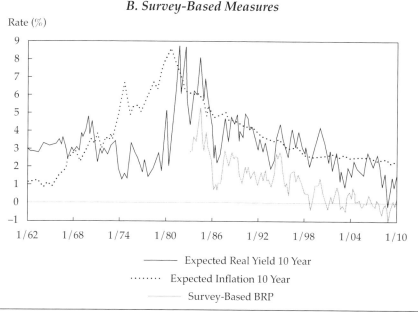

B. Survey-Based Measures

——— Expected Real Yield 10 Year

········ Expected Inflation 10 Year

———— Survey-Based BRP

Notes: Actual survey data on long-term inflation expectations start in 1978. I take an average of two to three available surveys over the past 30 years. Before 1978, I use the statistical estimate of long-term inflation expectations by central bank economists Kozicki and Tinsley (2006). Their article "Survey-Based Estimates of the Term Structure of Expected U.S. Inflation" goes beyond an exponentially weighted average of past inflation rates by also using information in consensus forecasts of next-year inflation.

Sources: Bloomberg, Federal Reserve Board, Federal Reserve Bank of Philadelphia, *Blue Chip Economic Indicators*, Consensus Economics, Sharon Kozicki, author's calculations.

The rate-expectation and risk-premium components in the YC are related in opposite directions to the rate level, a situation that weakens the overall link between the YC and the BRP. The YC has a net negative correlation with the level of short rates, unlike survey-based and many model-based BRP measures. Indeed, the empirical correlation between curve steepness and the three-month bill rate is −0.53. The linkage is even stronger if we use detrended bill rates (detrended by subtracting the past-decade average from the current level): the correlation is −0.79, as illustrated by the good fit in **Exhibit 3.7**. Detrending is consistent with the mean-reversion story because the past decade average is a plausible anchor for mean-reverting rate expectations. The wider the gap between the current short rate and this anchor, the stronger the market's

Exhibit 3.6.   Mean-Reverting Rate Expectations Dominate at Extreme (High or Low) Rate Levels

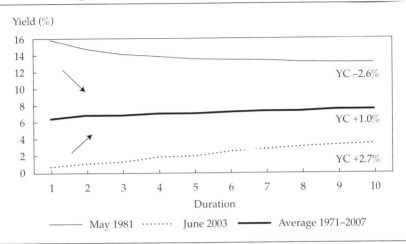

Sources: Bloomberg, Federal Reserve Board.

Exhibit 3.7.   Inversely Level-Dependent Curve Steepness Is Related to Mean-Reverting Short-Rate Expectations

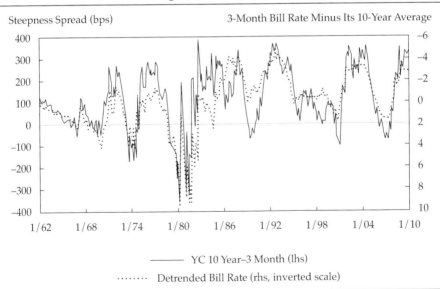

Sources: Bloomberg, Federal Reserve Board.

expectation of normalization (as long as the central bank has sufficient credibility that yields well above the past decade average are not taken as a signal for much higher future inflation).

So, my story is that record-high short rates around 1980, together with mean-reverting rate expectations, made the yield curve quite inverted, despite the fact that the *ex ante* BRP was positive and quite high. The level-dependent components offset each other in the opposite way during the early 1990s and early 2000s and also in 2009–2010: Short rates were exceptionally low, and the yield curve was exceptionally steep due to mean-reverting expectations of eventual rate normalization. During such times, the steep curves reflect expectations of rising rates more than they do high required BRPs.

Overall, these offsetting level dependencies (positive for the BRP, negative for mean-reverting rate expectations) help explain why the YC has been so range bound in past decades and why it has "missed" the secular trends in both the level and the volatility of inflation. We also better understand why over short horizons, the yield curve shape (forward rates) primarily forecasts excess bond returns, whereas over a five-year horizon the curve possesses little return-forecasting ability (but, rather, predicts future short-rate changes in line with the PEH).

One implication of the above analysis is that the YC's ability to foresee negative near-term excess returns in 1980–1981 may not be a sign of the YC being a good proxy for *ex ante* BRP. More likely the YC reflected mean-reverting rate expectations that proved wrong in the near term but correct in the long term. I emphasize below that bond return predictability may reflect irrational expectations and investor learning as well as a time-varying BRP.

3.5. Explaining the BRP Behavior: First Targets, Then Four Drivers

Identifying the BRP target series: There are numerous ways to disentangle the yield curve into (unobservable) rate-expectation and risk-premium components. My preferred approaches use survey data in some way. Without this anchor, the values can be quite silly—reflecting model specification or estimation errors as well as hindsight. To me, SBRP and the *ex ante* real yield are underutilized but useful real-time measures of *ex ante* risk premia.

Survey-based BRPs give the most direct estimates, albeit with measurement error. **Exhibit 3.8** uses the consensus forecasts in the semiannual economist survey of *Blue Chip Economic Indicators* to decompose the 10-year Treasury yield into three parts: expected inflation (over the next decade), expected average Treasury bill yield (over the next decade), and the required BRP.

Exhibit 3.8. **(A) Decomposing the 10-Year Treasury Yield Based on Survey Data and (B) Inflation-Level-Dependent Bond Risk Premium** (correlation 0.87)

A. Decomposing 10-Year Treasury Yield Based on Survey Data

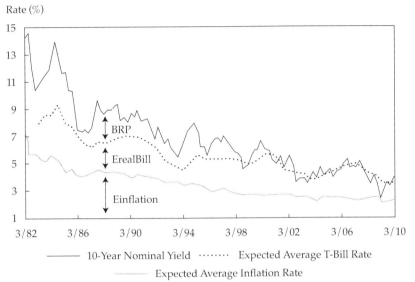

B. Inflation-Level-Dependent Bond Risk Premium

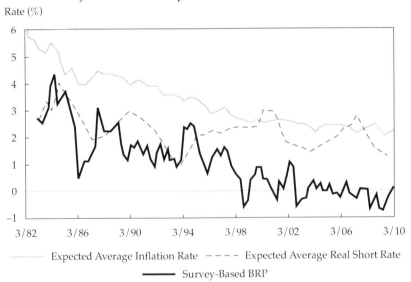

Sources: Bloomberg, Federal Reserve Board, Federal Reserve Bank of Philadelphia, *Blue Chip Economic Indicators*, Consensus Economics.

The various BRP proxies in **Exhibit 3.9** show broadly similar contours. Recall that the Kim–Wright model combines the discipline of a no-arbitrage term structure model with a survey anchor. The C–P BRP reflects yield curve curvature and is purely based on statistical estimation.

With some statistical tricks, we can even extend the survey-based BRP series to times before 1983 when the published long-term rate forecasts began. A Fed study by Rosenberg and Maurer (2008) splices different types of data and estimation methods (for periods when the Kim–Wright curves are not yet available) to create a long history of curve steepness split into its rate-expectation and risk-premium components. Their evidence, reproduced in **Exhibit 3.10**, is consistent with my argument that much of the curve's cyclical fluctuation reflects mean-reverting rate expectations while the risk premium exhibits the mountain shape that echoes inflation trends over the sample period.

The YC, K–W BRP, C–P BRP, and survey-based BRP all proxy for *ex ante* BRP without telling why. I now turn to the main explanations. I discuss in some detail four major drivers of *ex ante* bond premia and real yields:

• Level-dependent inflation uncertainty

• Equity- and/or recession-hedging ability

Exhibit 3.9. Comparing Various Bond Risk Premium Measures (smoothed)

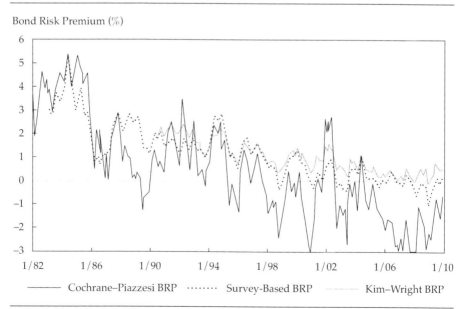

Bond Risk Premium (%)

———— Cochrane–Piazzesi BRP ⋯⋯⋯ Survey-Based BRP ———— Kim–Wright BRP

Sources: Bloomberg, Federal Reserve Board, *Blue Chip Economic Indicators*, author's calculations.

Exhibit 3.10. Curve Steepness (YC) and Its Split into Rate-Expectation and Risk-Premium Components

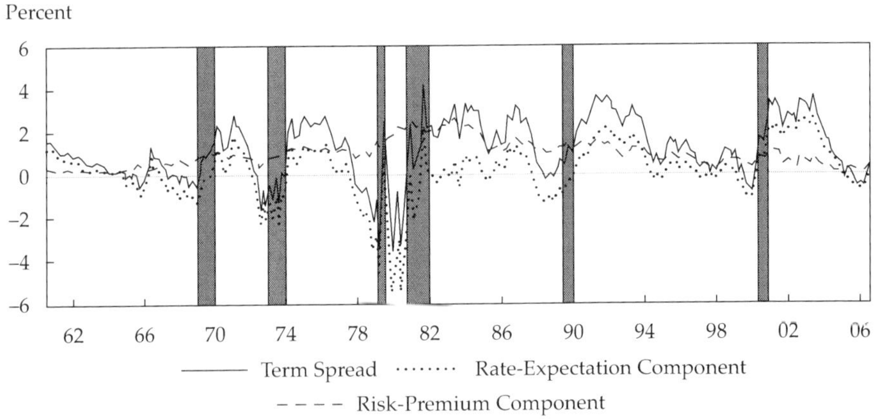

Note: The shaded areas indicate periods designated national recessions by the National Bureau of Economic Research.
Source: Rosenberg and Maurer (2008).

- Supply/demand factors
- Cyclical effects

The second and fourth factors, in particular, can be motivated by covariance with bad times, while the first and third factors are related to bonds' standalone risks. In my opinion, the long-run variation in the BRP has been primarily driven by a level-dependent inflation premium. This is the only premium that can move yields by several percentage points; the yield impact of other factors amounts at most to 1%. Over the past decade, given stable inflation expectations and near-zero inflation premia, real factors have mattered more: negative equity beta (the safe-haven role), supply/demand factors, and perhaps cyclical factors. The countercyclical pattern in the predictable component of bond returns has dominated the academic literature, but it might reflect systematic forecast errors as much as it does a time-varying BRP.

Inflation risk premium (IRP)

The IRP is the most important secular driver of required expected real bond yields and BRPs; it contributed 3% to 4% to nominal bond yields when they peaked in the early 1980s and subsequently fell close to zero. The story is simple and rings true with investment practitioners: higher inflation levels are associated with greater inflation uncertainty, which in turn warrants higher required premia for holding nominal bonds. Note the common trends in Exhibit 3.8.B.

This view is supported by multi-country evidence, as shown in the scatter plot of expected real bond yields and expected inflation in **Exhibit 3.11**. While the sample covers only the disinflationary period since the early 1980s, both the within-country pattern in each country and the multi-country pattern are consistent with a level-dependent inflation premium in *ex ante* real yields.

The view that the BRP history is primarily driven by time-varying inflation premia used to be nonstandard but has become increasingly accepted. The evidence in favor of this view is pretty strong, even if data limitations—unobservable market expectations as well as limited histories of long-term investor surveys and inflation-linked bonds—require us to provide several pieces of a jigsaw puzzle.

• Level of inflation expectations. Realized and expected inflation series share similar contours—the postwar mountain shape (the 1960s and 1970s uptrend and 1980s and 1990s downtrend). Before 1978, no forecasts of long-term inflation are available, so I use one-year-ahead inflation forecasts or time-series estimates by Fed researchers instead.

Exhibit 3.11. Expected 10-Year Real Yield Scatterplotted on Expected Long-Term Inflation Rates for G4 Markets, 1983–2009

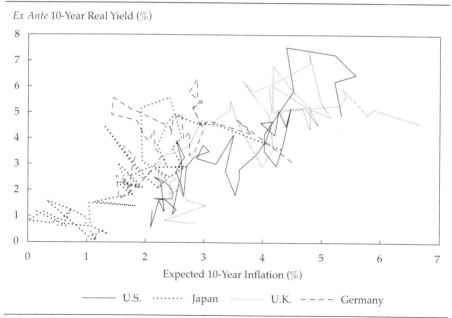

Ex Ante 10-Year Real Yield (%)

Expected 10-Year Inflation (%)

——— U.S. ········ Japan ——— U.K. – – – – Germany

Sources: Bloomberg, Haver Analytics, *Blue Chip Economic Indicators*, Consensus Economics.

- Inflation uncertainty. Realized time-series volatility of inflation and bond yields likewise show a peak around 1980 and later fall sharply. More relevant measures include option-based implied volatility, dispersion among many forecasters, and self-reported inflation uncertainty (individual forecasters' wide probability density).

- *Ex ante* real yields and BRPs. The mountain shape in the post-WWII period is also apparent in BRP proxies where data are available. The BRP appears to have moved nearly one-for-one with the expected inflation level, at least since 1983. Thus, changing (long-term) inflation expectations had a double-whammy impact on nominal bond yields both on the way up and on the way down, albeit with a slight delay.

While I just posit the positive relations between expected inflation, inflation uncertainty, and required bond premia, many Fed studies supply hard evidence. For example, D'Amico and Orphanides (2008) analyze the Survey of Professional Forecasters data between 1968 and 2006 and show that expected one-year inflation, self-reported inflation uncertainty, and disagreement across participants are all positively correlated with each other and with some BRP estimates. In addition, Wright's (2008) analysis of time-varying inflation risk premia using multi-country panel data documents a strong positive relation between time-varying premia and various measures of inflation uncertainty (including model-based time-series volatility, where the focus is appropriately on the volatility of the permanent component in inflation, dispersion among forecasters in a survey, and mean uncertainty as assessed by individual forecasters).

The inflation uncertainty explanation may appear simplistic to academics who link risk premia to covariances with major risks and not to assets' standalone risks. One reason to focus on standalone risk might be market segmentation between bond and equity investors: for bondholders, inflation is the primary risk. A theoretically more appealing explanation is that inflation has real effects, in that it exhibits predictable covariation with equities and real growth. Campbell, Sunderam, and Viceira (2009) present a model where temporary and permanent components of expected inflation uncertainty as well as real-vs.-nominal covariance (in addition to time-varying real rate and market risk aversion) cause time variation in required BRPs.

No studies have extended the empirical analysis of level-dependent inflation premia before World War II, but here is some speculation. Yield curves were typically inverted in the 19th century when real risks dominated and typically upward-sloping in the 20th century when inflation risks dominated. The gold standard implied low and well-anchored inflation expectations and stable long rates in the 19th century, while the lack of central bank smoothing of money market rates at the time exacerbated short-term (real) rate volatility.

The greater risk of rolling short-dated bonds may have given an (inverse) term premium for the front end (though bonds' different credit qualities across maturities may also have contributed to an *apparent* term premium for the front end if shorter-dated bonds were perceived as less creditworthy).

Conversely, explicit or implicit interest rate targeting smoothed short-term rate volatility after the Fed was created in 1913 and the gold standard was abandoned in 1933. Following centuries of flat long-term price levels, with inflation followed by deflation, in the 1900s, inflation became higher, less stable, and more persistent. Inflation risks began to dominate real risks, especially after the end of the postwar Bretton Woods regime in 1971 (which finalized the shift to fiat money), which was followed by large fiscal deficits, a productivity slowdown, and two oil crises. The economic costs of high and unstable inflation became apparent during the miserable decade following the Bretton Woods breakdown. The great disinflation began soon after Paul Volcker became the Fed chairman in 1979 and continued for over two decades as inflation expectations fell and became increasingly well anchored. Cochrane (2008) used this history to explain the 2005 "conundrum" of low and/or falling bond yields during a period of Fed tightening. The experience appeared consistent with low or even negative BRPs at a time of pronounced real risks and well-anchored inflation expectations. Thus, the experience of the mid-2000s looked like a return to the olden days, in the 19th century, when the BRP and the normal shape of the YC had a negative sign.

Covariance risk and safe-haven premium

In contrast to the standalone inflation risk stories told above, theoretically kosher stories relate the BRP to the covariance of inflation with marginal utility. In theory, covariances rather than variances determine risk premia. I will focus on the stock–bond correlation, whose time-variation and sign changes highlight dramatic changes in Treasuries' safe-haven qualities over time.

- During the negative supply shocks between 1973 and 1981, recessions, equity weakness, and high unemployment rates coincided with high inflation and poor bond performance, while during the 1930s in the U.S. and in the 1990s in Japan, the same real economic factors coincided with deflation and strong bond performance. (Nominal bond returns are inversely related to inflation developments.) So, at some times in history, Treasuries have been terrible investments that have lost money "at the worst possible time," while at other times, they have been wonderful recession hedges and safe-haven assets that smooth portfolio returns "just when it is most needed."

- The stock–bond correlation tracks government bonds' hedging ability almost in real time. Campbell, Sunderam, and Viceira (2009) use the stock–bond correlation to obtain information about the correlation between real and nominal assets (and between real activity and inflation). Over the past two centuries, the average stock–bond correlation has been mildly positive but the sign has not been constant. The stock–bond correlation was especially consistently positive between 1965 and 1997 during a period of large gyrations in expected inflation. During this period, changes in inflation expectations drove stock and bond returns in tandem. Periods of negative stock–bond correlations have been shorter: a decade between the mid-1950s and the mid-1960s and a few years around the 1929 crash. Then, during the past decade, the stock–bond correlation reached its most negative level ever, reflecting government bonds' role as the ultimate safe-haven assets (see **Exhibit 3.12**). The sign flipped to negative around 1998 in the U.S.

Exhibit 3.12. Stock–Bond Correlation, 1890–2009

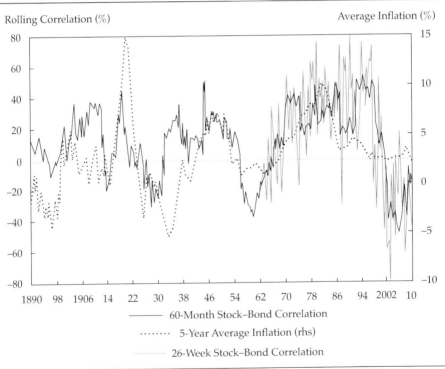

- 60-Month Stock–Bond Correlation
- ········ 5-Year Average Inflation (rhs)
- 26-Week Stock–Bond Correlation

Sources: Bloomberg, Robert Shiller's website (www.econ.yale.edu/~shiller), Ibbotson Associates (Morningstar).

- Measured correlations between real activity and inflation are noisier than asset return correlations. In theory, the growth-to-inflation relation is positive if demand shocks move the economy up and down a stable Phillips curve: nominal bonds are then valuable recession hedges that may even warrant a negative BRP. Conversely, the relation is negative if supply shocks shift the Phillips curve in and out: nominal bonds exacerbate losses for risky assets during stagflations and warrant a positive BRP. Strong central bank credibility and well-anchored inflation expectations support a stable Phillips curve, whereas weak credibility makes for an unstable Phillips curve—and riskier government bonds. The contrast between the 1990s and 2000s, on the one hand, and the 1970s, on the other hand, is clear.

We cannot be sure that the negative correlation will prevail, but we do know that it has sustained government bonds' high valuations in the past decade. Even the simple CAPM suggests that a negative stock–bond correlation can justify a negative risk premium for Treasuries. Losing the safe-haven characteristic would compound bonds' problems in the coming years as the loss would likely occur in an inflationary scenario and put further upward pressure on bond yields. In Ilmanen (2003b), I argue that the stock–bond correlation is likely to be negative in a world of low and stable inflation expectations—as well as during financial crises (high market volatility, flight-to-quality, and flight-to-liquidity episodes). Exhibit 3.12 supports this argument, with 60-month variation loosely tracking the inflation level. Higher-frequency fluctuations (26-week correlations) show broadly similar contours but better highlight the down spikes during financial crises (1987, 1998, 2002, 2008) when Treasuries served as great safe havens.

If it is true that the stock–bond correlation varies with the inflation level, any future rise in inflation expectations could have a triple-whammy effect on nominal bond yields. Besides the direct inflation-expectation impact, the required BRP would rise due to a level-dependent inflation premium and a lost safe-haven value. This logic reinforces the view that the inflation-induced BRP peaked around 1980 and was much lower both 20 years earlier and 20 years later. Not only was inflation uncertainty higher around 1980 than during earlier and later decades, but also inflation and poor bond returns coincided with various aspects of bad times.

Supply/demand factors

Various supply/demand factors that influence the pricing and required returns on bonds can also be viewed as contributing to the time-varying nature of risk premia. However, these factors imply some degree of market segmentation or imperfect asset substitutability (and possible irrationality). I discuss below three types of supply/demand factors: fiscal effects; regulatory effects and pension fund demand; and foreign flows. Other factors that occasionally influence yield levels include flight-to-quality flows (discussed in the previous section), yield-seeking demand, convexity hedging in the mortgage market, and potentially large demographic effects.

Fiscal supply effects

- One obvious example is the Treasury scarcity scare in 2000, where the prospect of continued fiscal surpluses raised a widespread concern that the Treasury bond market would disappear within a decade. (I know, this view seems hard to believe given how quickly those surpluses turned into deficits.) The substitutability of other assets for Treasury debt weakened, pushing yield spreads of near-riskless debt—U.S. agencies, interest rate swaps, and so forth—even higher than during the Russia/LTCM crisis in 1998. Note that, although there were some buybacks of U.S. Treasuries in the year 2000, the more important channel was the market *expectation* of continued large buybacks in future years (which, in the end, did not materialize). Similar richening occurred in other markets, though it was as pronounced only in the United Kingdom. Announcement effects provide interesting evidence: the plan to discontinue 30-year Treasury issuance in October 2001 had a large market impact within minutes of the announcement—the expected scarcity was instantly priced.

- The maturity structure of government debt influences expected excess bond returns, perhaps because long-duration issuance inflicts more interest rate risk on the marketplace. Looking at a 53-year history in the U.S., the share of long-maturity (greater than 10 year) bonds in outstanding government debt is positively correlated with both yield curve steepness and with next-year excess bond return. This fiscal variable is very slow moving, and its predictive ability is even better when used to forecast the next three years' average excess returns (see Greenwood and Vayanos 2010).

- Historically, the maturity structure of Treasury debt has mattered more than the level of indebtedness (say, divided by GDP). The latter variable may suffer from cyclicality that offsets its predictive ability: fiscal deficits and debt tend to expand during recessions, when low growth and low inflation keep bond yields low. Japan during the 1990s and 2000s is a major example of high debt ratios not boosting bond yields, thanks to ample domestic savings and a stagnating economy. The market's response may well be different in the coming years. Empirical studies with U.S. and global data suggest that a 1% rise in the public-debt-to-GDP ratio raises bond yields by 0.02% to 0.06%. The impact of rising debt and deficits on bond yields is greater when expected inflation is higher and initial fiscal conditions are poor; if the level of indebtedness is already high, the expectation of more debt issuance raises investor concern about debt sustainability and eventual debt monetization.

- Supply/demand effects have been especially important during and after 2009 as sharply rising public bond issuance (and the prospect of persistent fiscal deficits) battle with public purchases of financial assets (and other types of liquidity support). Gagnon, Raskin, Remache, and Sack (2010) estimate that the Fed's large-scale asset purchases in 2009 reduced 10-year Treasury yields by 0.4% to 0.8% and non-Treasury yields even more. However, yield curves are record steep, and in the future, unfunded pension and health care costs related to demographic challenges will be an even larger fiscal problem than the legacy of the 2008 crisis and recession. The creditworthiness of sovereign issuers—especially in developed markets— may be reassessed in the coming decade, and the fiscal outlook may become a first-order driver of bond yields.

Regulatory effects and pension fund demand

- The fact that the yield curve is typically flat or inverted at long maturities partly reflects demand from pension funds and other institutional inves- tors with long-dated liabilities (although some yield algebra issues also contribute). For such investors, nominal or real long bonds are the natural riskless asset.

- Such demand forces are hardly constant over time. In many countries, there are clear examples of regulatory or legislative changes quickly influencing the pricing of long-term bonds. For example, in the United Kingdom, the combination of the Minimum Funding Requirement (legislation that encouraged pension funds to shift from equities into bonds) and fiscal surpluses made long-term gilts extremely expensive at the end of the 1990s.

Foreign flows

- In the early 2000s, Asian central banks channeled their surpluses mainly into U.S. Treasuries. The "savings glut" view maintained that such demand was the main reason for the historically low real bond yields. Some estimates of the impact of foreign flows on U.S. Treasury yields exceeded 1 percentage point, but the consensus view was 0.3% to 0.5%. Near substitutes to Treasuries also benefited from this demand but to a lesser extent.

▨ Cyclical factors

Yield curve shape is closely related to (interrelated) business cycles, credit cycles, and monetary policy cycles. YC inversions predict recessions as defined by the National Bureau of Economic Research, but the YC tends to steepen fast during recessions and peak near business cycle troughs. A steep YC *coincides* with a high unemployment rate (correlation +0.45) and *predicts* fast economic growth. The YC's countercyclicality may explain its ability to predict near-term bond and stock returns: high required premia near business cycle troughs and steep YC; low required premia near business cycle peaks and inverted YC (see **Exhibit 3.13**). In addition, the Cochrane–Piazzesi, or C–P, BRP measure is distinctly countercyclical. However, survey evidence suggests that these countercyclical patterns in the curve shape have less to do with the rational required BRP than with systematic forecast errors.

The typical business cycle is closely related to the *monetary policy cycle* except for recessions characterized by deleveraging (the 1930s and 2008–2009). The Fed tends to tighten policy through the expansion (on average, the Fed has been tightening in 78% of months during the last third of expansions since the 1950s due to overheating and inflation pressures), and it then eases through the

Exhibit 3.13. Countercyclical Curve Steepness Moves with the Unemployment Rate—But Yield Curve Inversions *Predict* Recessions (as well as curve steepenings)

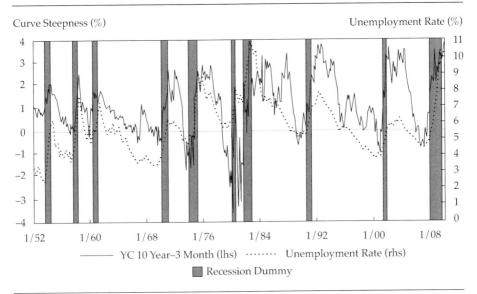

Sources: Bloomberg, Federal Reserve Board.

contraction (the same frequency falls to 36%, 16%, and 0% over the three thirds of the contraction). Inversion in the YC and negative C–P BRPs also ordinarily coincide with Fed tightening.

Vanishing monetary policy premium: It used to be the case that policy tightening initially raised the required BRP, due to what was then the Fed's lack of credibility as well as market uncertainty as to where the tightening would end. The disappearance of a monetary policy premium since the mid-1990s may reflect enhanced Fed credibility or enhanced transparency. As the Fed has influenced market expectations through its communication, any predictive ability that policy rate moves might have had in the past has vanished. In recent years, long yields have risen before the actual tightening started. Simple trading rules like "Follow the Fed" have not been successful since 1994. Recently, the information in the yield curve is distorted by the "zero interest rate bound" that has pushed the Fed to conduct large-scale asset purchases in lieu of rate cuts.

3.6. Tactical Forecasting—Duration Timing

I have focused on bond market predictability in Ilmanen (1994), which is my Ph.D. dissertation, and in several published articles on duration timing. Here, I just summarize, in **Exhibit 3.14**, the predictive correlations over short and long horizons for various generic risk-premium proxies and other predictors that are sorted into the four themes driving the *ex ante* BRP. (I remind the reader that there are valid econometric questions regarding long-horizon predictability because the effective sample size is small, the predicted return involves overlapping observations, and many series are quite persistent. As usual, the reported correlations are computed in sample.)

Comments

Generic BRP proxies have the best predictive correlations, and most work well for both short-horizon and long-horizon forecasting. Generic proxies have the advantage that they do not have to identify why prospective returns are high. *Ex ante* real yield shows the highest correlations. To give readers a sense of what the 0.31 correlation means in return terms, I sort the history of *ex ante* real yields and subsequent quarterly excess bond returns. Quarters forming the quintile with the highest (lowest) real yields were followed by +2.0% (−0.7%) quarterly excess bond returns, on average.

Inflation uncertainty: I don't have very good empirical proxies for this variable, but *a priori*, I would expect a positive relation only over long horizons. Indeed, expected long-term inflation and bond market volatility have high predictive correlations over the five-year horizon (0.31 and 0.64 respectively), consistent with the idea that high expected inflation and related uncertainty make the *ex ante* BRP high. Over short horizons, the correlations are low.

73

Exhibit 3.14. Correlations with Future Excess Return of (7-Year to 10-Year) Treasuries, 1962–2009

	Horizon		
	Next Quarter	Next Year	Next 5 Years
Generic			
Yield curve 10 year–3 month	0.21	0.34	0.06
Cochrane and Piazzesi BRP	0.24	0.44	0.32
Survey-based BRP (1983–)	0.19	0.38	0.67
Kim and Wright BRP (1990–)	0.25	0.43	0.34
Ex ante real yield	0.28	0.48	0.69
Inflation uncertainty			
Expected inflation 10 year	−0.02	0.01	0.31
Bond volatility (60-day)	0.11	0.22	0.64
Safe haven			
Equity market return (60-day)	−0.15	−0.14	−0.07
Equity market volatility (60-day)	0.11	0.08	0.27
Equity–bond correlation	0.01	0.06	0.22
Supply/demand			
Federal debt/GDP ratio	0.06	0.11	0.16
Debt share of >10-year Treasuries	0.13	0.28	0.66
Cyclical			
ISM Business Confidence	−0.10	−0.20	−0.30
CFNAI (real activity index)	−0.09	−0.19	−0.19
Corporate profits/GDP ratio	−0.13	−0.25	−0.52
Unemployment rate	0.11	0.18	0.24

Sources: Bloomberg, Haver Analytics, Federal Reserve Board, Federal Reserve Bank of Philadelphia, *Blue Chip Economic Indicators*, Consensus Economics, Sharon Kozicki (for statistical estimates of expected inflation in Kozicki–Tinsley 2006), Robin Greenwood (for Treasury debt maturity share histories in Greenwood–Vayanos 2010), Federal Reserve Bank of Chicago, Center for Research in Security Prices, Bank of America Merrill Lynch.

Safe-haven influences: These influences should be observed best at short horizons, perhaps even shorter than one quarter if they are related to brief flight-to-quality episodes and wealth-dependent risk aversion. Negative equity returns and high equity market volatility are bullish news for bonds both contemporaneously and predictively (with −0.15 and +0.11 predictive correlations to bonds for equity returns and volatility, respectively, over a one-quarter horizon). The negative coefficient on equity returns may also reflect an underreaction effect for growth news and not just risk aversion news. However, the absolute values of the correlations are not high, so the evidence on stock–bond correlation is weak.

Supply/demand factors: I do not have good data on demand factors, but I would expect the slow-moving supply factors to mainly influence long-horizon expected returns. The debt maturity share indicator has a 0.66 predictive correlation over the five-year horizon.

Cyclical: A strong economy—for example, captured by ebullient business confidence—empirically predicts low bond returns. I find the correlation signs consistent with this logic at all horizons but, surprisingly, the largest correlations for the longest horizon. Business confidence measures give pretty similar results. The Chicago Fed National Activity Index (CFNAI) is a summary measure of 85 economic announcements. The unemployment rate has the opposite sign because it is inherently countercyclical.

The fact that bond returns are predictable over a five-year horizon must reflect secular rather than cyclical features, such as the apparent inflation-level dependence of the unemployment rate and corporate profits. For example, the corporate profit share of overall GDP derives its forecasting ability for bond returns (−0.52 over a five-year horizon) largely from one observation, the profit trough in the 1970s followed by massively positive bond returns in the early 1980s. The same single observation may explain the significant correlations of the unemployment rate and business confidence with bond returns over the next five years.

For shorter-horizon tactical trading, I also assess predictive correlations for next-month excess bond returns. I just report here that the best predictors (which reach double-digit correlations) include several generic risk-premium proxies and carry/value measures as well as the past-month equity market return and bond return. Note that recent bond market momentum works well for very short-term trading but not over multi-month or multi-year horizons (thus not shown in Exhibit 3.14).

This chapter focuses on a single BRP, implicitly assuming that it is perfectly correlated across the curve. The working assumption that BRP varies across Treasuries in proportion to duration or volatility is reasonable; it is likely that most fluctuations in yield curve shape over time reflect investors' changing rate expectations. Empirically, one-factor models (roughly, assuming parallel shifts in the yield curve) do explain a large chunk of bond return variation, and the remaining factors (related to evolving curve steepness or curvature or even more maturity-specific details) may not earn significant long-run premia. The typical concave shape of the yield curve (a steeper curve at short durations than at long ones) does suggest that duration-neutral curve steepening positions earn a positive long-run premium. This empirical feature could reflect a single BRP because curve steepening is correlated with falling short rates.

4. Credit Risk Premium

- Bonds exposed to credit risk have outperformed Treasuries only marginally over long histories (by 0.2% to 0.5% annually for investment-grade credits), arguably giving poor compensation for their lower liquidity and poor timing of losses. Long-dated corporate bonds have performed especially poorly, while barely speculative-grade bonds (BB-rated) have performed best.

- In this generally bleak picture, short-dated top-rated credit bonds have given an attractive reward-to-volatility ratio. Levered arbitrageurs cannot remove this opportunity because of the financing rates they face. This group of bonds is also risky, with the largest losses occurring during financial crises.

- Credit spreads are observable measures of the prospective return advantage of risky assets over "riskless" Treasuries. However, spreads overstate this advantage because they do not include a decrement for expected losses from default or downgrading losses and because of embedded options.

- Historical average yield spreads for investment-grade debt have by far exceeded average default rates. Yet, it does not necessarily follow that investors have earned the bulk of the spread as excess returns. Indeed, evidence suggests the contrary. One explanation for the apparently contradictory sets of evidence is that index investors constrained by rating requirements, unlike buy-and-hold investors, sell exactly the types of corporate bonds that subsequently tend to perform well (BB-rated "fallen angels" and short-dated debt).

- Spread variation over time reflects the scarcity and liquidity edge of Treasuries over other issues as well as cyclical, volatility, and default developments.

- Credit spreads have some ability to predict excess returns, as do various cyclical and supply/demand indicators.

4.1. Introduction, Terminology, and Theory

Decomposing the Credit Spread

Government bonds such as U.S. Treasuries almost always have lower yields, and presumably lower expected returns, than comparable nongovernment debt. Credit spreads are a convenient measure of corporate bonds' prospective return advantage over Treasuries.[18] However, they clearly overstate this advantage. Besides presenting empirical evidence on historical experience, this chapter reviews pitfalls in equating credit spreads with expected excess returns.

Credit spreads would be positive even if investors only expected the same return from corporates as from Treasuries. The main reason, only recently challenged, is the perception that developed-country government debt is default-free. The uncertain repayments of bonds exposed to credit risk ("credits" for short) mean that these bonds have lower expected cash flows than matching Treasuries with the same promised yield. Risk-neutral investors will require a break-even yield cushion over Treasuries to offset the expected default losses. Risk-averse investors in the real world likely require further compensation (a higher return than riskless assets *after* losses from defaults, thus a credit risk premium, or CRP). If issuer-specific default risk could be perfectly diversified away, there would be no expected excess return in equilibrium and we could obtain risk-neutral pricing even given risk-averse investors. However, defaults are empirically correlated and tend to cluster in "bad times" (recessions, financial distress), so they contain significant systematic risk; so, corporate bonds should offer some credit risk premium beyond the break-even cushion.

Besides credit considerations (the break-even spread due to expected default or downgrading losses plus the credit risk premium), yield spreads over Treasuries likely reflect a premium for the lower liquidity of corporate bonds. Disentangling these unobservable components is an even greater challenge than disentangling the market's rate-expectation and required bond risk-premium components in Treasury yields in the previous chapter.

Raw yield spreads may further be boosted by the embedded options held by an issuer. For example, the issuer may have the right to call (repay) the bond at par before the maturity date. Since the 1990s, institutional investors have had access to option-adjusted spread measures that account for such embedded options (although the estimates do vary across models and especially depend on assumed volatility levels).[19]

---

[18]This chapter focuses on the credit spreads and excess returns of corporate bonds. Chapter 10 in Ilmanen (2011a) also discusses other nongovernment debt—mortgage-backed securities and emerging market debt as well as swap-to-Treasury spreads and credit default swap spreads. To save space, these topics are omitted from this book.

[19]Yet other considerations: in the past, yield spreads were not properly duration matched or maturity matched, creating noise in these spreads. Corporate bonds may also earn additional rolldown gains beyond the spread income if credit spread curves are systematically upward sloping, but this effect tends to be empirically small. Differential taxation of corporates and Treasuries (taxable holders pay state taxes on corporate bond income but not on Treasury bond income) may also contribute to yield spreads.

The stylized illustration below decomposes the raw corporate–Treasury yield spread into three parts: the true *ex ante* return advantage and two break-even cushions that offset the expected impact of default losses and optionality. Unfortunately, the terminology is used unevenly. Comments on yield spreads rarely mention whether the spread is option adjusted or not. Worse, the term "credit premium" (or "default premium") is sometimes used for the *ex ante* yield spread; at other times, for the *ex ante* excess return or even only its credit-related component (excluding the illiquidity premium); and yet elsewhere, for the realized excess return.

Ex ante return advantage + Offset for expected default/downgrading losses
+ Offset for short embedded options

Risk ↓	Credit/illiquidity ↓	Option-adjusted ↓	Raw yield
neutral	premia	spread	spread
0%	0.4%–0.6%	0.7%–1.0%	1.0%–1.3%

Before turning to empirical evidence on credit spreads and premia, I briefly discuss the huge literature on credit risk analysis and modeling. This literature is relevant for understanding both corporate bonds' expected cash flows and their discount rate (the excess returns that bond buyers may require for bearing default risk and related systematic risks).

There are different ways of analyzing credit risk, including statistical (purely empirical) and analytical approaches. The latter literature has split into structural and reduced-form models.

Statistical Credit Risk Analysis

The most common approach is to extrapolate historical loss experience for each credit-rating class. Refinements use financial ratios and market-based data to predict defaults.

The expected loss from default depends not just on the probability of default but also on its severity, where severity is measured by the recovery rate. By construction,

Expected default loss = Default probability × (1− Recovery rate).

A 40% recovery rate is commonly assumed for senior debt, broadly consistent with long-run experience. However, recovery rates vary over time and with debt seniority.

For top-rated investment-grade (IG) bonds, defaults are a remote possibility and rating downgrades are a more realistic risk. Downgrades may be analyzed in the same way as defaults. Downgrades are consistently associated with credit spread widening and thus capital losses. However, market spread changes typically predict rating changes several months ahead. Some rating agency actions (e.g., putting a credit on a watch list) that typically precede downgrades are also more forward-looking.

For example, Elton, Gruber, Agrawal, and Mann (2001) use the rating transition matrix (the historical frequency of rating changes or defaults) to estimate the long-term default probability for various rating classes. Combined with a recovery rate assumption, they compute the break-even spreads that would equal the market spreads in a risk-neutral world. These break-even spreads (0.14% for A-rated and 0.40% for BBB-rated bonds at a 10-year maturity, even lower for shorter bonds) are much below market spreads.

Analytical Models on Single-Name Risk

Academic and practitioner literature in the 1980s and 1990s focused on single-issuer credit risk (default probability, recovery value, and maybe also downgrading events), based on either structural models or reduced-form models.

Structural models price all corporate securities in a common framework, grounded in the pioneering theoretical models of Merton (1974) and Black and Scholes (1973). In the classic "Merton model," a firm's capital structure is particularly simple: a single zero-coupon debt and a single equity issue. The firm's equity can be viewed as a call option on the firm's assets (struck at the maturity value D of its debt), while the firm's debt consists of a riskless zero-coupon bond (that guarantees the payment of D) and a short put option on the value of the firm (struck at D). Thus, the bondholder is effectively writing a put on the firm's assets, being long equity but short equity volatility. The value of any option depends crucially on the volatility level of the underlying asset (as well as time horizon and leverage, where leverage is the difference between the firm's assets' current value and the value of its debt).

- While all corporate stakeholders tend to benefit from rising equity prices, a key difference between the exposures of equityholders and bondholders is that the former benefit from rising volatility while the latter are hurt by it. The alignment of management and shareholder interests makes debt-holders vulnerable to discretionary management decisions—such as sharp increases in leverage—that cause volatility to rise and redistribute wealth from the bondholder to the equityholder.

- Moody's KMV model is the most popular variant of the Merton model. It measures default risk by "distance to default" (the number of standard deviation moves required to push the firm value below the default point within the time horizon being evaluated). Instead of assuming a lognormal distribution of asset values as in the Merton model, KMV uses historical default experience to convert this distance-to-default measure into expected default frequency. Such measures of default probability and rating migration probability outperform the rating agencies' predictions.

- Standard structural models predict much lower credit spreads than observed in reality. These models often imply that short-dated spreads should approach zero. Some recent structural models are able to explain actual debt pricing by adding a jump component and an illiquidity premium.

Reduced-form credit pricing models bypass firm valuation and, instead, directly model the default probability. They treat default (or rating change) as a random event whose probability can be estimated from observed market prices in the context of an analytical model (or directly from historical default data). Useful indicators, besides equity volatility and leverage, include past equity returns, certain financial ratios, and proxies for the liquidity premium. This modeling approach is sort of a compromise between statistical models and the theoretically purer structural models. Reduced-form models can, naturally, match market spreads better than structural models can, but unconstrained indicator selection can make them overfitted to in-sample data.

Default Correlations and Portfolio Risk

In the past decade, credit risk modeling literature increasingly turned its focus from single-issuer default risk toward portfolio analysis, due to the growing importance of structured products (pooled composites of bonds and loans, either pass-through or tranched). The joint probability of defaults (default correlation) is a crucial factor in such portfolio analysis. Both the structured finance instruments and the related literature became increasingly complex in the 2000s, arguably going too far (ahead of the investor understanding), thereby contributing to the market turmoil when defaults began in earnest in 2007–2008, resulting in vanishing liquidity and the virtual extinction of many market sectors.

4.2. Historical Average Excess Returns

The realized average outperformance of credits should, in principle, be an accurate measure, not suffering from the overstatement of prospective return advantage that is an inherent characteristic of yield spreads. However, average returns can be contaminated by capital gains or losses from sample-specific spread trends—and excess returns are estimated with some noise. In any case, historical average returns are not very informative about the future if expected returns vary over time, but we study them in the hope of gleaning something useful about the long-run reward.

Dimson *et al.* (2002) estimate that long U.S. corporates outperformed long Treasuries by 0.5 percentage points between 1900 and 2000. This *ex post* default premium estimate is subject to the caveats that data sources vary, the average rating is ambiguous, and durations are mismatched. My reading of the evidence suggests an even lower number—about 0.3 percentage points.

The further back we look, the worse-quality data we have. Since about 1990, we have had access to properly duration-adjusted excess returns over Treasuries. Between 1973 and 1989, some interpolations are needed to compare corporate returns with matching Treasuries. Before 1973, the main data source is the Ibbotson Associates long corporate bond index; it has higher credit quality (only Aaa- and Aa-rated debt) and longer maturity (over 10 years) than the full Barcap (Barclays Capital, formerly Lehman Brothers) Index, and its monthly return is simply compared with the Ibbotson Long-Term (20 year) Treasury Index return. However, the returns on the Ibbotson corporate series are calculated from yields, with no allowance for defaults and/or downgrading. Thus, the Ibbotson estimates overstate high-quality corporate returns.[20] (Note that I use Moody's and S&P's ratings notation—e.g., Aaa and AAA—interchangeably because my diverse sources use both of them.)

For the longest history in **Exhibit 4.1**, the geometric mean (GM) *ex post* credit risk premium is 0.24%, and no better for the Barcap Index data available since 1973.[21] All excess return in the long series came in the first 42 years, nothing in the second 42 years. The Barcap IG Index shows a mild positive outperformance trend since 1973, despite sharp falls in 1973–1974, 1986, 1990, 1998–2002, and 2007–2008. Performance is better for HY bonds, but even this picture is not compelling, given deep drawdowns during the past three recessions. (The active original-issue HY market developed only in the late 1970s, but earlier data exist on low-grade bonds—fallen angels—all the way back to 1953.)

Exhibit 4.2 analyzes average excess returns across rating classes. Lower-rated IG classes have earned higher mean returns, but excess returns are small and inconsistent (with an information ratio of, at best, 0.16). The long-run record was unimpressive even before 2008, and as of late 2008, the cumulative outperformance over many decades was negative for most rating classes.

The BB-rated sector, just below the IG threshold, provides the best long-run performance of any bond rating category. This relative success likely reflects partial market segmentation caused by the constraints under which many portfolio managers operate. Fallen angels ("orphan" bonds downgraded from IG to HY, which IG portfolio managers are forced to sell) appear to outperform bonds originally issued as HY.

---

[20] Hallerbach and Houweling (2011) analyze maturity mismatches and other problems in the Ibbotson default premium series.

[21] The compounding of excess returns may exclude or include the base asset's return. The 0.24% GM is based on compounding the excess return without giving the corporate bond the benefit of earning "interest on interest" on the Treasury return. If I compound the total return of the credit index and that of the Treasury index and then compute cumulative excess return as the ratio, the GM for 1926–2009 is 0.41%. See the dotted line in Exhibit 4.1 compared with the dark solid line.

Exhibit 4.1. Cumulative Excess Returns of Corporate Bonds vs. Duration/Maturity-Matched Treasuries

Cumulative Excess Return vs. Matched Treasury
220
200
180
160
140
120
100
80
26
31
36
41
46
51
56
61
66
71
76
81
86
91
96
01
06
Corp AAA & AA Long vs. Tsy
Corp HY vs. Tsy (1953=100)
Same with Compounding Advantage
Corp IG All vs. Tsy (1973=100)

Note: IG = investment grade; HY = high yield; Tsy = Treasury.

Sources: Bloomberg, Barclays Capital, Ibbotson Associates (Morningstar).

Exhibit 4.2. Excess Returns of Citigroup Credit Indices over 7- to 10-Year Treasuries, 1973–2009

	IG Credit AAA/AA	IG Credit A	IG Credit BBB	HY BB	HY B	HY CCC (starts 1985)
Arithmetic mean	0.02%	0.33%	0.83%	2.34%	1.89%	—
Volatility	3.2	3.9	5.1	8.6	11.5	18.7%
Information ratio	0.01	0.08	0.16	0.27	0.17	—
Geometric mean 1973–2009	−0.03	0.25	0.70	1.99	1.24	—
Geometric mean 1985–2009	−0.34	−0.02	0.26	1.70	−0.14	−2.66

Note: IG = investment grade; HY= high yield.

Sources: Bloomberg, Barclays Capital (pre-1980), Citigroup.

The riskiest subsector has fared the worst. The lowest-rated sector, CCC, has clearly underperformed Treasuries since 1985. These surprisingly poor returns may have been caused by some combination of a reach-for-yield mentality, overoptimistic cyclical views, investors' excessive confidence regarding their timing and/or selection ability, and lottery-seeker preference for the riskiest assets. Admittedly investors only recently accumulated enough data on CCC-rated bonds from which to learn, since there were few issuers below a B rating until the 1990s.

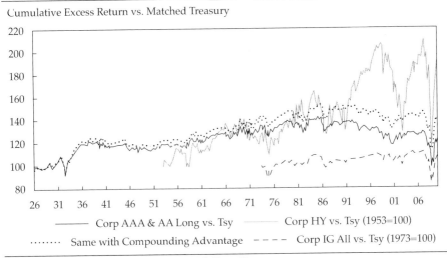

In the bull markets (2003–2004, 2009), CCC-rated bonds fared extremely well (after having lost nearly half of their value in 2000–2002 and in 2008). Low-rated bonds can be good tactical investments during economic recoveries and when initial spreads are wide—but apparently not great long-term investments.

Even with very limited outperformance, a simple argument could be made that corporates are superior investments to Treasuries: they offer slightly higher long-term returns and slightly lower volatilities. These facts hold for corporate bond indices and Treasury benchmarks over long periods. However, this naïve comparison ignores important considerations such as Treasuries' superior liquidity and better recession-hedging and equity-diversifying abilities. At a more mechanical level, corporate bond index volatilities, and correlations with equities and other asset classes, are understated because of stale pricing of corporate issues.

Why Such Low *Ex Post* Credit Premia?

Corporate bonds' *ex post* excess returns have only delivered a small fraction of their historical *ex ante* yield advantage, a fact that may not be widely appreciated. For example, the Lehman/Barcap investment-grade corporates earned a 0.30% average *ex post* excess return over comparable-maturity Treasuries between 1973 and 2009, compared with the 1.20% average option-adjusted (or yield-to-worst) *ex ante* spread and to an even wider average yield-to-maturity *ex ante* spread over those same Treasuries. Where did the rest of the spread advantage go? This question may surprise experts. The better-known puzzle in academic circles is about inexplicably *wide* credit spreads. Recall that the long-run historical default experience implies average default losses much lower than average yield spreads—perhaps just 0.2 percentage points of the long-run average credit spread, which exceeds 1.0%.[22]

Exhibit 4.3 highlights the tension between these two findings. The left bar says that because realized returns were so low, default and downgrading losses must have eaten much of the yield spread. The right bar says that because realized default and downgrading losses were so low, credit bonds must have earned the rest as true outperformance over Treasuries. Both the excess return analysis and the default rate analysis seem to say: "It is not me causing those wide spreads; it is that other part."

---

[22]Using the 1970–2009 default experience over a 10-year horizon and a 40% recovery rate assumption, an annual break-even spread of 0.15% would offset all default losses for IG rated debt. However, any number of changes would push this break-even spread wider. Switching to Baa-rated debt, the break-even spread would be 0.30%; using a 20-year horizon (and bond), it would be 0.21%; using 1920–2009 default data, it would be 0.26%; assuming a 20% recovery rate, it would be 0.20%. Adjusting for the tendency of recovery rates to be low when default rates are high would also widen the break-even spread. Finally, incorporating the downgrading bias (see main text) could double the break-even spread.

Exhibit 4.3.   Is the Puzzle Too Wide or Too Narrow Credit Spreads?

Long-Run Average Yield Spread for IG Corporate Bonds

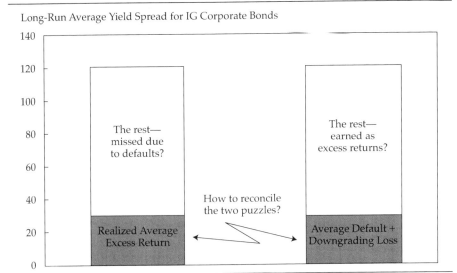

How can we reconcile the conflicting evidence? The key is to distinguish between investor types. For buy-and-hold investors, it is sufficient to adjust credit spreads for embedded options and expected default losses. However, for active investors, (1) downgrading bias and (2) trading activity due to index changes, discussed in detail below, can further reduce expected returns. Moreover, within-sample widening of general credit spreads can cause capital losses that reduce investors' realized returns. This repricing effect should be small over long data windows but can matter even over 20 years.

Downgrading bias: Among IG bonds, the impact of defaults is modest but the impact of downgrading bias can be significant for top-rated bonds. The expected capital losses due to downgrading bias reflect the relative likelihood of upgrades versus downgrades as well as the asymmetric spread and price outcomes of upgrades versus downgrades.

- Asymmetric probabilities of rating changes: For example, an A-rated bond is twice as likely to be downgraded next year to Baa as to be upgraded to Aa. The migration probabilities are more symmetric for lower ratings, but the asymmetry in outcomes still causes downgrading bias for most IG bonds.

- Asymmetric outcomes: More importantly, the cost of a downgrade is much greater than the benefit of an upgrade because the spread roughly doubles per full rating notch. Using average spreads since 1994, if an A-rated bond is upgraded to Aa, the spread narrows by 0.36% but a downgrade to Baa widens the spread by 0.56% and spreads widen even faster for further downgrades.

Trading activity: This explanation is important even if we ignore costs associated with active view taking and merely track the costs of trading according to index rules. The large excess returns in the second bar accrue to "buy-and-hold investors," who keep the credit bonds irrespective of their subsequent rating changes or aging. In contrast, the modest excess returns in the first bar accrue to "index investors," who hold credit bonds only as long as they satisfy the index criteria. Specifically, IG index investors are presumed to sell bonds that are downgraded below IG rating as well as bonds whose maturity falls below the usual one-year threshold. (Also, bonds with a small issue size, which no longer satisfy the liquidity criteria for the index, need to be sold.) Given the empirical evidence of the good performance of BB-rated bonds—especially of fallen angels—as well as short-maturity bonds, such actions damage long-run returns!

Ng and Phelps (2011) quantify these effects and show that IG corporate index investors would enhance their annual returns (based on experience over 1990–2009) by 0.38% per year by retaining all bonds that initially qualified for this index. Most of the gains (0.32%) accrue from retaining the fallen angels instead of selling with the crowd (index rules imply selling at the bid price at the end of the month when a bond is downgraded to a sub-IG rating).

Investment practices could clearly be improved. However, some institutional investors have no choice because regulatory requirements or investment mandates force them to sell non-IG bonds within a relatively short period.

All in all, the information in **Exhibit 4.4** can loosely account for the 1.20% average (option-adjusted) credit spread in recent decades. Any decomposition is further complicated by various interactions and compounding effects as well as by data mismatches. For example, the average default rates are based on the fraction of *issuers* in distress while the yields and returns of bond indices are weighted by *issues*. Other factors may also need to be taken into account: the market-cap weighting of indices may explain some of the gap between *ex ante* and *ex post* credit premia if average losses from default and downgrading are not similarly cap-weighted. Separately, the return impact of corporate "events" (leveraged buyouts, mergers and acquisitions, initial public offerings, and the withdrawing of bond ratings) may not be well captured in the empirical analysis of average yields and defaults.

Back to my original question: Why such low *ex post* credit premia? I wonder whether the highly visible *ex ante* yield advantage has outweighed much less visible negatives (embedded options, downgrading bias, agency problems, lower liquidity, bad timing of losses) in investors' minds and made credits *a structurally overpriced asset class*. Investors may be more aware of historical average yield spreads than of historical excess returns; the excess return analysis above is somewhat complex, and its unappealing evidence is rarely publicized in Wall Street research. More commonly, we hear how much wider average yield spreads have been than average default losses.

Exhibit 4.4. Reconciling the Twin Credit Spread Puzzles: Stylized Components of the Long-Run Spread

Realized excess return (credit + illiquidity premia)	0.3–0.4%
Losses due to within-sample spread widening	0.0–0.2%
Index investors' bad selling practices	0.3–0.4%
Losses from default and downgrading biases	0.2–0.4%

The appeal of credit to institutional investors is not universal. Swensen (2009), just to give one example, is highly critical of nongovernment debt and argues that the principal–agent problems in corporate bonds are underappreciated. Because firm managers' interests are better aligned with shareholders than with lenders, discretionary management actions are more likely to benefit the former at the expense of the latter. Finally, institutional demand may contribute to overpricing: banks are the largest asset managers and must hold credit risk disproportionately, while insurers often opt for high-yielding assets as long-term investments, adding to the oversubscription of corporate bonds.

4.3. Focus on Front-End Trading—A Pocket of Attractive Reward to Risk

There is one exception to the disappointing performance of credits. In the U.S. credit markets, the highest volatility-adjusted returns have accrued from overweighting top-rated credits (AAA/AA bonds, agencies, or interest rate swaps) against Treasuries at short maturities (one to three years, perhaps even better in money markets). The evidence is similar in U.S. agency markets and in swap-to-government spread positions in dollar, euro, sterling, and yen markets. For unlevered investors in traditional asset classes, overweighting short-dated credits was perhaps the best structural tilt on a risk-adjusted basis in the past 10 to 20 years.

Let us review the long-term evidence. Good data exist for U.S. credits since 1978 and even better since 1988.[23] Exhibit 4.5 shows that short-maturity credit carry trades gave much smoother outperformance than longer-maturity trades

---

[23] Bank of America Merrill Lynch corporate indices for one- to three-year (and longer) maturity subsector portfolios for AAA/AA versus Treasury (pretty similar durations) start in 1978. Duration-adjusted excess returns of the Lehman/Barcap Index one- to three-year (and longer) maturity subsector portfolios separately for each rating class start in 1988. The former series is analyzed in Exhibit 4.5; the latter, in Exhibit 4.6. Both exhibits analyze the returns of cash-neutral corporate–Treasury long–short trades, but the former series is maturity-matched and the latter more cleanly duration-matched against Treasuries. Indeed, Barclays Capital publishes these duration-adjusted excess return series for credit rating/maturity subsector portfolios, and the information ratios in Exhibit 4.6 are simply the annualized mean/volatility ratios for each series.

**Exhibit 4.5. Cumulative Excess Returns of Corporate Bonds vs. Duration/
Maturity-Matched Treasuries**

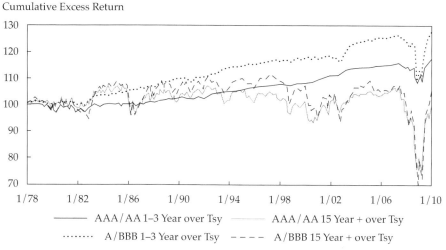

Cumulative Excess Return

——— AAA/AA 1–3 Year over Tsy   ——— AAA/AA 15 Year + over Tsy

········ A/BBB 1–3 Year over Tsy   – – – – A/BBB 15 Year + over Tsy

Note: Tsy = Treasury.
Sources: Bloomberg, Bank of America Merrill Lynch.

and ended up earning higher raw excess returns as well. The post-1988 duration-adjusted excess returns paint a similar picture, as does evidence on U.S. agencies and swap–government spread trades (not shown).

Drilling into the duration-adjusted excess returns from Lehman/Barcap across maturity and rating subsets, **Exhibit 4.6** shows that the one-year to three-year AAA/AA versus Treasury trades achieved an information ratio in excess of 0.5 (and above 1.0 before the 2008 crisis) while most lower-rated and longer-dated credit portfolios actually underperformed Treasuries over the past 20 or more years. The consistency of this pattern was exceptional as rolling two-year outperformance has been always positive since the late 1980s until late 2007 (not shown). In all rating classes, the short-maturity credit trade gave a higher return and (of course) lower volatility than a long-maturity trade.

What explains this superior risk-adjusted performance? I first give a mechanical answer and then turn to the economic questions—why the opportunity exists in the first place and why it has not been arbitraged away. The success has been quite predictable. *Ex ante* Sharpe ratios (e.g., spread per unit of volatility) have persistently been higher for top-rated front-end carry trades than for most other credit trades—and the *ex post* Sharpe ratios have broadly

Exhibit 4.6. Information Ratios for U.S. Credit vs. Treasury Strategies across Ratings and Maturities, 1988–2009

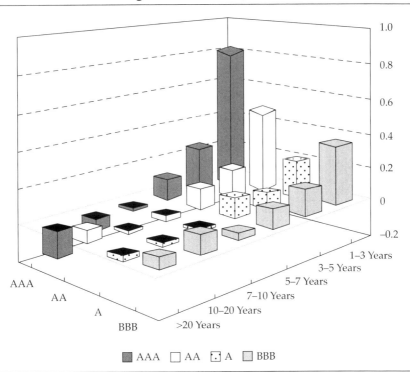

Sources: Bloomberg, Barclays Capital.

reflected delivery of these promised outcomes. Although yield spreads can be quite narrow at short durations, they are not zero, as standard structural credit models imply, and that is the key. A positive intercept (positive spread over Treasuries at near-zero maturity) and a relatively flat slope of the spread curve ensure that the spread-to-duration ratio peaks at the front end. Mechanically, the high *ex ante* Sharpe ratios reflect large spread-to-duration ratios (i.e., broad break-even cushions[24]) and relatively stable spreads at short maturities. Only if yield spreads rose one-for-one with duration would the break-even cushions be equal across maturities—see **Exhibit 4.7.** Thus, it is common to see the broadest break-even cushions at the front end, despite the narrowest spreads. Moreover, yield spread volatilities tend to be lower at short maturities, at least

---

[24]The break-even spread widening can be approximated by the annual yield spread divided by the duration at horizon. Break-even cushions are broad at the front end because a given spread widening causes only a small capital loss for short-duration assets.

for highly rated debt. Together, these features explain the high *ex ante* Sharpe ratios—and lesser *ex post* Sharpe ratios. Only an exceptionally dramatic spread widening (or actual default) can make short-dated carry trades underperform *ex post*, and since the 1980s this has occurred only in 1998 and 2007–2008.

Exhibit 4.7. **(A) Stylized Shapes of Empirically Typical and "Theoretical" High-Grade Spread Curves and (B) Corresponding Break-Even Spread Widening Cushions**

A. Stylized Shapes

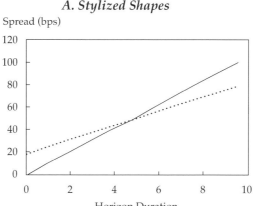

B. Corresponding Break-Even Spread

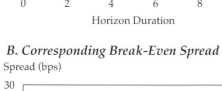

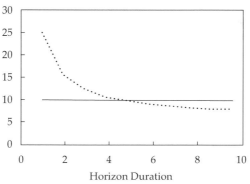

┈┈┈┈┈ Empirically Typical Spread Curve
───── Theoretical Spread Curve

Source: Citigroup, author's calculations.

Which Forces Have Given Rise to Such an Attractive *Ex Ante* Opportunity?

We can first rule out one plausible answer. Shorter-dated credit bonds have lower spread duration (price sensitivity to yield spread widening) than longer-dated bonds, but they have just as much exposure to pure default losses as longer bonds. This default risk could conceivably explain the wide front-end spread. However, the top-rated short-dated bonds hardly suffer from any default risk: historically, less than 0.3% of AA-rated issuers have fallen below IG status over a one-year horizon, let alone defaulted.

This opportunity may originate from the partial market segmentation and the convenience yields related to the higher liquidity of Treasuries. Some investors are constrained to hold Treasuries even if close substitutes with moderately higher risk offer consistently better performance. The number of such return-insensitive investors has declined over time and has reduced this opportunity; even foreign central banks have become more return conscious and less constrained. For active investors, Treasuries offer superior liquidity and real savings in trading costs. Finally, Treasuries perform especially well during flight-to-quality episodes, and most investors value this safe-haven feature.

Why Has This Opportunity—With Persistently High *Ex Ante* Sharpe Ratios—Not Been Arbitraged Away?

The above analysis ignores *funding rate spreads* that would make carry positions less attractive. Financing rates have limited impact for long-only managers (who only hold investments without explicit leverage), for whom the decision is whether to hold an unlevered long position in Treasuries or in corporate bonds.

But any levered trader needs to take into account Treasuries' below-LIBOR financing rates. Loosely speaking, a leveraged corporate–Treasury trade involves funding the long corporate bond position at a high rate (near the LIBOR deposit rate) while borrowing Treasuries (for the purpose of shorting them) at a less advantageous repo rate (near the Treasury bill rate). (When Treasuries are borrowed, cash must be left at the bond lender as security; it is compensated with the general collateral repo rate or an even lower special repo rate.) To proxy for this effect, I subtract from the positive carry of the asset pair (say, two-year corporate bond minus Treasury spread) the negative carry in these assets' relative financing rates (using one-month repo minus LIBOR). If the funding spreads at money market maturities were as wide as the longer-dated bond spreads, there would be no opportunity for levered traders. Incorporating funding rate spreads cuts the information or Sharpe ratio of the aggregate trade from 0.7 to 0.4 and makes the proposed strategies less compelling for levered traders.

After the funding-cost adjustment, the average return advantage is relatively modest (about 0.4%) compared with other available opportunities. When leverage is restricted, less capital gets devoted to front-end trades that lack inherent volatility (and thus require leverage to achieve meaningful returns), so arbitrage opportunities are less fully exploited and Sharpe ratios are higher.

More generally, the best trading opportunities that markets offer often involve levering up low-volatility positions. In the mid-2000s, *ex ante* Sharpe ratios declined both because Treasury holders gradually became more conscious of the opportunity cost of their low-returning holdings and because more levered capital became available to pursue any remaining "arbitrage" opportunities. The strategy of buying corporates and shorting Treasuries suffered unprecedented losses in 2007–2008, but these losses, of course, improved the subsequent *ex ante* opportunity. Some evidence suggests that this opportunity can be "market timed": the *ex ante* spread has had some ability to predict the next year's performance. A strategy of sizing positions based on the *ex ante* opportunity would have helped in the long run but would have stumbled in 2008.

Besides the financing rate gap and unexciting unlevered returns, obstacles faced by capital-constrained arbitrageurs include limited liquidity in short-dated corporate bonds and the poor performance of this trade in serious flight-to-quality episodes. While losses from this strategy are rare, they tend to materialize just when it hurts the trader the most. Arguably, the strategy's payoff profile resembles that of writing put options on a systemic catastrophe.

4.4. Understanding Credit Spreads and Their Drivers

So much for average returns. A key theme in this book is that expected returns vary over time so we should study the *ex ante* opportunities. With corporate bonds, it is harder than with equities to believe that the *ex ante* premium is constant when the observable spreads vary so much and so visibly over time. Indeed, history tells that wide spreads predict higher future returns. Between 1973 and 2009, the correlation between the spread level and the next-month (next-year) corporate sector excess return was 0.12 (0.48).

While I recognize that historical credit spreads overstate the expected return advantage, these spreads are a natural starting point for assessing corporates' likely expected return advantage over governments. **Exhibit 4.8** displays spread histories dating back to 1926 to show that the Depression era spreads have still not been matched or exceeded even during the stagflationary recessions between 1973 and 1982 or during the 2008 credit crunch. I include a recession "dummy" variable (recessions are shaded) to highlight the strong countercyclicality in spreads. While the Baa–Aaa and Aaa–Treasury spreads move together, the lower-rated bonds (as shown by the Baa–Aaa spread) exhibit more pronounced countercyclical variation than the top-rated bonds.

91

Exhibit 4.8. Long-Dated Credit Spreads since the 1920s

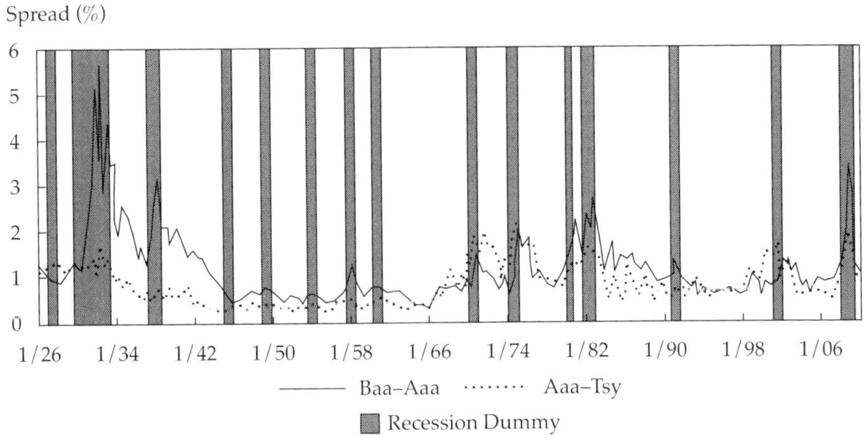

Spread (%)

```
1/26   1/34   1/42   1/50   1/58   1/66   1/74   1/82   1/90   1/98   1/06
```

——— Baa–Aaa   ········ Aaa–Tsy

▨ Recession Dummy

Note: Tsy = Treasury.
Sources: Bloomberg, Moody's, Ibbotson Associates (Morningstar), Federal Reserve Board, National Bureau of Economic Research.

These Moody's and Ibbotson yield indices (the Treasury yields are from Ibbotson and represent a roughly 20-year maturity) are the best-known long histories. In addition to data quality concerns regarding individual bonds, we caution that the yield spreads are not option adjusted and that there may be duration mismatches between these indices that matter when the curve is steep (all indices are for long-dated bonds). Given the embedded options, and the perhaps longer maturities of Aaa-rated corporates, the graphed spreads may be overstated.

With the introduction of bond indices by Lehman Brothers (now Barcap) and others, better-quality data have become available, including option-adjusted spreads (OAS). Starting in 1973, we have access to crudely option-adjusted yields ("yield-to-worst") and since 1990, to OAS data that also are naturally duration matched. The broad contours of the results using modern data are similar to those obtained using the Moody's yield spread data, but details differ. While the OAS model adjusts for embedded options and for duration mismatches, it remains in various ways an imperfect measure of expected returns—even if the OAS model's term structure specification and volatility assumption were correct. The OAS model ignores, on the one hand, expected capital losses due to downgrading bias and defaults and, on the other hand, expected gains or losses from rolling along the credit spread curve. It is possible, if tedious, to adjust for these shortcomings based on historical experience.

Despite their shortcomings, credit spreads are the most directly observable measures of risky assets' prospective return advantage. Thus, it is worth drilling into their drivers. Recall the spread decomposition at the beginning of this chapter. The yield spread over Treasuries for straight corporate bonds or the OAS for bonds with embedded options reflects (1) the break-even spread needed to offset expected capital losses from defaults and the downgrading bias and (2) the true risk premium, consisting of the excess return required mainly to compensate for default risk and illiquidity. Corporate bonds also have a tax disadvantage and trading cost disadvantage compared with Treasuries. These features would require a further break-even spread for actively trading taxable investors, but if the marginal investor in corporate bonds is a passive, nontaxed institution, taxes or costs should have no impact on market spreads.

Overall, key explanatory variables for corporate spreads include:

- Liquidity premium proxies and Treasury scarcity measures;
- Cyclical indicators;
- (equity and spread) Volatility measures; and
- Default rates.

Different aspects dominate the determination of spreads for (1) top-rated credits, (2) most IG corporates, and (3) high-yield bonds.

1. For top-rated (AAA/AA) credits, the default probability is minimal, and even the downgrading bias appears to be a small part of the yield spread. The ratio of the yield spread to expected credit losses is very high (> 5) for top-rated bonds. In contrast, liquidity, tax, and systemic factors dominate. Top-rated bonds are more exposed to (rare but toxic) systemic risks and less to easily diversifiable idiosyncratic default risks.

2. For A– and BBB-rated bonds, various economic factors are important but the actual default risk remains moderate. Cyclical effects as well as (equity and spread) volatility are important drivers. Spreads are wide in economic downturns and in periods of high volatility.

3. For speculative-grade (HY) bonds, the expected default rate is the most important driver of spreads. These bonds behave most like equity.

More details on 1–3 are given in the following subsections:

1. Top Rated

It is difficult to disentangle the credit and liquidity components in corporate yield spreads. **Exhibit 4.9** tracks yield spreads that involve minimal default risk and that consequently can be viewed primarily as liquidity spreads. For example, government-guaranteed Resolution Funding Corporation (Refcorp) bonds offered an average yield spread of 0.5% over Treasuries but widened to 2.0% in late 2008. Swap–government spreads did not widen out as much because the market's supply concerns cheapened Treasuries.

Exhibit 4.9.   Liquidity Spreads Vary over Time

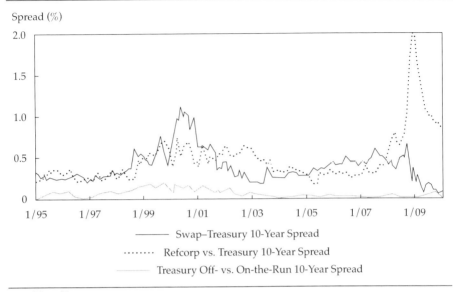

Spread (%)

Note: Tsy = Treasury.
Sources: Bloomberg, J.P. Morgan.

The tax effect reflects the fact that corporates are taxed at the federal, state, and local levels, while Treasuries are only taxed at the federal level. The impact of the differential tax effect on yields might be 0.3%, but it has declined over time with falling yield levels.

For top-rated bonds, the uniqueness of Treasuries may be a more important pricing factor than the risk in the credits (and is accentuated whenever Treasuries are relatively scarce and less substitutable). The AAA–Treasury spread has been inversely related to the federal debt/GDP ratio since the 1920s (see **Exhibit 4.10**). The scarcity premium on Treasuries was especially pronounced in 2000 amidst the concern about disappearance of the Treasury market, while the spread troughed after World War II amidst record high debt/GDP levels.

2. A & BBB

Cyclical effects

Below the top-rated bonds, cyclical influences are the primary drivers of yield spreads. Recall Exhibit 4.8, which shows spreads widening during recessions. In addition, **Exhibit 4.11** shows the close relation of the BAA–AAA spread and a composite of a broad set of real activity indicators published by

Exhibit 4.10. Credit Spreads Also Reflect Treasury Scarcity or Abundance, 1952–2010

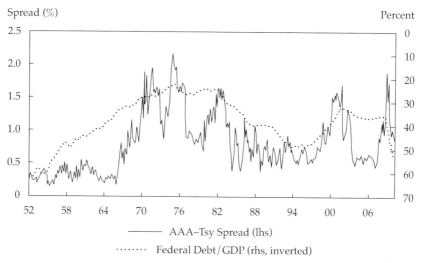

Notes: Tsy = Treasury. Correlation = −70%.

Sources: Bloomberg, Moody's, Ibbotson Associates (Morningstar), Federal Reserve Board, Haver Analytics.

Exhibit 4.11. Credit Spreads Are Wide When the Real Economy Is Weak, 1973–2010

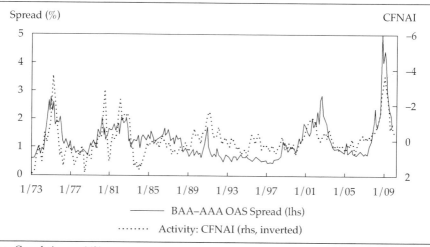

Note: Correlation = −64%.

Sources: Bloomberg, Barclays Capital, Federal Reserve Bank of Chicago.

the Chicago Fed (the CFNAI). Academics emphasize the correlation of spread widening with bad times as a reason for a required default premium. Credit spreads are often widest during recessions when they hurt the holder the most, consistent with habit formation models in which consumers are closest to their time-varying subsistence level during recessions.

The link between *ex ante* equity yields and corporate yields is weak. Corporate spreads appear more closely related to equity market volatility and to recent realized losses in equity markets.

Volatility

Many equity volatility measures—from rolling historical volatilities and idiosyncratic volatilities to implied market volatility—move in synch with credit spreads (see **Exhibit 4.12**). So do other proxies for uncertainty, such as analyst disagreement (the dispersion of beliefs in earnings forecasts). The standard Merton-model story of default risk rising with equity volatility is especially applicable to lower-rated bonds. Moreover, recessions and flight-to-quality episodes tend to be associated with both higher equity volatilities and wider credit spreads. These features may explain the link between Baa–Aaa spreads and equity market volatility. The importance of idiosyncratic volatility may reflect either firm-specific fundamentals or discrete events (for example, acquisitions or leveraged buyouts) that can suddenly change the riskiness of the firm's debt.

Exhibit 4.12. Credit Spreads Widen Amidst Higher Realized Equity Market Volatility

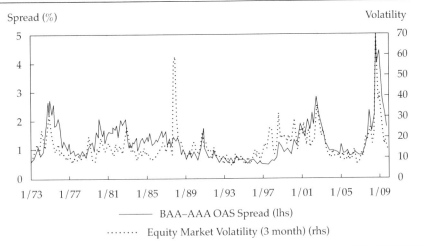

Note: Correlation = 0.69.

Sources: Bloomberg, Barclays Capital.

Cross-sectionally, spread volatilities increase nearly linearly with the spread level. This pattern is useful in risk management and hedging. Conversely, spread levels vary directly with spread volatilities, perhaps reflecting differences in assets' credit risk premia. Spread widening and rating downgrades tend to boost an asset's measured riskiness and maybe its required relative risk premium (the causality can work both ways). The evidence for this story is primarily cross-sectional, but time series evidence appears consistent with it: higher spread volatilities over time tend to coincide with wider aggregate spread levels and, presumably, higher required risk premia.

Yield level dependence

The empirical relation between the *levels* of yields and spreads is ambiguous and period specific; I argue that the cyclical effect dominates any level dependence. Any rate level dependence for spreads is a coincidence, depending on whether recessions were inflationary or deflationary. During the stagflationary 1970s, recessions, rating downgrade waves, and wide spreads coincided with high inflation and bond yields, whereas in the 1930s and in the various economic slowdowns since 1998, downgradings and wide credit spreads have coincided with low inflation and bond yields. Perhaps the true relation is U-shaped. Both deflation and high inflation are bad news for corporate profits and valuations. The sweet spot of low and stable inflation that we found for equity market valuations may also support narrow credit spreads.

One key factor causing the yield level to affect spreads in a positive direction is the tax effect. Corporates need to provide additional yield to offset their state and local tax disadvantage—and the related break-even spread varies directly with the yield level. The key factor causing the yield level to affect spreads negatively is optionality. Lower yields make the (short) options more valuable and widen the credit spreads. Structural credit models imply a negative relation because corporate bonds are effectively short the volatility of the firm's assets. Short options embedded in callable bonds exacerbate this feature. The negative relation between *changes* in yield levels and corporate spreads is consistent with this story.

3. High-Yield Bonds

When defaults matter

High-yield bond market performance is primarily driven by changing default rates (see **Exhibit 4.13**) that tend to cluster, peaking near economy-wide recessions. Default rates are backward looking while rating changes suffer from inertia, so it is no wonder that HY spreads lead both modestly. Despite loss clustering, long-term bond spreads could look "through the cycle" in the way that rating agencies do, but in practice, spreads are more sensitive to current conditions than simple default arithmetic suggests, due to time-varying risk

Exhibit 4.13. Moody's Annual Investment-Grade and Speculative-Grade Default Rates, 1920–2009

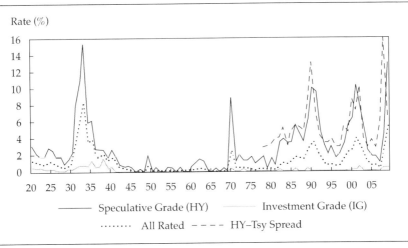

Note: Tsy = Treasury.

Sources: Moody's, Bloomberg, Barclays Capital, Citigroup.

premia, human nature, and capital constraints among HY specialists and financial intermediaries. Moreover, credit market deterioration is not only reflected in rising default rates; downgrading rates (the net downgrading bias in rating changes) and spread volatilities also rise near recessions, while recovery rates in defaults decline.

Exhibit 4.13 shows Moody's annual issuer-weighted default rates since 1920 for both investment-grade and speculative-grade debt. The long-run averages are 0.15% and 2.8%. However, looking at data only since 1970, the average is lower for IG (0.08%) but higher for the HY sector (3.9%). The Great Depression experience was more exceptional for IG than for HY, but the postwar stability of IG was also exceptional—with no IG defaults between 1941 and 1969. HY debt has seen spikes in the default rate comparable to the 1930s spike on several occasions since 1970—perhaps because the growth of the original-issue HY market in the 1980s has made this segment riskier. The graph also plots the HY–Treasury spread for reference. Since 1978, this spread has averaged 5.3%, compared with a 4.3% default rate and default losses of roughly 2.6% after the recovery rate is included. Roughly speaking, investors realized half of the *ex ante* spread, but it has been a roller-coaster ride, and the cumulative 30-year excess return evaporated fully in the depths of the 2008 crisis.

It is important to recall that actual default losses are smaller than the default rates. Annual losses can be computed by multiplying the default rate by 1 minus the recovery rate. The typical recovery value for all seniorities averages near 40%—and this is the base assumption in many analyses. However, lower annual recovery rates clearly coincide with higher annual default rates, compounding the adverse effects of clustered defaults. Thus, long-run average default losses are higher than the product of the average default rate and average amount not recovered (that is, the average of [1 − Recovery rate]). Adjusting for the recovery rate (but ignoring downgrading bias or rolling down the spread curve) and apportioning the losses evenly across years gives us the break-even yield spreads that would have exactly offset the default losses. **Exhibit 4.14** gives an example of such calculations based on Moody's default data over 1-, 5-, and 10-year horizons, using a 40% recovery rate assumption and the 1970–2009 global default experience (except for the last columns, which use 1920–2009 data for comparison).

Giesecke, Longstaff, Schaefer, and Strebulaev (2010) have collected the longest available database of defaults—a history covering 1866–2008 for U.S. nonfinancial bond issues, irrespective of their rating or even being rated. Long histories are interesting, notwithstanding problems with very old data. Unlike Moody's statistics that capture the fraction of *issuers* in default, the default rate is computed here by the fraction of *issues* (par value of debt) in default, thereby better matching market yields. The authors find an average annual default rate of 1.5%, with a clear downtrend (4% in the late 19th century, 1.4%

Exhibit 4.14.   Cumulative Default Rates and Corresponding Break-Even Yield Spreads, 1970–2009

Rating	Cumulative Default Rate				→	Break-Even Spread (assuming 40% recovery rate)			
	1 yr	5 yr	10 yr	10 yr (1920–2009)		1 yr	5 yr	10 yr	10 yr (1920–2009)
Aaa	0.00%	0.11%	0.50%	0.9%		0.00%	0.01%	0.03%	0.05%
Aa	0.02	0.23	0.54	2.2		0.01	0.03	0.03	0.13
A	0.05	0.72	2.05	3.3		0.03	0.09	0.12	0.20
Baa	0.18	1.93	4.85	7.2		0.11	0.23	0.30	0.45
Ba	1.17	10.40	19.96	19.2		0.70	1.32	1.34	1.28
B	4.55	25.90	44.38	36.4		2.79	3.60	3.52	2.71
Caa-C	17.72	52.29	71.38	52.8		11.70	8.88	7.51	4.50
IG	0.08	0.97	2.50	4.3		0.05	0.12	0.15	0.26
HY	4.53	21.36	34.01	29.0		2.78	2.88	2.49	2.06

Note: IG = investment grade. HY = high yield.

Sources: Moody's Investors Service (2010), Reid, Bhimalingam, and Burns (2010).

for 1900–1945, and only 0.3% after World War II). Default rates at the peak of the 1870s railroad bust exceeded 30%, much worse than during the Great Depression. The long-run default rate matches the 1.5% average estimated corporate spread over Treasuries for this long sample. Assuming a 50% recovery rate, investors earned a 0.8% annual excess return over Treasuries, measured as the difference between the spread and average default losses. Note that this crude estimate is for all bonds (whether investment grade, speculative grade, or unrated) and is not tainted by index investors' tendency to sell fallen angels.

4.5. Tactical Forecasting of Corporate Bond Outperformance

While my focus is on long-term expected returns, I also discuss tactical forecasting models. I focus only on the period where we have good-quality excess return data. **Exhibit 4.15** shows simple correlations between a kitchen-sink list of predictors and the subsequent excess returns of the IG corporate bond index for the period 1990–2009.

Wide credit spreads are the strongest bullish indicators. High implied volatilities—both equity market volatility and interest rate volatility—are also bullish, partly reflecting the contemporaneous correlation between volatility and spread levels. Weak real activity and a low profits/GDP ratio are bearish predictors. The two best growth predictors in financial markets give a mixed message—

Exhibit 4.15. Correlations in Predicting Corporate Bond Excess Returns, 1990–2009

	Next-Quarter Corporate Bond Excess Return	Next-Year Corporate Bond Excess Return
Corporate spread (option adjusted)	0.25	0.46
MOVE implied Treasury volatility	0.19	0.40
VIX implied equity volatility	0.28	0.39
Yield curve 10 yr–2 yr	0.20	0.27
Equity market momentum	−0.07	−0.37
Corporate bond excess return momentum	0.15	−0.32
Treasury yield momentum	−0.10	−0.11
Chicago Fed real activity index	−0.25	−0.35
Corporate profit/GDP	−0.19	−0.37
Forecast fiscal balance/GDP	−0.34	−0.31

Sources: Bloomberg, Barclays Capital, Federal Reserve Bank of Chicago, Federal Reserve Board, Haver Analytics, Consensus Economics.

steep yield curves predict high credit returns, while strong equity markets (somewhat unexpectedly) predict low credit returns. Credit bonds appear to exhibit short-term momentum and longer-term reversal patterns. Finally, fiscal deficit concerns predict corporate bond outperformance versus Treasuries. Many of these predictive correlations have the same sign contemporaneously, suggesting that corporate bonds may suffer from underreaction effects.

4.6. Concluding Remarks

Corporate credits have only mildly outperformed Treasuries in recent decades, if at all. The long-run return advantage for IG bonds is roughly 0.30%. Only fallen-angel bonds just beyond the IG threshold and short-dated top-rated credits have outpaced government bonds in a reasonably consistent manner. The disappointing performance of corporates applies to some extent to other non-government bonds. They all went through a roller-coaster ride in 2007–2009. The newer securitized debt classes—asset-backed and commercial mortgage-backed securities—fared worst during the subprime crisis.

I have some sympathy with David Swensen's (2009) extreme view that nongovernment bonds may not deserve a *strategic* allocation in institutional portfolios. Yet, corporates certainly can be useful tactical investments, as they were in 2003 and 2009 when spreads narrowed from extremely wide levels during an economic recovery. If one wants to tactically time the corporate bond market, credit spreads give good insights about medium-term prospects, despite their shortcomings. For reasons discussed below, I expect credits to outperform governments over the next 10 to 20 years. Leverage constraints should sustain the risk-adjusted rewards for short-dated credits.

Swensen's argument is clouded by growing sovereign risk. Future credit spreads may be as much influenced by markets' questioning of the default-free status of government bonds as by any default concerns about corporate bonds. Sovereign credit risk became a hot topic after 2008 as governments bailed out banks, guaranteed risks taken by the financial sector, and committed to unprecedented fiscal expansion, while tax revenues were dropping off the cliff due to economic recession. Arguably, the crisis only brought the focus on public debts forward in time, so current rather than just future investors need to consider them. Demographic developments are an even larger problem, at least for the aging nations of the developed world. Sovereign credit default swap spreads for major economies rose from hundredths of a percent in early 2008 to almost 1% for the best credits (and much wider for peripheral developed economies) at their early-2009 peak. As the appetite for risk revived, all credit spreads narrowed, but sovereign spreads began to widen again in 2010.

5. Alternative Asset Premia

- Alternative asset classes improve portfolio diversification, at least in normal times, and may enhance returns.

- Alternative assets are often less liquid and less transparent than traditional assets.

- Alternative assets became increasingly popular in the 2000s, which inevitably reduced their prospective returns. In 2008, the quintessential bad times, most (but not all) alternatives failed both to diversify and to enhance returns.

- Real estate can be accessed directly through less liquid physical markets or indirectly through listed REITs and property stocks. The long-run return of real estate is between that of bonds and stocks, although starting valuations clearly matter. Long-run real price growth is negligible, but rental yield income can be significant.

- Commodity futures are perhaps the best diversifiers of financial assets and also the best inflation hedges. Long-run average returns are more reflective of futures' roll returns than of spot price appreciation. Oil-related futures have given the highest returns and have had the best diversification and hedging properties in recent decades.

- Hedge fund (HF) index data suggest that HFs have been able to add value, even as a group and after fees, unlike traditional managers. Critics question how much the documented outperformance reflects biases in reported fund returns (reflecting the voluntary reporting into HF databases) or various risks (traditional and alternative betas, illiquidity, tail risks). I review attempts to quantify these biases and risks.

- Private equity funds have a less impressive track record as a group, according to academic studies. Adjusting for reporting biases and some risks, they appear to underperform listed equities, despite their liquidity disadvantage. To outperform after fees, investors need to be able to pick top-quartile managers.

5.1. Introduction to Alternatives

The definition of alternative asset classes is fuzzy, but a useful definition can be crafted based on what they are not. Stocks, bonds, and cash in any country in the world, held directly or in a long-only fund, are viewed as *traditional* asset classes, while all other investments are alternatives. At this time, alternatives consist mainly of real estate, commodities, hedge funds, and private equity. The boundary between traditional and alternative assets has shifted over time, with some alternative assets becoming familiar and migrating into the traditional category. As recently as the 1980s, all non-U.S. assets may have been deemed alternative by U.S. investors, but all public markets are now regarded as traditional (even including "frontier" equity markets and local-currency emerging debt markets). Within U.S. markets, traditional asset classes might now include less liquid and riskier pockets of stocks, bonds, and cash—such as high-yield bonds and small- and micro-cap stocks. Based on current industry practice, I would also include index derivatives—based on various indices of stocks, interest rates, and credits—as traditional investments.

The big-four alternatives that I'll dwell on below are real estate, commodity futures, hedge funds, and private equity funds. The first two are added to traditional portfolios more for their diversification and inflation-hedging properties, while the latter two are perhaps brought in more as return enhancers (perceived, or hoped-for, alpha providers). The first two are real assets, more so than any traditional financial assets, and are clearly distinct asset classes—but they have been around so long that some criticize use of the term "alternative" to describe them. The latter two may be better characterized as active investment strategies, implemented by specialist managers who earn fees that are higher and more performance related than those earned by traditional ("long-only") asset managers. The question of whether hedge funds constitute an asset class has especially been debated, but in practice, end-investors allocate part of a capital budget and/or a risk budget to them, effectively delegating active decision making to them—for a fee—and thus causing them to function as a kind of asset class.[25]

Common characteristics of all four alternatives include:

- They were not part of most institutional investment portfolios even 20 years ago, but they now increasingly are.

- They are rarely exchange traded and typically are *less liquid* than traditional assets, involving higher costs and fees and requiring a longer investment horizon (commodity futures are an exception to these key characteristics).

---

[25]Note that traditional (long-only) asset managers are not viewed as distinct asset classes. Even if these managers have an active mandate, they typically have a clear benchmark in one asset class of publicly traded securities (equities, bonds, or a narrower subset) and are not expected to deviate too much from the benchmark's performance. (Their target tracking error is often much lower than the asset class volatility.) Thus, investors can view an investment in a traditional large-cap U.S. equity fund manager and in the S&P 500 Index itself as nearly equivalent from a risk-budgeting perspective.

- They are less scalable than traditional assets (capacity constraints apply especially to newer alternatives).

- They are less transparent and more plagued by information asymmetries than traditional assets. Even historical performance data may be limited and of questionable quality.

- They are good diversifiers of traditional portfolios and might enhance returns (due to illiquidity premia, risk premia, and the potential alpha of the asset manager); however, both advantages have decayed over time and, on average, failed in 2008.

- They are a source of various risk and illiquidity premia—including both traditional equity and bond betas and "alternative betas" that investors could not access using traditional public markets. Illiquidity premia may be especially important for some alternatives.

- They all boomed between 2002 and 2007 and were crushed in 2008.

The growing popularity of alternative investments reflected diverse factors. Risky assets had disappointed investors badly in 2000–2002, and *ex ante* indicators pointed to single-digit future returns on all traditional asset classes. (Some observers argued for negative expected returns on equities in the short run.) David Swensen's *Pioneering Portfolio Management* (Swensen 2009) showcased Yale's success in using alternative managers to diversify and boost returns. As institutional interest in alternatives grew, assets under management ballooned. With hindsight, the period 2001–2007 may be viewed as the golden age of alternatives.

Beyond the big four, the list of alternatives has grown and become increasingly diverse. It includes privately held infrastructure, timber, and farmland; art and other collectibles (fine wines, rare coins, stamps); and more-novel securities, such as catastrophe bonds, carbon credits, intellectual property rights, viatical or life insurance settlements, longevity swaps, and others. If hedge funds can be characterized as an asset class, then the list of alternatives may be extended to include managed futures (typically, momentum-oriented commodity trading advisors or CTAs), global tactical asset allocation managers (typically contrarian investors), active FX, volatility trading, and alternative betas and hedge fund replication, as well as investments focused on corporate governance, sustainable development, and shareholder activism.

Exhibit 5.1 shows the cumulative returns of the big four alternatives since 1984. Note that historical returns on actively managed asset classes (HF, private equity) may be misleading because of survivorship and other reporting biases that can overstate actual returns. Moreover, standard risk adjustments don't capture all risks to which these active strategies are exposed. Finally, asset

Exhibit 5.1. Cumulative Total Returns of Four Alternative Asset Classes, 1984–2009

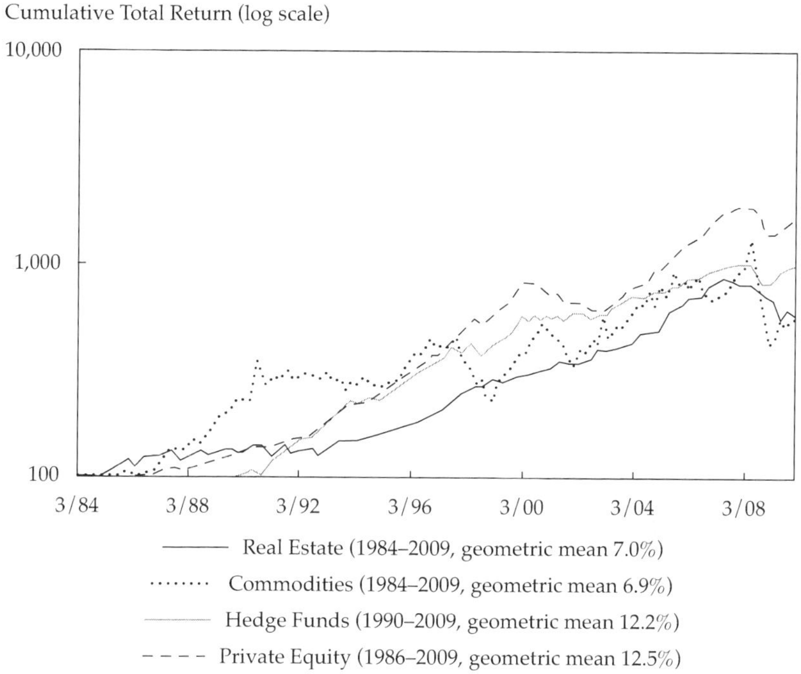
Cumulative Total Return (log scale)
10,000
1,000
100
3/84
3/88
3/92
3/96
3/00
3/04
3/08
Real Estate (1984–2009, geometric mean 7.0%)
Commodities (1984–2009, geometric mean 6.9%)
Hedge Funds (1990–2009, geometric mean 12.2%)
Private Equity (1986–2009, geometric mean 12.5%)

Sources: Bloomberg, MIT-CRE, S&P GSCI, Hedge Fund Research, Cambridge Associates.

inflows and growing competition have shrunk the available alpha opportunities, so even if past fund performance was not overstated, future performance may be less exciting.

This chapter relies more on historical returns than the other chapters of this book because forward-looking indicators (such as yields or valuation ratios) are rarely available for alternative asset classes. Given such data limitations, there is little tangible evidence on time-varying expected returns, but it seems safe to say that the various premia found in alternative investments vary strongly over time. Alternatives generally appear to excel amidst flush liquidity and high risk appetites—and suffer amidst tougher conditions. This procyclical tendency disappoints investors who look to broad-based portfolios of alternatives for diversification of equity and bond risk and suggests that such investors should choose alternatives more carefully for their diversification potential. It looks like short-term momentum and long-term reversal patterns work here as well. Some *ex ante* valuation signals as well as money-flow (overcrowding) signals may be useful contrarian indicators.

5.2. Real Estate

Introduction

Real estate is an important real asset that, for institutional investors, is a *good diversifier and better inflation hedge* than most financial assets. Real estate is a relatively *illiquid* asset class; private real estate holdings, especially, cannot be traded actively, and any performance comparisons need to take into account the consequences of illiquidity.

I will focus on the two types of commercial equity real estate available for investors: private real estate (traditionally, measured in the U.S. by the NCREIF Index) and publicly traded real estate investment trusts (listed REITs).[26]

There are no definitive figures for the size of the global real estate market. The investable commercial real estate equity universe amounts to several trillion dollars, and the listed segment is just a fraction of that. Total real estate wealth is even larger: Francis and Ibbotson (2009) estimate that in 2007, U.S. residential real estate amounted to $18 trillion and commercial real estate to $16 trillion. McKinsey Global Institute (2009) gives much higher estimates—that U.S. residential real estate value exceeded $30 trillion in 2007, a third of the global total. In any case, residential real estate is a huge market, but most institutional investors focus on commercial real estate.

Commercial and residential real estate markets are inextricably linked, so I present data from both markets, especially because house price histories date back further than commercial property indices. I should stress, however, that real estate investors treat the commercial and residential markets differently, and the two markets can move out of lockstep for extended periods.

Historical Performance

A recent study by Francis and Ibbotson (2009) presents comprehensive evidence on U.S. real estate (RE) returns between 1978 and 2008. Here are the geometric average total nominal returns over this 31-year span when inflation averaged 4%:

- Private RE: commercial RE 10.0%, residential RE 5.7%, farmland 8.8%
- Listed RE: equity REITs 11.9% (in contrast, debt-focused mortgage REITs earned only 4.9%)
- For comparison, large-cap U.S. stocks earned 10.8%, small caps 13.1%, short-term Treasuries 6.7%, long-term Treasuries 9.8%, long-term corporates 9.1%, and commodities 7.8%.

---

[26]NCREIF is the National Council of Real Estate Investment Fiduciaries and constructs an appraisal-based (not transaction-based) index of commercial properties likely to be held by institutional investors.

Private RE returns likely overstate what investors actually could have achieved, because fees, costs, and taxes may be understated. Even so, residential RE gave a disappointing performance (a 1.7% real return, including rental income), while commercial RE's 6% real return looks appealing. Equity REITs fared best, but they benefited from leverage, a favorable time period for small-cap stocks (which they resemble, with a correlation of 0.74), and the growing institutional demand for this segment.

Exhibit 5.2 compares long-run average returns for many of these real estate categories. The bars in the exhibit show average returns since 1978 or since 1984, for which I have more data series. These averages hide two boom markets (around 1980 and in the early 2000s), a slowdown (around 1990), and a crash (2008–2009). Private real estate (both the NCREIF and MIT-CRE indices) have earned a bit over a 7% annual return since 1984, while listed holdings (REITs and other property stocks) all earned over 8%. Although the MIT-CRE index and the NCREIF index have comparable long-run returns, the former has twice as high volatility as it is not as artificially smoothed, so its measured Sharpe ratio is lower—but more realistic.[27]

Exhibit 5.2. Compound Average Returns of Private and Publicly Traded Real Estate Investments

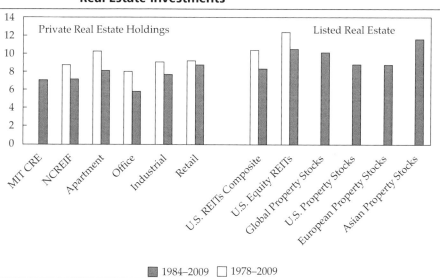

■ 1984–2009 □ 1978–2009

Sources: Bloomberg, MIT Center for Real Estate, NCREIF, FTSE, Global Property Research.

[27] Appraisal-based returns are excessively smooth, reducing their measured volatilities and correlations with other assets. The listed REIT return series are arguably excessively volatile. The MIT Center for Real Estate (MIT-CRE) index relies on actual transactions in the NCREIF database and is somewhere between appraisal-based and listed indices. For details on these indices and their return calculations, see websites www.ncreif.com and web.mit.edu/CRE/.

Between 1984 and 2009, Asian property stocks were the best performers, but if we had started the sample in 1990 after the Japanese bubble ended, they would have had the lowest return (4%). During that 20-year period, timber (11.8%) and infrastructure stocks (9.3%) would have been the stars (these series were not yet available in 1984, so they are not shown in the chart). Timber was also the only category that earned positive returns in 2008–2009 (at least on paper, pun intended); most others lost 10% to 15% in each of the two years.

I do not have good-quality data on global private real estate or house prices, but it is well-known that the early 2000s housing boom and the subsequent bust were global phenomena. Some of the hottest property markets in the 1990s and 2000s were the U.K., Ireland, Australia, Spain, and South Africa, while Japan and Germany were major laggards.

Long histories only available on house prices: NCREIF data extend back to 1978, and REIT returns, a bit earlier. Earlier data estimates are available for U.S. house prices but not for commercial real estate. The best-known series is the composite real house price series since 1890 that Robert Shiller and Karl Case created from various data sources (see **Exhibit 5.3**). Shiller's result has been summarized as saying that house prices barely kept up with inflation, except for the bubble run-up. This finding is surprising but consistent with other evidence that Manhattan and Amsterdam land, both in great locations, barely maintained their real value over 100 and 400 years, respectively.

Net real house price appreciation (HPA) was minimal over the 120-year window (0.3% per annum), but there were two big rallies—the late 1940s (due to the postwar return of soldiers) and the early 2000s—and two big falls—a real

Exhibit 5.3. Real House Prices Estimated by Robert Shiller, 1890–2010

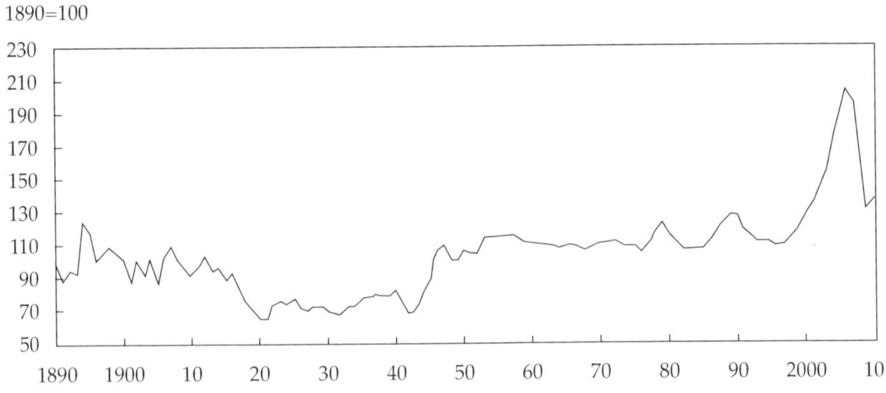

Source: Robert Shiller's website (www.econ.yale.edu/~shiller).

fall during the 1910s inflation and the recent crunch. For comparison, Davis and Heathcote (2007) report real HPA of 1.4% for 1930–2000, 0.5% higher than the Shiller data show for the same window.

Because these studies do not include yield income, to get estimates of total returns, I turn to the history of rental yields for U.S. owner-occupied housing since 1960 compiled by Davis, Lehnert, and Martin (2008). For the 1960–2008 period for which Davis *et al.* rental yields are available, the Davis–Heathcote (2007) nominal (real) HPA is 5.7% (2.0%). Combined with an average rental yield of over 5%, the estimated total nominal (real) return for 1960–2008 is 11.5% (7.0%). This gives a more benign picture of historical housing returns than Shiller's analysis, though the rental yields may overstate the benefits investors would earn because only regular utility expenses, not repairs or other capital expenditures, are subtracted from income.

Ex Ante Value Measures

The most popular real estate value indicator is the *rental yield, or the inverse of the price-to-rent ratio.* It is often thought of as the real estate market equivalent to earnings yield in the equity market (the inverse of P/E), but it can also be viewed as equivalent to dividend yield (D/P or carry). The difference between these concepts in real estate is arguably small because over very long horizons, the real growth of house prices has been negligible; that is, there are almost no "retained earnings," so $E \approx D$. The nominal (real) total return on housing reflects the rental yield (net of unreimbursed utilities, taxes, and other recurring expenses as well as capital expenditures) plus nominal (real) house price appreciation.

Capitalization or cap rate is a concept closely related to the rental yield and income return—these can even be exactly the same, but the detailed usage varies (cap rate is used in commercial RE, rental yield in residential RE). Cap rate is the ratio of a property's recurring earnings or net operating income to its price. Recurring earnings are primarily rent payments less expenses. The subtracted expenses exclude extraordinary items (lumpy capital expenses, etc.). When all capex is subtracted from cap rates, we get *cash flow yield,* which is a better indicator of the cash income an investor can expect from a property. The average gap between the cap rate and cash flow yield between 1979 and 2004 in NCREIF data was almost 3% (8% vs. 5%). The income return before capex is close to the cap rate, but the return series after capex subtraction is more realistic.

Exhibit 5.4 plots the rental yield for U.S. housing from Davis *et al.* (2008) as well as cap rates and income returns for commercial real estate from NCREIF. The rental yield fell from about 5% in the 1990s to 3.1% in 2006 before returning to 5% by 2009. Just as with financial assets, short-term changes in asset prices are primarily driven by valuation changes; the correlation between year-over-year changes in real house prices and year-over-year changes in rental yields is −0.88. Comparing the three series, it is visually clear that the housing

Exhibit 5.4. Rental Yield in U.S. Housing and Cap Rate and Income Return in Commercial Real Estate

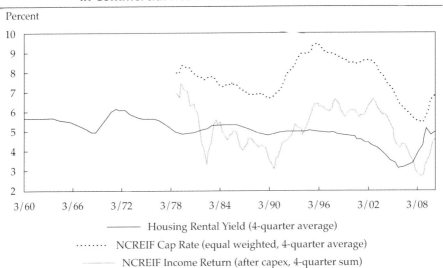

Percent

——— Housing Rental Yield (4-quarter average)

········ NCREIF Cap Rate (equal weighted, 4-quarter average)

——— NCREIF Income Return (after capex, 4-quarter sum)

Sources: NCREIF and Davis, Lehnert, and Martin (2008); data located at Land and Property Values in the U.S., Lincoln Institute of Land Policy (www.lincolninst.edu/resources/).

market led the commercial real estate market both in the early 2000s rally phase and especially in the late 2000s bust. The NCREIF annual income return before capex (not shown) closely tracks the cap rate, so the gap between the two NCREIF series in Exhibit 5.4 largely reflects capex. The gap between the housing rental yield and the NCREIF income return tells something about fluctuating relative valuations between housing and commercial real estate, but the series are not directly comparable.

As with other asset classes, in addition to making comparisons of absolute valuation (the *ex ante* attractiveness of an asset versus its own history), it is useful to look at the relative attractiveness of the asset class. For example, we can compare the cap rate of a private real estate index or the dividend yield of a REIT index with the dividend yield of a broad equity index or with the (nominal or real) yields in fixed-income markets.

Ruff (2007) tracks the risk premium for commercial real estate over time by comparing with the Treasury yield the estimated total *ex ante* real estate return that consists of the following three components, each shown along with the assumptions used to estimate it:

- Income (i.e., cash flow yield) = (Cap rate − 2% capex)
- Income growth = Expected long-run inflation
- Expected valuation change = 0

110

The cap rate averaged 9.6% for 1965–2006, rising from 8% in 1965 to double digits between 1978 and 1985 (higher than the NCREIF estimates above) and back down to 7% by 2005. Subtracting capex (assumed to be fixed at 2% per year) and adding expected inflation gives an expected total return series that rose from 8.5% in 1965 to 19% in 1981 before falling back and ending at 7.5% in 2006. The *ex ante* real estate risk premium over the 10-year Treasury averaged 4% over 42 years, peaking at 8% in 1980 and troughing at 2% in 1984 and then again at 2.9% in 2006.

Overall, the long-run real return reflects mainly the cash yield. However, the cash yield may be overstated because capex could well amount to more than 2%. To balance this possibility, the income growth assumption is conservative. While Shiller as well as Ruff (2007) assume no *real* HPA or income growth, in line with the very long-term empirical record, others estimate a 1% to 2% real HPA.

This long-run analysis assumes no valuation changes. However, after the boom–bust cycle and some evidence on mean-reverting valuations, it appears that starting valuations matter even for medium-term expected returns.

Some words on value indicators are in order in the context of the recent real estate bubble. Real house prices, price-to-rent ratios and price-to-(labor-) income ratios, all shot up to unprecedented levels, far from long-run trends. Because of low mortgage rates, the proportion of one's income required for housing debt service was not as extreme, relative to its own history; affordability of financing thus served as one fundamental justification for the rising house prices. The *user cost of housing* is a broader concept that takes into account the financial returns from owner-occupied housing (including expected HPA and financing costs) as well as risk differences, tax benefits, property taxes, depreciation, and maintenance costs. In equilibrium, the expected total cost of renting and owning a house should be equal over the life of the house, after accounting for the above features. Thus, higher price-to-rent ratios may reflect lower financing costs or changes in any of the features listed above. Such comparisons are one way to assess how much of the housing market rally was based on fundamentals and how much was irrational, perhaps reflecting extrapolative expectations and the naïve belief that house prices cannot fall. General liquidity, high risk tolerance (complacency), securitization innovations in mortgage markets, and lax lending standards also contributed. Wallison (2009) has also blamed government policy intended at expanding the proportion of homeowners, but his argument explains only the housing boom in the U.S., not the rest of the world. Rajan (2010) argues that U.S. politicians promoted home ownership and, especially, the easy availability of mortgage financing for low-income households as a palliative against stagnating real wages and rising income inequality.

Real estate returns also exhibit short-term momentum and long-term reversal tendencies. The momentum effects are stronger, but it is hard to ascertain how much they reflect smoothed and/or stale prices and how much they identify tradeable opportunities. In part, the observed momentum likely reflects extrapolative expectations. Clearly, many house buyers in the mid-2000s expected continued price rises. Even after the well-publicized U.S. housing bust and double-digit price falls in the U.K., if you tell Londoners who experienced real HPA of 6% between 1995 and 2009 (excluding rental income) that the long-run expectation is near zero or that valuation ratios have some predictive ability, a shrug is perhaps the most common response.

Main Determinants

Property market fundamentals (which affect income growth) and capital market forces (which affect cap rates) both determine the *ex ante* attractiveness and *ex post* returns of real estate investments. Fundamental determinants include economic growth (HPA is clearly procyclical), inflation, demographics, and population migration as well as shorter-term supply-and-demand factors. REITs are driven more by equity market movements. Financing rates (Treasury yields and mortgage spreads) influence RE prices both instantly and with a lag. Apparently, a unique RE factor exists beyond stock and bond market influences. One reason for a premium over Treasuries is the relative illiquidity of real estate.

Fluctuations in cap rates and rental yields are important drivers of real estate prices, often overwhelming the fundamental impact of income growth. A time-varying housing premium in rental yields may have irrational as well as rational origins. Property income in the U.S. grew nearly monotonically in the 1980s and 1990s. It then *fell* 20% between 2001 and 2004, but the negative effect of the fall on real estate prices was overwhelmed by the sharp fall in cap rates between 2002 and 2006. Rational capital market influences—growing liquidity, low bond yields—explained the early part of the cap rate decline, but at later stages, naïve extrapolative expectations of house price appreciation, combined with securitization and lax lending standards, likely dominated.

Besides real yields, corporate spreads and economy-wide leverage and liquidity can empirically explain the time-series behavior of cap rates. The narrowing credit spread and the growing availability of debt capital could explain the fall in cap rates in the mid-2000s, while the trend reversals in these series coincided with the rise in cap rates after 2007. Such empirical evidence says nothing about the rationality of these valuation changes, but a widespread interpretation is that a liquidity- and sentiment-driven real estate bubble and a credit bubble reinforced each other. Arguably, real estate is more prone to bubbles than other asset classes, due to the difficulty of pinning down fair value and the near impossibility of selling the asset short, as well as the cost and infrequency of transactions.

Some academics argue that the trend decline in global real bond yields fed the equity and housing market rallies (of the late 1990s and early 2000s, respectively), helping to reduce discount rates in competing asset classes. This explanation is at best partial. While real yields in all asset classes fell from the 1980s to the 2000s, the downtrends were hardly synchronous. Rental yields only started to fall around 1997, and the major decline occurred after 2001. Moreover, real yields fell much less than nominal yields. In theory, the rental yield is a *real* measure and should vary with real rather than nominal yields.

Money illusion may also have contributed to the rapid HPA of the early 2000s. The *Economist* frequently warned about the folly of aggressive mortgage borrowing inspired by exceptionally low inflation and nominal yields. Brunnermeier and Julliard (2008) argue that multi-decade evidence in both the U.K. and U.S. housing markets is consistent with money illusion. Empirically, rental yields—and, based on the authors' decomposition, especially their mispricing component—move with inflation and nominal bond yields while exhibiting scant relation to real yields. It is harder to explain why house prices also rallied during the inflationary 1970s. Piazzesi and Schneider (2007) propose a model where disagreement between rational and inflation-illusioned investors can cause housing rallies when inflation is both abnormally low *and* high. During the 1970s, rational investor buying was behind the housing boom, while the latest boom saw the financially less sophisticated (illusioned) investors as key buyers.

A recent study emphasizes demographic influences on housing markets. Using panel data from 22 advanced countries between 1970 and 2009, Takats (2010) estimates that both real GDP-per-capita growth and total population growth boost real house prices one-for-one (a 1% increase in either series raises real house prices by 1%) while ageing has a negative impact (a 1% increase in the dependency ratio—the ratio between old-age population to working-age population—reduces real house prices by 0.7%). These factors are not the only drivers of house prices, but they partly explain the lagging performance of Japan and Germany. More generally, the study argues that the multi-decade tailwinds on housing and other asset prices are now turning into multi-decade headwinds.

I have little to say about the active management of real estate investments, or skills needed for it, partly due to my lack of expertise. I can only note that performance measurement and separating alpha from beta returns are inherently more difficult for illiquid asset classes than for liquid ones. Investable performance benchmarks with frequent mark-to-market pricing are simply not available, and it will take "forever" to distinguish whether returns earned reflect the risks taken (beta exposures) or particular active management skills (alpha).

5.3. Commodities

Return Decomposition and Theories of Expected Risk Premia

Most financial investors do not hold spot commodities outright—just consider the inconvenience and storage costs that would be involved—but rather gain commodity exposure through futures contracts. This chapter does not focus on the fundamental drivers of spot commodity prices (which are quite diverse across commodities, say, for gold versus oil versus wheat) but on the more technical determinants of commodity futures returns.

For each commodity, there are several futures contracts with different maturities. The nearest-dated ("nearby") contract is often the most liquid. Therefore, even investors who plan to maintain a commodity exposure over several years often hold the actively traded nearby futures contracts.

Commodity futures returns are often decomposed into three elemental parts: spot price change, collateral return, and roll return. Collateral return refers to the margin income earned when buying futures contracts, typically earning the Treasury bill return. Roll return depends on the shape of the futures term structure, as explained below. The change in the spot price (often proxied by the nearby futures price) is the most visible and volatile part of return. However, the long-run *average return* for commodity futures investing largely reflects the two more stable components.

To understand roll returns, consider an investor who wants to maintain long exposure to commodities over time through a sequence of short-dated futures contracts. For example, investing in the popular S&P GSCI involves holding a long position in the nearby futures contract until it is close to its expiry date. Index managers then sell the soon-expiring first contract and replace it with a long position in the second contract. That is, they "roll their position." The gain or loss from rolling the position is zero only if the first and second futures contracts have the same price—that is, if the term structure of futures prices is flat. If the term structure is downward sloping ("backwardated" in commodities jargon), the roll return is positive as the second contract can be bought at a lower price than the first contract was sold. Conversely, when the term structure is upward sloping ("in contango"), the roll return is negative.[28]

It is tempting, and not unreasonable, to think of the three components of the commodity futures return thus:

- Collateral return ≈ riskless return.
- Roll return ≈ *ex ante* risk premium.
- Spot price change ≈ unexpected return.

An extensive literature reviews the decomposition of commodity returns. The mechanical decomposition into collateral, roll, and spot returns is easy. However, equating spot price changes with unexpected returns is not completely correct because markets may have expected a part of the spot price change.

An analogy of the commodity term structure with the term structure of interest rates may help us see the limitations in this approach. Recall that any term structure reflects some combination of expected rate changes and required risk premia. If we equate steep backwardation and a high roll return with a high *ex ante* risk premium, we effectively assume that the market expects the current spot rate to remain unchanged forever. The roll return measures expected excess return only if the spot price and the term structure of constant-maturity futures prices follow a random walk and thus are expected to remain unchanged. This empirical assumption may work well on average (see Exhibit 5.9), but sometimes it is too extreme.

---

[28] If we focus on specific calendar-month contracts— say, for crude oil futures—the cumulative annual (excess) return of the proposed strategy can be measured by chaining the distinct returns of 12 monthly contracts. For example, if the strategy design involves rolling into a new contract just at each month-end, we can chain the January return of the contract that expires in February, the February return of the contract that expires in March (e.g., Bloomberg ticker CLH1 for the March 2011 contract), and so on. If we, instead, focus on the price evolution of the *generic* nearby contract (e.g., ticker CL1 in Bloomberg), the cumulative annual (excess) return of this strategy reflects the price change in the generic nearby contract over the year *as well as* the return impact of rolling positions each month. The main text takes the latter approach because focusing on generic nearby contracts leads to a convenient decomposition of excess returns into roll returns and spot price changes.

Both perspectives—chaining actual calendar-month contract returns and the generic nearby contact series—give the same returns when used correctly. However, investors sometimes mix the two approaches. When investors want to see a longer history of crude oil prices, it is common to plot the time series of the generic nearby contract prices (CL1). This is fine as a visual tool, but I stress that the price change should not be confused with the excess return of any investment strategy because this generic price series ignores roll returns. (All serious performance analysis begins with creating a proper excess return series that includes roll.) For example, the nearby futures price of crude oil ended up being virtually unchanged between mid-2007 and mid-2009 (near $71 per barrel), but the realized excess return was −36% due to persistently negative roll return.

What drives the shape of the commodity term structure and expected commodity returns? The classic commodity pricing literature focuses on the former and only indirectly addresses the latter (expected risk premia).

The oldest idea, attributable to John Maynard Keynes, is that the term structure of commodity prices is normally inverted (backwardated: S > F) because producers create more hedging pressure than consumers do. Producers' selling of futures—to lock in the prices of the commodities they produce—pushes the futures price below the level of the expected spot price. The net hedging pressure hypothesis stresses that speculators take the other side of this trade so as to earn an insurance (or risk) premium for the service of bearing the price risk. Speculators earn this premium by buying at lower futures prices and expecting to sell at higher spot prices. Then, F = E(S) + RP (risk premium RP is negative due to the hedging or insurance activity of producers), so on average S > F. However, if consumers have greater hedging needs than producers, the futures price curve can slope upwards (be in contango).

Alternatively, the theory of storage can explain a backwardated or contangoed term structure shape by considering the role of storage and financing costs and the "convenience yield" of holding inventory. The convenience yield is the intangible benefit (or potential profit) from having commodity supplies on hand when they are needed or wanted. The convenience yield lets inventory holders (of the spot commodity, not the futures holder) benefit from temporary price increases due to temporary local shortages or from the ability to maintain a production process despite interruptions in the supply of a commodity used as raw material. The spot price thus reflects both the consumption value (convenience yield) and the deferred value (expected future asset value); the futures price reflects only the latter. The theory of storage thus says that:

Spot price – Futures price = Convenience yield – Storage cost – Financing cost.

Backwardation (S > F) is likely when the convenience yield is high, storage costs are low, and financing costs are low. Conversely, high storage costs (or high interest rates) can make spot prices systematically low relative to futures. High storage costs also reduce inventories and thus make spot prices more important in balancing supply and demand, resulting in greater seasonal variation in prices (and in the S–F gap).

The convenience yield depends inversely on inventory levels, because the potential to profit from having ready supplies is greatest when inventories are low. For example, agricultural commodities display a greater tendency for backwardation (S > F) just before the harvest season; low inventories imply high convenience yields, high spot prices, and steep backwardation. That is, when a seasonal scarcity-induced spike in the spot price makes the whole futures term structure steeply inverted, it seems likely that the inversion partly reflects the temporary nature of the richness in the spot price and the market's expectation of mean-reverting (falling) prices once seasonal pressures have abated.

Standard asset pricing models indicate that required risk premia reflect covariances with marginal utility (which is, perhaps, proxied by major systematic factors capturing economic or market conditions). Using this logic, commodities may or may not warrant high risk premia. Their correlation with financial assets has historically been low. Unlike financial assets, commodities (especially energy) tend to be good inflation hedges. However, some commodity prices (notably industrial metals) are quite procyclical, perhaps increasingly so. Finally, all commodities tend to benefit from loose monetary policy and easy credit and liquidity conditions. This last feature may explain why the correlation between commodities and equities increased in the 2000s, making commodities less effective diversifiers. The inflation-hedging ability points to negative risk premia, whereas the growth, equity, and liquidity betas point to positive required premia.

Interestingly, Erb and Harvey (2006) document a strong cross-sectional relation between average roll returns and sensitivities to unexpected inflation. That is, commodity sectors that have been the best inflation hedges—notably, energy—have also produced the highest roll returns (and, over many time periods, the highest realized returns). Perhaps because of its inflation-hedging ability, energy (with negative equity and bond betas) also has been a better diversifier against equities and bonds than other commodity sectors. This confluence of desirable characteristics seems too good to be true. I suspect that a fortuitously benign sample is part of the story—the increasing scarcity of oil and the growing demand from China and other emerging markets have boosted oil prices, resulting in persistent upside surprises.

One can try to assess commodities' expected returns from a supply-and-demand perspective if standard finance models do not apply well. As just noted, the growing developing-world demand for energy contrasts with finite supplies. In addition, inventory conditions influence commodity prices in the short term, but at least for oil, what lies in the ground matters more for the medium term. The main speculative stores are held underground by oil producers—much more cheaply than in any above-ground storage facilities. Owners will not rush to pump these supplies out of the ground if they expect fast oil price appreciation in the future. Given OPEC's partly monopolistic pricing power, oil exporters can adjust their production and inventories until the expected spot oil price increase just equals the risk-adjusted interest rate. Finally, a debate continues regarding the role of growing institutional demand for commodities as an investment, as well as speculative demand from trend followers, in feeding the long-term commodity bull market. This debate has been reflected in Congressional hearings.

Fundamentally, it is useful to think that the long-run anchor for commodity prices reflects the marginal cost of production—albeit estimated with large uncertainty—while spot prices and the term structure largely reflect inventories and thus demand-and-supply conditions, which are more cyclical. Long-dated forward prices of oil, in particular, were quite stable around $20 per barrel for a long time but became unhinged after 2003, gyrating almost as much as spot prices. Discretionary traders who take views on commodities must take into account structural, cyclical, and technical drivers.

Historical Average Returns on Commodity Investing

I will focus on the experience of investing in commodity futures and not investing outright in commodities or commodity-related stocks. Over the past 40 years, commodity futures (as represented by the S&P GSCI) earned a 10% annualized total return, of which more than half reflected the Treasury bill return that would be earned on collateral required by futures exchanges to be deposited as margin. The excess return over Treasury bills reflects spot price change and roll return. Spot price changes dominate short-term return volatility, but the roll return has been a significant component of long-run *average* excess returns. The roll return was only mildly negative over long time periods but contributed to 8% annual losses in the 2000s due to the prevalence of contango (akin to negative carry), which offset most of the 10% annual spot price increases.

Exhibit 5.6 splits the cumulative annual excess return of the S&P GSCI into its two components: spot price changes and roll returns. Roll returns used to be positive, on average, but between 2005 and 2009, the annual roll losses ranged between −8% and −25%. As a result, the cumulative advantage from roll since 1970 had all been lost by the end of 2009. The general shift of the oil term structure from backwardation to contango has been the main reason, but the increasing role of institutional commodity index investors and the temporary market impact of index investors rolling their contracts in synchrony (that is, at the same predictable time each month) accentuated the roll losses.

The right half of **Exhibit 5.5** shows the average excess returns of index subsectors for the full 1970–2009 time period and for each decade. Since 1983, industrial metals and energy were the best-performing sectors. The agriculture sector had the lowest returns, and livestock and precious metals also underperformed cash. Among individual commodities, unleaded gas and crude oil had the highest geometric excess returns in recent decades, while natural gas has fared very poorly.

Exhibit 5.5. Compound Annual Returns of S&P GSCI and Its Subsectors

	S&P Total Return	GSCI Excess Return	Index Spot Return	Subsector Excess Returns				
				Agriculture	Livestock	Precious Metals (1973–)	Industrial Metals (1977–)	Energy (1983–)
1970–2009	10.0%	3.8%	4.2%	−1.3%	1.7%			
1983–2009	7.4	2.3	3.6	−3.7	−0.9	−1.3	5.7	3.8
1970s	21.2	13.7	9.0	12.6	11.2			
1980s	10.7	1.0	−1.4	−6.2	4.9	−13.7	−0.2	
1990s	3.9	−1.2	−0.6	−5.4	−1.5	−6.6	−0.6	−0.7
2000s	5.1	2.2	10.4	−5.0	−6.7	10.7	7.6	3.8

Sources: Bloomberg, S&P GSCI.

Exhibit 5.6. Cumulative Excess Returns of the S&P GSCI and Its Two Components, 1970–2009

Cumulative Excess Returns (log scale)

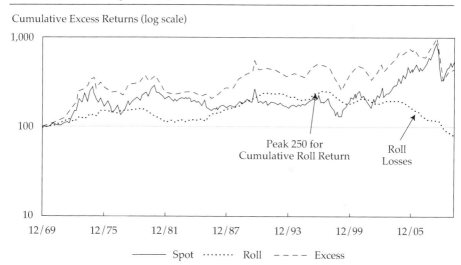

Sources: Bloomberg, S&P GSCI.

Eyeballing the cumulative performance in **Exhibit 5.7**, agriculture, live-stock, and precious metals saw their heyday in the 1970s, energy in the 1970s (not shown) and 1998–2007, and industrial commodities in the 2000s (up to mid-2008). The overall S&P GSCI has time-varying constituent weights but has long been dominated by the energy sector.

Exhibit 5.7. Cumulative Excess Returns of the Subsectors of the S&P GSCI Index, 1970–2009

Cumulative Excess Returns (log scale)

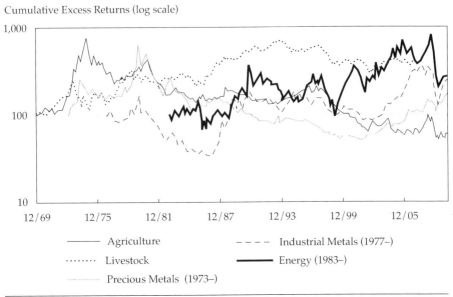

——— Agriculture			— — — Industrial Metals (1977–)			
········· Livestock			▬▬▬ Energy (1983–)			
········· Precious Metals (1973–)						

Sources: Bloomberg, S&P GSCI.

While the S&P GSCI is the oldest and still the most popular index of commodity futures (it was launched in 1991, and the overall return index history was back-populated to 1970), numerous new indices have come to the marketplace. Some have better performance than the S&P GSCI, perhaps partly reflecting hindsight in index construction. Nonetheless, the changes made in the new indices appear *a priori* reasonable: less weight in the energy sector; changes in roll schedules (because monthly rolling from nearby to second contract according to the S&P GSCI's schedule puts one-sided pressure on market prices and causes temporary price distortions that other traders can exploit or avoid); and, increasingly, a shift from holding only the most liquid nearby futures contract toward including a basket of deferred contracts.

The annualized return *for the index* also includes a so-called *diversification return*. The geometric mean return of the index can be several percentage points higher than the average geometric mean return of the constituents. The reason is that diversification reduces the volatility of the index; lower volatility (smoother returns) has no impact on the arithmetic mean but does boost the geometric mean. For the S&P GSCI, the gap between arithmetic and geometric means is 2% (12% – 10%), reflecting 20% volatility. For most constituents, this gap is even wider, reducing the geometric means of narrow subsectors or single commodities relative to their arithmetic means.

For a longer history, Hong and Yogo (2010) show that the mean excess return of an aggregate commodity futures portfolio between 1965 and 2008 was 7.08% per year, roughly half of which came from spot price growth and half from roll gains. The Sharpe ratio was 0.50. The portfolio was an equally weighted composite of four commodity sectors: agriculture, livestock, energy, and metals.

Broadly speaking, very long histories of real spot prices show a downtrend in agricultural commodities, an upward trend in energy, and a limited trend in metals. Roll returns and diversification returns are important long-run additions to commodity index returns. If anything, roll returns have exacerbated these spot price trends, boosting the returns of the energy sector and detracting from the returns of the agricultural sector. Overall, commodity sector data do not appear consistent with theories that say that the term structure shape reflects the market's spot rate expectations, although expectations of spot rates reverting to their long-term mean play a role during scarcity-induced spot price spikes.

Expected Commodity Returns

As noted above, long-run average returns across commodities are strongly influenced by the roll return. Typically, commodities with positive roll have earned positive excess returns (e.g., oils, nickel, and sugar tend to have back-wardated term structures and earn high returns), whereas commodities with a negative roll have earned negative excess returns (e.g., natural gas, aluminum, and corn tend to have term structures in contango and low average returns). Scatter plots of long-term average total returns and average roll returns across commodities line up nicely near a 45-degree line (see **Exhibit 5.8**). Such evidence has reinforced the idea that the roll return measures commodities' *ex ante* risk premium. Incidentally, the averages in this graph conceal interesting time variation; for example, the average roll return for crude oil fell from positive, +6% per year for 1992–2000, to negative, −3% for 2001–2009.

The roll return has been less useful for *short-term* market timing, perhaps because occasional scarcity-induced spot price spikes have coincided with an extreme backwardation and subsequent cheapening. Yet, even a dynamic cross-commodity strategy based on the roll return—overweighting commodities with a currently backwardated term structure and underweighting those with a contangoed term structure—has added value over time. The aforementioned Hong and Yogo (2010) study also notes that the aggregate roll across commodities has historically been useful for market-timing an aggregate commodity portfolio (general backwardation of commodity term structures predicts higher near-term returns), as have certain interest rate indicators (low short rates and an inverted yield curve both predict high near-term commodity returns).

Exhibit 5.8. Long-Run Average Returns Are Closely Related to Average Roll Returns, 1992–2009

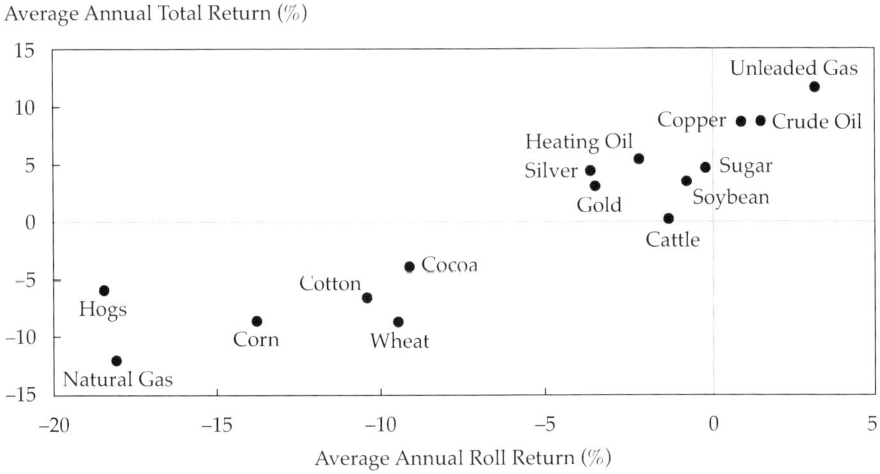

Average Annual Total Return (%)

Sources: Bloomberg, Brevan Howard, author's calculations.

Momentum-based dynamic strategies, such as trend following, have been even more successful. Empirically, extrapolating recent performance has been the best predictor of commodities' near-term returns. This result may reflect irrational influences, but Gorton, Hayashi, and Rouwenhorst (2007) argue that the profitable momentum and roll strategies may proxy for inventory effects, in line with the theory of storage. Low inventories, rising spot prices, and steep backwardation—all predict high near-term returns.

For commodities, it is often hard to come up with implementable value anchors. The most common value indicator is simply mean reversion: deviation from fundamental value is proxied by the deviation of the current price from a longer-term trend. Given that some commodities follow persistent trends for good reasons, this measure was not a useful value indicator for years until 2008. For many commodities, the fair value is the marginal production cost (extracting, refining, storing, and transporting), but these costs are often extremely hard to pin down, given uncertainty about technology, taxation, and politics.

The modest returns of standard commodity indices, such as the S&P GSCI, in recent years—notably, the negative roll return offsetting most of the spot price gains in 2000s—have raised interest in more dynamic indices that try to enhance performance in various ways. A plethora of such "second-generation" indices are now offered to investors. Rallis, Miffre, and Fuertes (2011) systematically review three approaches from the perspective of a long-only investor: overweighting upward-trending commodities, overweighting positive-roll commodities, and extending futures maturity to longer (deferred) contracts from the most liquid front contracts. All approaches appear to boost returns and Sharpe ratios, but they also involve higher trading costs (and, likely, fees).

5.4. Hedge Funds

5.4.1. Introduction

Hedge funds (HFs) are pools of money run by HF managers, who face less regulation and have much greater flexibility than traditional managers, notably, in their use of short selling, leverage, and derivatives. HFs face limited disclosure requirements, although transparency demands are growing from both customers and regulators. HF management contracts typically involve exceptionally high compensation arrangements with a large performance-related component; a 1½% to 2% fixed management fee plus an incentive fee consisting of 20% of returns are the norm. Managers are further incentivized by holding significant parts of their wealth in their funds. Absolute return mandates and restricted withdrawals are also characteristic of many HF contracts. Assets allocated to HFs grew quickly in the 2000s, peaking above $2 trillion in early 2008 and then falling by nearly half over a year of losses and redemptions, before rebounding again.

An investment in a HF is primarily a bet on the manager's skill in identifying and exploiting profit opportunities. The number of HF management styles and approaches is almost without limit. Collectively, HF managers cover all asset classes and all conceivable investment approaches—from discretionary decision making to purely systematic strategies, from betting on the market direction to fine-tuned relative value or risk arbitrage trades, from simple linear exposures to highly nonlinear exposures, from superfast, automated, high-frequency trading to nearly static long-term investing, from the most liquid assets with transparent pricing to highly illiquid markets with ambiguous valuations. In reality, hedge funds do not hedge away *all* risks; nor do most of them even hedge away all systematic (market) risks. Instead, they identify attractive market opportunities, try to isolate the exposures they want to assume, and hedge away the undesired exposures.

Many different classifications of HFs exist—each index provider, many funds of hedge funds (FoFs), and many end-users have designed their own classification systems. The obvious distinctions are between direct investing in single-manager HFs versus indirect investing via FoFs. Some newer vehicles, such as investable HF indices, HF replication products, and HF beta products, are also noteworthy.

Single-manager HFs are often classified into some asset or style bucket and are expected to focus on investments in their area of specialization. Funds may be classified by asset class (mainly, equity versus fixed income, but narrower domains are also used) and styles (directional, arbitrage, event-driven, opportunistic). The most popular categories have tended to be equity long–short and global macro/multi-strategy. One interesting dimension involves convergent strategies (which benefit from normalization of relative values and declining volatilities: many arbitrage and market-neutral strategies fit this description) versus divergent strategies (which benefit from momentum, new trends, and volatility: macro and CTA). This book will not cover specific strategies—for a discussion of them, see, for example, Jaeger (2008) and Anson (2006). Even within any one strategy, there are specialists in every asset and/ or trading approach, and each of the specialists may have enough proprietary expertise to fill a book.

5.4.2. Assessing Hedge Fund Performance—Balancing Two Opposite Views

I contrast two opposite readings of the HF industry's track record *as a group*. The positive spin—the industry's marketing line—is mainly about skillful alpha providers. The skeptics, in contrast, argue that high industry Sharpe ratios reflect various reporting biases that overstate returns as well as overlooking various risks that the Sharpe ratio does not capture well. (I will later return to the quite different questions of whether *individual managers* can predictably beat the markets and, if so, which ones.)

■ *The positive story involves some empirical facts and some* a priori *reasons for HF outperformance*

Empirical facts: standard reported results show that HFs have produced higher net returns and higher risk-adjusted returns than traditional equity/bond portfolios and have certainly outperformed cash, which is arguably the right benchmark for an "absolute return" manager. For example, the Hedge Fund Research (HFR) hedge fund index earned a compound average return of 12.3% and a Sharpe ratio of 1.1 over 1990–2009. Even the more realistic representation in the HFR FoF index achieved a Sharpe ratio of 0.7. In short, HFs have produced positive net alpha after fees. Because fees are high, this finding implies very high before-fee (gross) returns. Such apparent skill stands in contrast to the well-documented finding that mutual funds and pension funds tend to lag their benchmarks, at least when returns are calculated net of fees and other costs. So, the simple story is that alpha is transferred not just from some smart or lucky investors to less smart or lucky ones—but that this transfer happens systematically and persistently across sectors, from long-only and/or retail investors to absolute-return managers.

Some *a priori* reasons to expect HF managers to outperform include the following:

• HF managers face fewer constraints than long-only managers. In particular, they can sell short, lever up their positions, and use derivatives more freely than long-only managers (even if the latter have acquired some flexibility on all these fronts as part of the two-sided convergence between long-only and absolute-return managers). Depending on the mandate, they may also have more flexibility to exploit opportunities between asset classes or "silos" (subsets of asset classes). And they may have lock-ups, side pockets, and other arrangements that constrain investor redemptions and give managers a better chance to extract liquidity premia from the markets.

• HF managers are more motivated and better incentivized than long-only managers. Performance fees and managers' personal stakes in the funds should align their interests with those of their investors. Indeed, HFs with "skin in the game" lost less in 2007–2008 than banks and traditional managers.

• The most skilled and experienced traders and fund managers are enticed to start or join HFs because there they can best exploit their edge and extract the best rewards for it. HFs can often afford the best employees.

• As a group, HFs provide extreme breadth. Diversification across many hedge fund managers in a variety of asset classes and investment styles cannot be matched even by a broad set of equity- and bond-only managers.

• HFs may be earning fair rewards for various economic functions they offer: capital provision, risk sharing, liquidity provision, and market completion (offering alternative beta exposures not otherwise available for investors).

▦ The negative story focuses on biases and risks

The negative stories come in two forms: biases and risks. First, recall that *all reporting to HF indices is voluntary*. The high Sharpe ratios discussed earlier partly reflect various reporting biases (survivor, backfill, etc.) that almost surely result in overstated reported returns and understated risk measures. FoF numbers are more realistic, but they contain a double layer of fees, which could explain a good chunk of the observed return difference between HF and FoF indices. Also FoF index returns may be subject to the same biases as indices of single funds, although to a lesser degree (FoFs have less scope to benefit from certain biases discussed below; see Fung and Hsieh 2002). Second, many HFs load up on various risks that the Sharpe ratio does not capture well. Simple risk adjustment may thus be insufficient—volatilities, correlations, and betas are understated and other risk factors are ignored. Among these other risk factors are a large number of alternative betas, plus illiquidity, lack of transparency, leverage-related risks, adverse skewness and kurtosis, and related hidden tail risks (such as being short volatility, which resembles selling financial catastrophe insurance).

Skeptics also raise counterpoints to the positive *a priori* arguments. The benefits of unconstrained investing and restricted redemptions were less obvious during the 2007–2008 market turmoil. There are dark sides to the incentive question: asymmetric payoffs may motivate excessive risk taking, managers may hoard assets to maximize management fees, and managers may close a fund after a large drawdown and, shortly thereafter, open a new one. Being smart also does not necessarily translate into consistent performance: LTCM is the most famous case in market history where high IQs met with catastrophic losses, but it is only one of many. Any outperformance HFs showed in the past decades as a group might reflect their aggressive risk taking during a long tailwind environment. In 2008, most HFs suffered double-digit percentage losses—better than most equity managers but not exactly capital preservation. The marketing myth of HFs as absolute return products came back to haunt the industry.

Even if HF managers have the skill to earn positive alpha and risk-adjusted returns, they have been able to keep much of the value added for themselves. HF investors have kept tolerating exceptionally high fees for several reasons: innate optimism and overconfidence as well as lottery preferences; inability to distinguish luck from skill among past outperformers; and, perhaps, underappreciation of biases and risks.

By now, there is a consensus that HF excess returns over the riskless rate are not purely alpha. Some observers even argue that after adjusting for reporting biases and various risks as well as high fees, HFs *in the aggregate* may not provide *any* alpha to their investors. Top-quartile funds do, but these are hard to identify *ex ante*. Even to the extent that some performance persistence exists, consistent top-quartile funds may be closed to new investors and their fees sometimes even exceed the 2-and-20 norm; and successful managers may capture most of the gains through these fees. Given the fact that some of the past successes reflect more luck than skill, the deal is seldom compelling to end-user investors, say critics. The critics conclude that the popularity of active funds, and especially hedge funds, reflects a triumph of hope over reason.

Let the data speak: a study on decomposing HF index returns

Ibbotson, Chen, and Zhu (2011) analyze HF returns as reported in the TASS database (1995–2009) and adjust the net returns for survivorship and backfill biases. This is an update of an earlier study to include the 2008 experience, but the results are broadly similar to those obtained in the original study. First, the authors explore the impact of two well-known biases discussed below.

- Equally weighting all funds that were live at the end of the sample, they get a 14.9% annual return.

- Including both "live" and "dead" funds removes the survivorship bias: the net return falls to 11.7%.

- Adjusting for the backfill bias (by only including returns starting from the date each fund first reports to the database) further reduces the equally weighted average return to 7.7%.

As **Exhibit 5.9** shows, the two biases can be summed in two ways. The combined impact is 7.2%, but it can be seen as the sum of 3.2% and 4.0% survivorship and backfill biases or as the sum of 5.1% and 2.1% (or something in between). Given the overlap in biases, one cannot add up the two higher bias estimates.

The results are better for a value-weighted composite, which produced 11.8% average return after both bias adjustments. Large HFs dominate the value-weighted composite, and it turns out that large HFs have outperformed small ones (albeit at higher volatility). In particular, the backfill bias has been a negligible 0.3% for the value-weighted composite, which makes sense because large funds typically have longer histories.

The authors then turn to risk adjustments. They add back typical fees (1.5% and 20%) to the equally weighted 7.7% return to get an average gross (before-fee) return of 11.1%. They regress monthly gross returns on three factors (the S&P 500, a bond return index, and a cash return index) to assess how much of the HF return reflects traditional beta sources. Using this risk model, they find a 3% intercept (alpha or average unexpected return). Thus, they can decompose the bias-adjusted 11.1% gross return into a 3.4% fee earned by HF managers, traditional beta return of 4.7% (including cash income), and alpha return of 3.0%. Even after adjusting for biases and risks, the alpha is statistically significant—apparent evidence that, even as a group, HF managers exhibited skill over this

---

Exhibit 5.9. Equally Weighted Average Returns over 1995–2009 for Subsets of Hedge Funds in the TASS Database

	Only Live Funds	Live and Dead Funds
Including backfilled returns	14.9%	11.7%
Excluding backfilled returns	12.8%	7.7%

Note: Survivorship bias (between columns) is 3.2% or 5.1%, and backfill bias (between rows) is 2.1% or 4.0%.

Source: Ibbotson, Chen, and Zhu (2011).

sample period. The authors also document positive alpha for each year in the 2000s, including 2008, and for all HF subsectors they study. Again, the results would be even more compelling for a value-weighted composite.

According to a more skeptical view, further bias and risk adjustments are warranted. While this study captures survivorship and backfill bias, it is unable to quantify selection, liquidation, and lookback biases. Moreover, the risk adjustment is deliberately simple. No alternative betas are adjusted for, because the authors do not want to penalize HF alphas-as-measured for typical alternative betas that are part of HFs' value added compared with traditional managers. However, when the authors use the Fung and Hsieh (2004) seven-factor model, which includes alternative betas, as a robustness check, they find a higher alpha of 5.2%. This result still leaves the possibility of unaccounted liquidity premia or tail risks.

▧ *Details on return biases due to voluntary reporting*

HF indices are not as comprehensive or neutral as market-cap-weighted equity market indices. They are manager composites, not universes of securities. Any HF database, or a combination of them, covers only a subset of funds—and likely a flattering subset. The main quantifiable biases in published hedge fund returns are survivorship bias and backfill bias. Underlying most biases is the voluntary nature of reporting to such databases and the flexibility that database providers give to reporting funds. Individual funds are likely to be motivated by marketing considerations because there is plenty of evidence that fund inflows are strongly (and unduly) influenced by past performance. These biases lead to overstated published returns—and understated risks—for individual funds and for the industry as a whole. Although these biases are discussed and quantified in numerous academic papers, they perhaps are not fully appreciated by HF investors.

The list of biases is long and partly overlapping.

- *Survivorship bias*: funds leave databases when they die. There is strong evidence that the extinct funds in the "graveyard" module of HF databases earned lower average returns than the live (surviving) funds.

- *Backfill bias* (also called incubation bias and instant history bias): when funds submit performance histories to the database for the first time, they can include as much of their earlier history as they want. Given this option, funds with superior histories are more likely to report them. It is also natural that among many incubated funds, the more successful ones will eventually be reported while poorer performers will not be. Empirically, it is clear that average returns are lower if backfill filters (to be explained below) are used.

- *Selection bias*: funds report mainly for marketing reasons. They may opt out because of poor performance but also because an established fund is closed and has no need to attract new capital. Because many large funds do not report to databases and are among the most successful, the sign of the bias, net of these two effects, is ambiguous.

- *Liquidation bias*: funds often stop reporting before shutting down. The last few months' performance of liquidating funds is typically poor and will not be captured in the HF index, even in the graveyard module, unless a special detective effort is made.

- *Lookback bias*: funds can even ask to have their entire historical records removed. The impact could be quantified by studying all vintages of databases, but these are rarely available. More subtly, funds can delay reporting poor performance and keep the option open whether to restart reporting.

- *Lookahead bias*: many analyses only include funds that persisted some minimum number of months. Short-lived funds that are ignored tend to have lower returns.

Only the first two biases have been extensively quantified. Several studies indicate that the survivorship bias is between 2% and 3%. That is, using only "live" funds at the end of the sample overstates industry returns by 2% to 3% (because there are nearly as many defunct funds as live ones and the defunct ones tend to have 5% to 6% lower returns than live funds). This bias can be corrected by comparing the average return for both live and defunct funds if such data are available.

Since HFs can backfill their whole return history (or a part of it) when they start to report to a database, it is conceivable that the backfilled histories in databases contain only the successful half of all funds from a true universe of fund start-ups. As a remedy, some studies adjust for the backfill bias by filtering out the first one to three years from each fund's reported returns. This adjustment may be too small (if backfilled histories are even longer) or too large (if it leaves out successful young funds without backfilled returns). Since many HF databases have added a "first reporting date" data field, it has been possible to assess the backfill bias more accurately (though perhaps too aggressively, given that this date may reflect a change in the fund's reporting policy and may occur years after the fund launch). Overall, adjusting for the backfill bias appears to reduce (equally weighted) average HF returns by 2% to 4%. The bias is milder for value-weighted averages because backfilling is more often done by small young funds.

While many studies make adjustments for survivorship and backfill biases, few studies are able to quantify selection, liquidation, lookback, and lookahead biases.

More investors read published HF index returns than academic studies about biased returns. How biased are the major indices? All HF databases capture only a subset of HFs, and HF indices capture only a subset of the database, but the hope is that indices contain less systematic biases than broader databases do. At least the more recent index data are of better quality.

For example, the Dow Jones Credit Suisse (DJCS) HF index data (based on the Lipper TASS database) starts in 1994, the same time that the graveyard module became available. Moreover, since 2000, the DJCS index has been run on a real-time basis, so there should be little survivorship or backfill bias after that point. The HFR index goes further back (published data start in 1990), but at least in the early years, it is not adjusted for survivorship bias.

One could also expect the value-weighted DJCS index to exhibit milder biases than equally weighted fund indices such as the HFR, so it may not be surprising that the 1994–2009 average return of the former index is slightly lower (9.3% versus 9.8%). Both indices easily beat the HFR FoF index (6.0%). Moreover, adding the 1990–1993 returns to the HFR index boosts its long-run average return from 9.8% to 12.2%; a significant part of this increase may be due to reporting biases. **Exhibit 5.10** shows that, while the broad contours are similar, calendar-year returns of the two indices have diverged by as much as 9%; at least the gaps have become smaller over time.

Exhibit 5.10. Contrasting the Annual Returns of Two Hedge Fund Indices

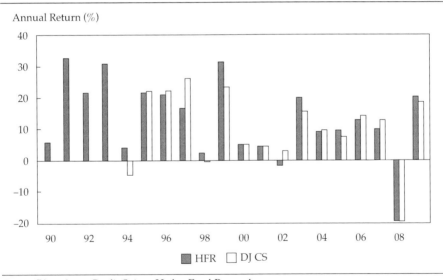

Sources: Bloomberg, Credit Suisse, Hedge Fund Research.

Here is one more concern that must be blamed on HF investors rather than on their managers: Dichev and Yu (2011) show that typical HF investors have earned 3% to 7% lower (dollar-weighted) annual returns than buy-and-hold investors in the same funds would have earned. This gap reflects HF investors' return-chasing tendency, in which they load up after good performance and reduce allocations after bad performance.

Details on understated or neglected risks

Hedge funds are sometimes criticized for charging alpha fees for beta production. In addition to any true alpha provided, HF returns reflect both traditional betas and various alternative betas and tail risks. HFs as a group may have higher returns because of their complex risks, which warrant significant risk premia and liquidity premia. **Exhibit 5.11** shows that, even when it comes to simple equity market correlations, HF index returns are highly market directional, in contrast to the ideals of market neutrality and absolute returns. All single HFs do not of course share this embarrassing characteristic. Among HF subsectors, short sellers and trend followers have a negative equity market correlation; of the other subsectors, global macro and equity market-neutral funds have the lowest—but still positive—equity correlations.

Exhibit 5.11. 24-Month Rolling Correlation of Hedge Fund Indices with Global Equities

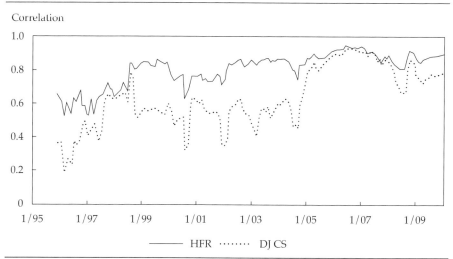

Sources: Bloomberg, Credit Suisse, Hedge Fund Research, author's calculations.

Downside beta: Simple equity market correlations may underestimate the propensity of HFs to lose money in bad times. Looking at the worst 12 months for the HFR index between 1990 and 2009, half occurred in 2008 (starting with the worst: October, September, January, November, July, March) and the other half included August 1998 (Russia/LTCM), November 2000 (the broadening equity market bust), August 1990 (Kuwait invasion, recession), July 2002 (corporate scandals, recession), April 2000 (the first down leg of the tech stock bust), and September 2001 (the 9/11 attacks). All were especially bad times to lose money; global equities earned negative returns in all of these months, falling by 6% or more. Conversely, looking at the worst 12 months for global equities over the same period, the HFR index was down in every one of them.

Asymmetry: HF index returns are significantly related to selling variance risk or correlation risk. It turns out that, while diversification across individual HFs reduces volatility, it boosts the negative skewness and the fat tails property. Operational risk, lack of transparency, and complexity are all features that increase tail risks. Such tail risk enables funds to show misleadingly long periods of solid profits at the expense of rare disastrous losses. Indeed, many arbitrage-oriented HF strategies resemble selling lottery tickets that pay off to the buyer in bad times. (That is, an investor in the strategy collects small periodic payments from selling the tickets and pays out a large amount only rarely; the timing of the large payout correlates to bad times.) Such strategies can be valid sources of long-run return, but the questionable part would be in concealing the return source and in excessive risk taking motivated by the asymmetric incentive fees.

Illiquidity: Many HFs trade in illiquid assets and/or restrict investor redemptions via notice periods, lock-ups, and gates. These features represent an optionlike cost to HF investors in terms of reduced flexibility. Moreover, illiquid assets tend to suffer during liquidity droughts. Infrequent and/or stale pricing of illiquid assets causes understated volatilities, correlations, and betas for these assets and for the fund. HF risks may be better measured by incorporating lagged betas into risk models and by desmoothing autocorrelated returns. Recent studies use positive return autocorrelation as a proxy for a fund's illiquidity. Some studies suggest that less liquid HFs (that is, funds with higher autocorrelation, with lock-ups, and with greater sensitivity to liquidity risk) tend to provide higher returns—presumably reflecting illiquidity premia that investors require—but it is not clear that this result will survive after the 2008 data are added. Investors should not blindly demand better liquidity terms: funds that promise more liquidity (favorable redemption terms) to investors than their asset base truly supports are especially prone to forced selling at fire sale prices, and thus poor performance, if liquidity evaporates and investors redeem capital.

5.4.3. Other Topics

Selecting outperforming managers

Even if HFs as a group might not add much value after adjustments for biases and risks, some managers do add value. Historically, there are always some managers who outperformed (although quite long track records are needed to statistically distinguish luck from skill and more so with HFs, given their non-normal return distributions). A more interesting question is whether it is possible (for anyone? for you?) to identify those outperforming managers in advance. Manager picking can be as hard as stock picking.

Past performance is the most commonly used guide, but it is useful only if performance persistence exists. Fortunately, there seems to be more performance persistence among alternative managers than among long-only managers.

Can we say anything useful beyond past returns? Manager selection is more an art than science, and avoiding big losers may be more important than identifying the winners. Still, here are some pointers from academic research. The literature is mixed on the impact of fund age and size, but recent research suggests that young and small funds have a slight performance edge. The main difference is between very small and medium-sized funds, so presumably many very small funds ("minnows") trade poorly scalable strategies (which hit capacity constraints if the fund size increases). Other favorable attributes include fund distinctiveness (funds with low correlations with peers outperform those with high peer correlations by 6% in the following year) as well as greater managerial incentives and discretion.

Ammann, Huber, and Schmid (forthcoming) show that performance persistence exists up to two- or three-year horizons (which are longer than most funds' notice or redemption periods). Beyond return and alpha persistence, fund distinctiveness is the main other characteristic that helps identify superior future performance. (The study uses fund data from 1994 to 2008.)

Sectors—no consistent patterns: **Exhibit 5.12** shows the performance of HFR index style subsets between 1990 and 2009. Most styles earned double-digit returns, and all styles except short selling equities achieved a high Sharpe ratio. Various reporting biases, together with standard concerns about sample-specific findings, make it unclear whether this graph tells us anything useful about future returns. Limited data hint at relative mean-reversion tendencies across sectors: if a style is successful over multiple years and there are substantial inflows into it, future return potential may be reduced. It seems likely that these sectors exhibit time-varying expected returns—occasional tailwinds for each sector—but fund access and liquidity issues make tactical allocation difficult in practice.

Exhibit 5.12. Average Returns and Sharpe Ratios of HFR Hedge Fund Sector Subindices, 1990–2009

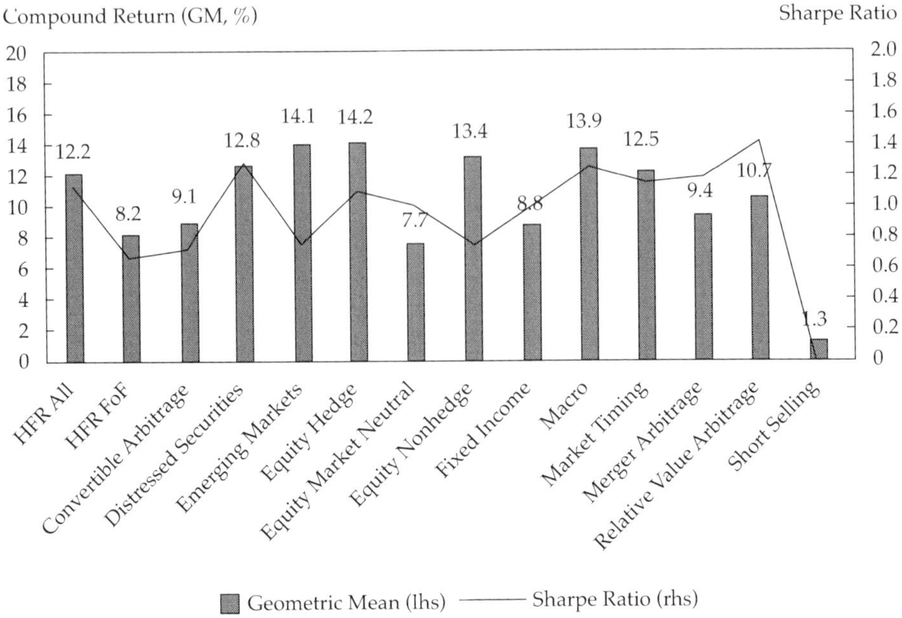

Compound Return (GM, %)   Sharpe Ratio

Geometric Mean (lhs) ——— Sharpe Ratio (rhs)

Sources: Bloomberg, Hedge Fund Research.

There is limited literature on time-varying expected returns for HFs. Tightening liquidity conditions and falling equity markets are bad environments for most hedge funds, as seen in 2008, but these are hard to predict. Seasonally, December has been clearly the best month for HFs as a group. One suggestion is that managers of illiquid assets have some flexibility in marking their assets to market; early in the year, such managers may price holdings conservatively to create some cushion for smoothing returns, but near the year-end, they want to benefit fully from performance fees, so they use up any cushion. Whatever the reason, the pattern is hard to exploit, given limited liquidity (notice periods, penalties for short holding periods). The most feasible approach is for investors to accelerate their HF investments intended for January and buy in November/December instead.

▦ *Different ways to access HF returns: direct HFs vs. FoFs*

The classic distinction in implementing a hedge fund investment program has been between direct investing in HFs and indirect investing via funds of funds or managed accounts. (Managed accounts are single-investor, separately managed portfolios of hedge funds bearing the same relation to FoFs that

134

separately managed accounts in traditional asset classes bear to mutual funds.) Newer vehicles, such as investable HF indices, HF replication products, and HF beta products, have become additional possibilities.

FoFs have been an extremely popular way to access HFs, despite their second layer of fees (say, 1 and 10 on top of the underlying funds' 2 and 20). FoFs provide diversification, oversight (due diligence, though questioned after the Madoff scandal), and maybe access to popular funds that are effectively closed to new investors. They may also offer skill in fund selection and risk management but do not offer much fund timing (because of lock-ups and costs and because FoFs may fear they will lose access to top HFs once they sell them). The returns on FoF indices have lagged those measuring direct HF investing due to the double layer of fees and because of dispersion risk (a FoF must pay incentive fees to the winning managers in its portfolio even if the net performance across all of the FoF's holdings is flat or negative). A more positive take is that (1) part of the apparent gap reflects smaller reporting biases in FoF returns and that (2) FoFs as a group have provided a respectable risk-adjusted track record since 1990, with diversification making the returns smoother than with single-fund HF investments. The year 2008 was the first with a double-digit negative return for the HFR FoF index.

Investable HF indices are really portfolios of HFs that perhaps tried to take advantage of the marketing allure of the word "index." Investable indices offered lower costs, better transparency, and better liquidity than nonindex investments. However, top HFs had little incentive to participate, leading to adverse selection bias, and investable HF indices have consistently underperformed broader HF indices. After a brief detour, I will return to other HF alternatives.

Alphas, betas, alternative betas, and alpha–beta separation

The demarcation line between alpha and beta is quite fuzzy. It is useful to think of the grey area between them as "alternative beta," a catch-all term for all common factors beyond traditional equity, term, and credit premia.

Alpha–beta separation is a concept that became popular about a decade ago, following growing realization that traditional or "long-only" active managers had a very large beta component in their returns and yet charged active management fees. (This could have been accepted had they not as a group consistently underperformed index funds.) Lumping alpha and beta together in a tie-in sale made sense for the sellers, who could add some long-run value by providing access to the equity premium (and camouflaging any underperformance) but not for the buyers, who could access the equity premium much more cheaply through index funds or index derivatives. Add a notion that HF managers are more likely than traditional managers to provide positive alpha even after their costs and fees and, voilà, alpha–beta separation is the way to go: a barbell of very cheap index funds (beta providers) and more expensive hedge funds (alpha providers) can be more cost-effective than an investment in a traditional long-only fund.

This argument became a great defense against institutional investors' qualms about high HF fees: the blended fee in a portfolio of index funds and hedge funds is arguably competitive with a traditional active long-only manager's fee if we consider the alpha/beta mix of each type of manager (both contain equity beta but HFs much less than traditional long only) and insist that beta exposure should earn only an index fund fee. Not surprisingly, most institutional inflows after the millennium have gone into the index fund–hedge fund barbell and not to traditional managers.

A variation on this strategy is alpha transport (portable alpha). A beta position is established using index derivatives, which do not tie up very much capital. Then, a portfolio of HFs is assembled to add alpha. (HFs do require that the investor put up capital.) This blend substitutes for the more traditional strategy of selecting active managers with the beta position as their benchmark.

For years, the HF industry had a wonderful marketing story, especially as long as investors believed that all returns produced by a "good" HF manager were pure alpha. Over time and certainly by 2008, investors learned that HF returns are a mixture of alpha and a variety of betas and that, for the industry in aggregate, the net alpha could not be very large.

What exactly is alpha? Alpha is often defined as "the return from skillful active management." This definition is convenient for alpha producers because it perpetuates the alpha myth (superior investors making money irrespective of market conditions). Arguably, a better definition of alpha is "the part of (asset or fund) return that cannot be explained by common risk factors." This definition helps us see that alpha is always defined with respect to a particular asset pricing model (the model specifies which factors drive expected returns; alpha is the intercept or the average unexplained component).

The latter definition also helps us appreciate the continuous process by which alpha sources morph into beta over time. As academics and the industry come up with ever more factors that explain returns, the alpha pool shrinks and gets reclassified as beta. Berger, Kabiller, and Crowell (2010) illustrate the evolution of the concept of manager value added from the total return of a fund (all of which was typically attributed to the manager in the days before the CAPM, the market model, and performance measurement) to CAPM alpha; from CAPM alpha to alpha as the intercept in Fama–French three- or four-factor regressions; and thence, to alpha as the intercept in even broader models in which the factors explain even more of the return. At each step, we commodify

136

return generation and put downward pressure on fees because well-known systematic factors do not justify as high a fee as pure alpha does. This process will help the end-investor's net returns and understanding, albeit gradually.

There could be infinitely granular classifications, but the current state of the art appears to follow the three-part classification: *traditional betas, alternative betas, alpha*. Even here, the boundaries are fuzzy, but I would say that the three premia—equity risk premium, bond risk premium, credit risk premium—accessed by static long-only holdings in traditional asset classes belong to the category of traditional betas. Examples of alternative (or HF) betas include the value, carry, momentum, and volatility strategies reviewed in Ilmanen (2011a) as well as mechanical merger arbitrage or convertible arbitrage strategies.

The demarcation line between alternative beta and alpha is especially blurry. I like a demarcation line that says that any static (average) exposure to a nontraditional factor is alternative beta, while any dynamic factor timing, other fine tuning, or discretionary security selection is alpha. This definition lumps most systematic strategies into alternative beta but not all. One could be even tougher on systematic strategies and argue that anything that can be written down as a set of rules or procedures may be characterized as (alternative) beta—including any trading rules for factor, market, or style timing.[29]

These definitions matter because they have *fee implications*—very large ones. Most observers agree with Asness (2004) that true alpha—that elusive, scarce, perhaps capacity-constrained component of excess return that is truly due to skill—deserves the highest fees; traditional betas deserve only index-fund fees; and alternative beta deserves something between the two. The fact that systematic strategies can be written down has the advantage of transparency and intuition but the disadvantage of being easily replicable (quickly becoming subject to competitive pressures and eventually to overcrowding risks).

HF replication strategies and HF beta products

Recall the empirical findings that (1) HFs as a group appear skillful enough to add alpha in gross returns but their high fees leave little of this alpha for fund investors (especially after adjusting reported returns for various biases) and (2) most excess returns are not pure alpha but reflect equity market beta and other common factors, notably volatility selling and the collection of liquidity premia. Combining (1) and (2) logically makes the business case for HF replication and HF beta products. Not surprisingly, many firms have offered these alternative

---

[29]This definition makes it easy for discretionary managers to claim that they are alpha producers (no one can replicate what is going on in their minds or write down their full subjective decision-making process), whereas any systematic manager can at most create alternative beta. Despite the transparency and replicability of their approach, systematic managers are the ones called "black boxes." The world is unfair!

products in recent years, but no one has yet made it a major business success or a performance success. Investors who buy into these products will, by design, miss pure alpha (but it is known to be exceedingly rare and highly priced); instead, they try to capture the other good things that HFs can offer, and they pay lower fees.

HF replicators try to identify HFs' aggregate exposures to relevant rewarded systematic factors, often identifying them with the help of multi-factor regression models. Initial factor models explained HF returns using only static linear exposures to major asset classes. Dynamic risk allocation was addressed (clumsily) by regressing past 24-month HF index returns on selected factors to find current weights. Such approaches with static asset classes could only capture, in a rearview mirror, HFs' recent average exposures. To better proxy HFs' current exposures, some studies broadened the menu of factors to include nonlinear exposures (such as synthetic lookback options) and/or dynamic trading strategies (such as a trend-following proxy, merger arbitrage proxy, and convertible arbitrage proxy). The in-sample fit to HF index and HF sector index returns can be often surprisingly good, but out-of-sample results less so. Such analyses show that, as a group, HFs often have significant risk exposures (albeit time varying) to equities, the small-cap premium, interest rates, and credits.

Besides lower fees, the benefits of using replicators include better liquidity, capacity, and transparency; less single-manager risk; and greater flexibility and granularity, which can be useful in risk budgeting and tactical sector allocations. However, there are also disadvantages to using replicators. Many HF replicators mainly capture equity market exposure (a traditional beta) rather than the alternative beta exposures that investors really desire. Jaeger (2008) argues that the latter are best captured by a bottom-up collection of dynamic trading rules and that the simple equity market exposure may be hedged away (or captured more cheaply with liquid products).

HF beta investing (or rules-based investing) differs from HF replication mainly by trying to capture only the part of HF returns that consists of alternative, as opposed to traditional, betas. There is little reason to mimic the "bad" part of HF returns: traditional beta exposures for which a HF fee is charged.

Capturing the HF betas requires skill, both in defining them (identifying smart strategies: inclusion, weighing, rebalancing) and in implementing them cost-effectively and with effective risk management. With HF betas, we can structure a diversified portfolio with an especially attractive reward-to-risk ratio—for example, combining value and momentum strategies that both have a positive alpha but that are often negatively correlated with each other. Truly original proprietary strategies have a special premium in today's competitive environment where fears of being in overcrowded trades are not unreasonable.

138

Both HF replication and HF beta strategies try to capture (some of) the predictable part of HF industry returns. Another approach to assessing time-varying expected returns for HFs explores the broad macro-financial environment (headwinds or tailwinds for the industry or certain subsets), the volatility level, signs of crowding, and other factors.

To convey the big picture, a stylized summary table in **Exhibit 5.13** decomposes net HF returns into building blocks. Given some risk model, returns can be first split into the contribution of diverse betas and "the rest." In the messy real world, "the rest" is not only skill-based alpha but also reflects contributions of luck (randomness), omitted (yet unmodeled) risk factors, and reporting biases. Isolating these components of measured alpha is extremely difficult. (We might include fees as a factor and thus also distinguish between gross and net alpha.)

■ Capacity and prospective returns

Large inflows into HFs have raised questions about capacity. The simple story is that greater competition will reduce excess profits in the sector. That is, we should expect lower returns and lower Sharpe ratios than in the past, merely due to competitive pressures. (Other critics add that the average quality of HFs has deteriorated and that this too has reduced the industry profitability. Yet, others stress that institutional investors required lower volatility and accepted lower Sharpe ratios than traditional HF investors, making single-digit returns and volatilities the new norm.) The capacity question can be raised for HFs overall and for specific HF sectors or strategies. Sectors involving less liquid assets appear especially capacity constrained.

The realized HF alpha has fallen over time, in line with the stories above. It is harder to say which mechanisms caused the alpha decay. Hindsight tells us that leverage was excessive and many strategies were overcrowded in 2006–2007.

Exhibit 5.13. Stylized Decomposition of Hedge Fund Net Return

Returns Explained by Systematic Factors
Equity market beta
Other traditional betas
Alternative betas

Returns Not Explained by Systematic Factors (measured alpha)
Skill (true alpha)
Luck
Omitted factors
Biases

Reduced profitability was the first and more innocuous consequence of HF inflows. The nastier consequence was evident in August 2007 and late 2008 when liquidations from overcrowded positions (everyone trying to rush through the same narrow door) caused extreme price dislocations. Cheap assets got ever cheaper, rich assets got richer (an echo of a similar situation in late 1998), and many funds imploded. After the deleveraging phase, opportunities were more abundant for the lucky survivors as there were higher risk premia and larger market inefficiencies to exploit and less competition in capturing them. This situation did not last long because unprecedented fiscal and monetary stimulus and bailouts worked all too well in reviving speculative animal spirits.

Leverage constraints, whether forced by regulators or self-imposed, may have a special impact. Low-volatility assets and relative value trades that have low standalone volatility when not levered are likely to be shunned by arbitrageurs, resulting in mispricings and illiquidity but also better investment opportunities for those able to put on these trades.

The statement "Too much money chasing the finite dollar supply of alpha will reduce the HF Sharpe ratios" initially sounds plausible but, upon reflection, is problematic.

- There have been some attempts to estimate this finite alpha supply; one might, for example, suppose that smart alpha hunters can extract some fraction, say 50 bps, of the aggregate capitalization of the global capital market each year before the hunters' activity triggers a regulatory backlash. Given a capital market of $100 trillion at the market peak, 50 bps amounts to $500 billion in alpha supply using this method.

- A more nuanced view recognizes that the *measured* alpha pool is shrinking as more factors are added (recall the process of alphas being reclassified as betas).

- One observation is that the rising appetite for risk reduces the *ex ante* return premia on alternative betas. While traditional betas have nearly limitless capacity and alpha supply is finite, alternative betas are somewhere between these extremes. If we associate alpha with the gains from market inefficiencies and alternative betas with rational risk premia, the latter are less capacity constrained and more sustainable. Market inefficiencies disappear when many investors learn about them and more smart capital is allocated to exploiting them—a standard "competitive pressures" story. In contrast, alternative betas related to risk factors may well end up with a lower *ex ante* premium than before, but in equilibrium, the premium should remain positive (people require some long-run compensation for bearing the risk) rather than zero.

- Moreover, the *gross* alpha pool among all investors is zero, by definition ("the arithmetic of active management" according to Sharpe 1991). The *net* alpha among all active investors is negative due to trading costs and fees. Thus, active management or active trading is a negative sum game. Any systematic gains the HF sector makes must come from a large population of active investors that tolerates poor performance. Worse is the unpleasant fact that your most likely counterparty when you trade in today's markets is not a retired dentist but a HF manager. Admittedly, the zero-sum-game argument is clearest when all investors have the same benchmark; in the real world of segmented markets and multiple benchmarks, this argument is more complicated. I am not sure how the zero-sum-game argument works in a technical sense if all benchmarks used by investors do not add up to the global all-asset market portfolio, but the argument is sound conceptually, in that we cannot collectively be worth more than the sum of what we are worth individually.

- There are *some* superior HF managers with reasonably consistent profits after fees and other costs. However, the profits of any truly superior investor must imply net losses for other active investors, where the losses for the other investors include all the trading costs and fees for both sets of investors. Thus, the capacity question really boils down to asking about the quality of competition among active investors. Environments where some peers are more willing or prone to lose money are the pockets where alpha seeking can be more fruitful. But it should always be remembered that any gains come at the expense of other active managers.

5.5. Private Equity Funds

Private equity (PE) funds come in many varieties. At one end, venture capital (VC) firms finance startup companies (hoping to eventually go public), while at the other end, leveraged buyout funds help public firms turn into private companies (by repurchasing all outstanding shares). In addition, there are funds specializing in angel investing, mezzanine financing, and distressed debt investing. The term "private equity" sometimes covers all these types, or it may be exclusively used for buyout funds. Many original buyout specialists have broadened into mega-funds active in all these fields.

The typical investment vehicle or structure is a partnership in which the PE firm serves as the general partner and acts as the investment manager while external investors provide funding as limited partners. Some large institutional investors may also act in the capacity of co-investors with the PE firm. PE investments are made in two stages: (1) a commitment of capital by the limited partner to the general partner (PE firm) and (2) deployment of the capital by the general partner. The general partner can make a call on the committed capital when good investment opportunities arise. In a buyout context, the best rewards for deployed capital tend to come from initial public offerings (IPOs), in which the PE firm takes the company public again, completing the cycle. Selling the company to a strategic investor is often the next-best exit channel, but of course, not all deployments prove profitable. Underperforming investments are eventually written off.

The PE asset class boomed in the 1990s and 2000s. Assets under management grew from under $100 billion in 1990 to over $600 billion in 2000 and peaked above $2 trillion in 2007, largely driven by the perceived performance edge. The VC sector was especially popular and successful in the 1990s, but the 2000s belonged to broader PE funds. Investor inflows into PE funds (following well-known success by Yale University and some other pioneers), and apparently attractive investment opportunities and cheap debt financing, made 2003–2007 very strong years for the sector. The U.S.-centric activity expanded quickly to Europe and to the rest of the world. The year before mid-2007 has been hailed as the golden age—one that inevitably led to excesses and to a hard landing in 2008.

The main advantage of private equity over public markets is in better corporate governance, including closer supervision of management. PE funds can create wealth by improving operating efficiency and exploiting the tax deductibility of interest payments through leverage; thus, PE is not subject to the zero-sum-game argument of most active managers.

Yet, PE also involves risks. PE and VC funds have especially high equity market betas if the artificially smoothed returns are adjusted for, so they offer less diversification to an equity-dominated portfolio than do other alternatives. The characteristics of low liquidity and long holding periods have some advantages in enabling the PE fund to accomplish its goals with the companies it holds but surely warrant some premium as compensation. It is rarely noted that when buyout funds convert liquid listed firms into illiquid private investments, this should make the investment less attractive (create a price discount for illiquidity). All the improvements in monitoring, operations, and financing of PE investments must first overcome this discount before the net impact is positive.

The 2008–2009 experience painfully revealed one danger in PE investing: multi-year capital commitments reduce portfolio liquidity, and capital calls during liquidity droughts may force investors to sell other assets at inopportune times to satisfy the calls; see Siegel (2008). (An investor who does not meet a capital call may lose his prior investment or be sued.) This particular illiquidity risk—commitments implying lost flexibility and implicitly sold options—had been underestimated in good times. Finally, Franzoni, Nowak, and Phalippou

(2010) find that PE fund annualized returns are 7 to 12 percentage points higher during periods of improving aggregate liquidity than during normal times. A liquidity risk premium—compensation for funds' sensitivity to aggregate liquidity fluctuations rather than for the illiquidity of investments—can explain 3 percentage points of an average PE fund's long-term average return.

Other risks include leverage for buyout funds and the fundamental uncertainty of immature businesses for VC funds. The underlying fund positions tend to be concentrated and activist, implying opportunity and risk. Finally, lack of transparency is a concern: although the management of private firms by their PE-fund owners reduces agency problems and information asymmetries between the PE fund and its investments, there remains a misalignment of interests between the PE fund (general partner, GP) and its investors (limited partners, LPs), perhaps more so for mega-funds than for other funds.

Historical Performance

PE funds are famously opaque and secretive, but industry sources point to strong reported performance in the past decades. Based on Cambridge Associates data, PE funds earned 12.4% annually between 1986 and 2009 while VC funds earned 14.5%. These results clearly exceed the 9.2% return on publicly listed U.S. equities, and the VC edge looks even better if arithmetic means are studied. The Leitner, Mansour, and Naylor (2007) report quotes more detailed sector data from Thomson Venture Economics for 1986–2006: VC earned 21% per year with 45% volatility (higher returns for the volatile early-stage strategies than for later-stage strategies), whereas mezzanine and buyout funds earned about 12% at much lower volatilities. These numbers look attractive, but academic studies that drill deeper into the data are generally not impressed, for reasons that are discussed below.

First, performance is typically quoted as an internal rate of return (IRR), which is not directly comparable with the time-weighted rate of return (total return) quoted for more liquid asset classes in this book. IRRs are used partly because regular mark-to-market prices are not available for illiquid holdings and partly because the use of dollar-weighted averaging in the IRR calculation is appropriate given that an important part of PE fund managers' skill is choosing *when* to deploy the capital investors have committed.

While practitioners clearly like what they see, given the large inflows in recent years, the academic assessment of PE fund performance is lukewarm at best. In the best-known study, Kaplan and Schoar (2005) report after-fee average returns for limited partners no better than those from investing in the S&P 500 over 1980–2001. Given the tailwinds environment during those two decades, such performance is disappointing.

Ludovic Phalippou's research and surveys are not great marketing material for the industry. Phalippou and Gottschalg (2009) find even worse results after adjusting for selection biases related to voluntary reporting. Empirical analysis reinforces the suspicion that funds not opting to report to the fund databases tend to have worse performance than reporting funds. Adjusting for their estimate of nonreporting fund performance, the PE sector seems to have lagged the S&P 500 by about 3% per year. High fees largely explain this underperformance; by adding back standard fees, the authors find that gross PE returns *exceed* S&P returns by 3%. Apparently PE managers are skillful, even on average, but the benefits accrue disproportionately to themselves. PE funds charge a variety of fees that raise the hurdle of delivering value for end-investors (limited partners); fees on undrawn committed capital have received perhaps the most criticism.

In other studies, Phalippou (2007, 2009) drills into PE funds' visible and less visible fees and costs and discusses various ambiguities in performance reporting (for example, widely quoted IRR performance data can be misleading if bad IRRs last longer than good IRRs, as seems to be the case). Presenting data on arithmetic means (which do not penalize for volatility) or gross returns (rather than net), as is often done, further enhances the sector's *apparent* attractiveness. Unsurprisingly, most industry commentary focuses on the better reported results, as well as even more positive anecdotal evidence, rather than on these academic studies.

Even if we ignore the reporting biases and assume that PE funds matched or even modestly exceeded the performance of the S&P 500, the results are hardly exciting. Given the higher risk (high leverage, high volatility, and high equity market betas, even before upward adjustment of the beta to counteract the smoothing in IRR data) and much lower liquidity in private equity than in public equity, a significant required average outperformance by PE would seem warranted. In the aforementioned study, risk adjustment doubles the measured underperformance versus the S&P 500, from −3% to −6%.

▓ *Interpreting the returns and looking beyond the average*

Phalippou wonders why investors keep allocating so much money to this asset class despite the disappointing performance and then proposes several possible explanations: learning (experienced funds tend to perform better, but to participate in them, investors need to first buy into novice funds); mispricing due to misunderstanding (investors believe the historical track record is much better than it really is); overpricing due to investors' lottery preferences (VC investors, especially, are enchanted by the possibility of finding "the next Microsoft"; indeed, VC performance data are highly right skewed); side benefits (the LP may be motivated by a broader commercial relationship with the GP; this may be especially relevant for banks as LPs, which are shown to underperform other LPs); and other agency problems.

Whatever the reason, the average or median PE fund does not seem able to outperform public equities after fees. More positively, brand-name funds can stress the distinction between average performance and top-quartile performance. Empirical evidence shows clearly that both performance dispersion and performance persistence are higher among PE funds than among other funds. Thus, being a top-quartile fund implies a large degree of outperformance—and being a top-quartile fund *in the past* makes outperformance *in the future* more likely. Admittedly, part of this persistence reflects illiquidity and smoothed returns, but part of it is real.

Some fund characteristics other than past performance are helpful for manager selection. Tenure and vintage year have some predictive ability. Investors should prefer experienced GPs and avoid funds in hot years when too many funds are chasing the good deals. One reason for the tenure advantage is that established funds can behave tactically and accelerate their investments when investment conditions improve, competitive pressures for deal flow ease, and credit market conditions loosen. Younger funds cannot afford to be as sensitive to market conditions, and they tend to invest in riskier buyouts in order to establish a track record. Perhaps surprisingly, smaller funds earn higher returns. Anecdotally, funds with more focused holdings tend to outperform funds with broader holdings.

Lerner, Schoar, and Wongsunwai (2007) present intriguing findings of heterogeneous investor success in this field: PE funds with *endowments* as limited partners outperform the average fund by nearly 14% (and this can only partly be explained by their earlier exposures). Yale is the most famous example but by no means the only successful PE investor among endowments. In contrast, funds with *banks* as limited partners underperform the average fund by 10%. This finding is consistent with the side-benefits explanation above; banks may be motivated more by their broader banking revenues with the GP than by the profits of the fund.

I am not aware of useful value indicators for PE investing. However, the *ex ante* returns are likely to be better at early stages of bull markets when investment opportunities and financing conditions are attractive but competition for deals is not yet excessive. Investors chase performance and commit capital to PE funds after strong years, a pattern that then hampers subsequent performance. Heavy money flows into PE around the times of the 2000 and 2007 peaks were a warning signal; prospective returns are lower when every fund wants to "act like Yale." Conversely, the recession-ending years 1991 and

2001 turned out to be good vintages; the same may be true for 2009. The performance of the PE and VC sectors over time can be pretty well explained by public equity market performance (positive beta), the cost of financing (low yields on low-grade bonds help), and competitive pressures (larger number of funds raising capital hurts).

Despite apparent predictability in fund performance, PE fund investors' ability to exploit any regularities is limited. Access to the most attractive funds requires personal contacts and, often, past participation in less popular funds.

Overall, it seems that published PE fund returns are overstated and published risks understated (and underappreciated). The typical PE manager is skillful enough to outperform public indices on a gross basis, but the benefits of these skills accrue primarily to the manager and not to the investor. The Yale endowment's David Swensen concludes that the only way to justify active PE/VC investing, given risks and costs, is by an ability to invest in top-quartile funds. Identifying them in advance is not easy but perhaps not as difficult as in liquid markets.

Source Notes

Chapter 2

The equity premium is covered in major books such as Siegel (2002), Cornell (1999), Dimson, Marsh, and Staunton (2002), and Goetzmann and Ibbotson (2006). Surveys of the topic include AIMR Conference Proceedings (2002), Ilmanen (2003a), Fernandez, Aguirremalloa, and Liechtenstein (2008), Damodaran (2010), and Hammond, Leibowitz, and Siegel (2011). The contrast between historical averages and forward-looking expected returns was a theme in three influential papers after the 2000 equity bust: Fama and French (2002), Arnott and Bernstein (2002), and Ibbotson and Chen (2003).

The equity premium puzzle was introduced in Mehra and Prescott (1985); the subsequent academic literature is thoroughly reviewed in Mehra (2008). Explanations of the puzzle that I regard as notable include Rietz (1988), Barro (2006), Gabaix (2008), Weitzman (2007), Bansal and Yaron (2004), Cogley and Sargent (2008), Malmendier and Nagel (2011), Benartzi and Thaler (1995), and Barberis and Huang (2001). The failure of a beta pricing relation among stocks is discussed in Campbell and Vuolteenaho (2004), Fama and French (2004), Polk, Thompson, and Vuolteenaho (2006), Falkenstein (2009), and Frazzini and Pedersen (2010).

For broadening equity yields beyond dividend yields, see Allen and Michaely (2003), Boudoukh, Michaely, Richardson, and Roberts (2007), Lei (2006), Fama and French (2001), and Robertson and Wright (2006). For extensions of earnings yields, see my survey (Ilmanen 2003a) as well as Campbell and Shiller (1998) and Wilcox (2007). For explanations of valuation ratios involving money illusion and other factors, see Modigliani and Cohn (1979), Ritter and Warr (2002), Asness (2000, 2003), Bekaert and Engstrom (2010), and Berge, Consigli, and Ziemba (2008).

Demographic influences on stock markets are considered by Goyal (2004), Favero, Gozluku, and Tamoni (2010), and Reid and Burns (2010). For extending the DDM, see Campbell and Shiller (1988a). For the low trend growth rate of EPS and DPS, see Arnott and Bernstein (2002), Bernstein and Arnott (2003), Dimson, Marsh, and Staunton (2005), and Cornell (2010). For survey evidence on equity premia, see Graham and Harvey (2010), Vissing-Jorgensen (2004), Amromin and Sharpe (2009), Welch (2000, 2009), and Fernandez (2009).

For the academic debate on stock market predictability, see Welch and Goyal (2008) for a skeptical view and Campbell and Thompson (2008) and Rapach, Strauss, and Zhou (2009) for more positive views. I will not list the pioneering research on return predictability but mention a few more recent contributions: Lettau and Ludvigson (2001) on "CAY" or the deviation of consumption from asset wealth and labor income, Pollet and Wilson (2010) on correlation, Cooper and Priestley (2009) on the output gap, Baker and Wurgler (2006) and Edelen *et al* (2010) on sentiment, Longstaff and Wang (2008) on credit market size, Adrian *et al.* (2010) on broker-dealer leverage, and Chava *et al.* (2010) on the tightening credit conditions. Among practitioner work, Ned Davis's book *The Triumph of Contrarian Investing* (Davis 2003) lists several sentiment indicators used in the Ned Davis Research Crowd Sentiment Poll.

Chapter 3

This chapter differs from others by being more subjective. I have contributed to the bond risk premium (BRP) literature for two decades as an academic and a practitioner (Ilmanen 1994, 1995, 1997, 2003a, 2003b, and Best, Byrne, and Ilmanen 1998). In this chapter, I argue that a level-dependent inflation premium and a safe-haven premium are key drivers of the BRP; that the survey-based BRP captures relatively well the "true" *ex ante* BRP while historical variation in the yield curve shape is contaminated by mean-reverting rate expectations; and that the predictable time-variation in bond returns reflects both time-varying risk premia and systematic forecast errors.

Key academic works on this topic are Fama and Bliss (1987), Campbell and Shiller (1991), Cochrane and Piazzesi (2005), and Campbell, Sunderam, and Viceira (2009). Much interesting work has also been done in the Fed and other central banks; see the survey of Kim and Orphanides (2007).

On the macro-finance literature, see Ang and Piazzesi (2003) and surveys by Kim (2008) and Rudebusch (2010). On empirical models with survey data, see Kim and Wright (2005), Kim and Orphanides (2005), and Rosenberg and Maurer (2008). On the relation between the yield curve and economic growth, see Harvey (1989) and Estrella (2005).

Recent works that discuss the idea of a level-dependent inflation premium include Backus and Wright (2007), Kim and Orphanides (2007), Wright (2008), and D'Amico and Orphanides (2008). The models of Campbell, Sunderam, and Viceira (2009) and Ulrich (2010) combine both standalone inflation risk and covariance-based risk. The role of safe-haven demand and stock–bond correlation on the BRP was noted in Ilmanen (2003b), Li (2002), and Connolly, Stivers, and Sun (2005).

For supply/demand factors, see Krishnamurthy and Vissing-Jorgensen (2010), Greenwood and Vayanos (2010), Laubach (2007), Baldacci and Kumar (2010), Warnock and Warnock (2009), and Gagnon *et al.* (2010). For cyclical influences as well as survey evidence, see Fama and French (1989), Froot (1989), Cochrane and Piazzesi (2005, 2008), Bacchetta, Mertens, and Van Wincoop (2009), and Piazzesi and Schneider (2008). For return predictability, see Fama and Bliss (1987), Cochrane and Piazzesi (2005), Naik, Balakrishnan, and Devarajan (2009), and my own research listed above.

Chapter 4

Books on credit risks are more theoretical than empirical and often focus on credit risk modeling and management instead of the reward for bearing credit risk. On the Merton (1974) model and its extensions, see Kao (2000) and Kealhofer (2003). On analysis of rating data and default histories, see Reid *et al.* (2010) and Giesecke *et al.* (2010).

On empirical drivers of credit spreads, see Elton *et al.* (2001), Longstaff *et al.* (2005), Churm and Panigirtzoglou (2005), Chen (2009), and Cremers, Driessen, and Maenhout (2008). On return patterns, see Kozhemiakin (2007), Ng and Phelps (2011), Naik and Devarajan (2009), and my analysis on short-dated credit trades in Ilmanen and Fumagalli (2003) and Ilmanen, Byrne, Gunasekara, and Minikin (2004).

Chapter 5

For good overviews of alternative assets, see Swensen (2009), Anson (2006), and Leitner *et al.* (2007).

On real estate, Francis and Ibbotson (2009) and Hoesli and Lizieri (2007) are excellent sources. So are the three special issues in the *Journal of Portfolio Management* (2005, 2007, 2009), with many good articles, such as Conner and Liang (2005), Ruff (2007), and Clayton, Giliberto, Gordon, Hudson-Wilson, Fabozzi, and Liang (2009). Some useful long data histories are introduced in Shiller (2005), Davis and Heathcote (2007), and Davis *et al.* (2008). Besides the articles above, determinants of real estate pricing are discussed in Plazzi, Torous, and Valkanov (2010), Campbell, Davis, Gallin, and Martin (2009), Brunnermeier and Julliard (2008), Piazzesi and Schneider (2007), and Takats (2010).

On commodities, the book *Intelligent Commodity Investing* (Till and Eagleeye 2007) is a good starting point, especially the editor Hilary Till's surveys. Key articles include Erb and Harvey (2006), Gorton and Rouwenhorst (2006), Gorton, Hayashi, and Rouwenhorst (2007), Hong and Yogo (2010), and Rallis *et al.* (2011).

On hedge funds, books by Andrew Lo (2008), Lars Jaeger (2008), Alexander Ineichen (2002, 2008), and Francois Lhabitant (2007) are all useful. For a story with more flair (on hedge funds and hedge fund managers), see Mallaby (2010). Adjusting HF returns for risks and biases is a topic led by Fung and Hsieh (1997, 2002, 2004, 2009) and followed by Ibbotson *et al.* (2011), Malkiel and Saha (2005), Stulz (2007), Bhardwaj, Gorton, and Rouwenhorst (2008), Amenc and Goltz (2008), and TerHorst and Verbeek (2007).

For relative returns associated with different HF characteristics, see Kosowski, Naik, and Teo (2007), Aggarwal and Jorion (2008), Ammann *et al.* (forthcoming), Teo (2009), Avramov, Kosowski, Naik, and Teo (2011), Agarwal, Daniel, and Naik (2009), and Sun, Wang, and Zheng (2009). Liquidity-related issues are discussed in Asness, Krail, and Liew (2001), Getmansky, Lo, and Makarov (2004), Aragon (2007), Ang and Bollen (2010), Gibson and Wang (2010), Khandani and Lo (2009), and Teo (2010). For HF investors' returns, see Dichev and Yu (2011). For HF replication and HF beta strategies, see Asness (2004), Jaeger (2008), Lo (2008), and Berger *et al.* (2010).

On private equity funds, see Swensen (2009), Anson (2006), and Leitner *et al.* (2007), as well as surveys by Phalippou (2007) and Schoar (2008). Academic analyses of PE returns include Cochrane (2005), Ljungqvist and Richardson (2003), Kaplan and Schoar (2005), Lerner *et al.* (2007), Ljungqvist, Richardson, and Wolfenzon (2007), Phalippou and Gottschalg (2009), Phalippou (2009), Franzoni, Nowak, and Phalippou (forthcoming), Lopez, Phalippou, and Gottschalg (2009), and Kaplan and Strömberg (2009). On VC fund returns, see Cochrane (2005) and Smith, Pedace, and Sathe (2010).

References

Adrian, Tobias, Emanuel Moench, and Hyun Song Shin. 2010. "Financial Intermediation, Asset Prices and Macroeconomic Dynamics." Federal Reserve Bank of New York Staff Report No. 422 (January).

Agarwal, Vikas, Naveen Daniel, and Narayan Y. Naik. 2009. "Role of Managerial Incentives and Discretion in Hedge Fund Performance." *Journal of Finance*, vol. 64, no. 5 (October):2221–2256.

Aggarwal, Rajesh K., and Philippe Jorion. 2008. "The Performance of Emerging Hedge Fund Managers." Working paper (23 January).

AIMR Conference Proceedings. 2002. *Equity Risk Premium Forum*. Charlottesville, VA: Association for Investment Management and Research.

Allen, Franklin, and Roni Michaely. 2003. "Payout Policy." In *Handbook of the Economics of Finance*. 1st ed., vol. 1. Edited by George M. Constantinides, Milton Harris, and René M. Stulz. Amsterdam: Elsevier:337–429.

Amenc, Noel, and Felix Goltz. 2008. "Revisiting the Limits of Hedge Fund Indices: A Comparative Approach." *Journal of Alternative Investments*, vol. 10, no. 4 (Spring):50–63.

Ammann, Manuel, Otto R. Huber, and Markus M. Schmid. Forthcoming. "Hedge Fund Characteristics and Performance Persistence." *European Financial Management*.

Amromin, Gene, and Steven A. Sharpe. 2009. "Expectations of Risk and Return among Household Investors: Are Their Sharpe Ratios Countercyclical?" Working paper (20 February).

Ang, Andrew, and Nicolas P.B. Bollen. 2010. "Locked Up by a Lockup: Valuing Liquidity as a Real Option." *Financial Management*, vol. 39, no. 3 (Autumn):1069–1096.

Ang, Andrew, and Monika Piazzesi. 2003. "A No-Arbitrage Vector Autoregression of Term Structure Dynamics with Macroeconomic and Latent Variables." *Journal of Monetary Economics*, vol. 50, no. 4 (May):745–787.

Anson, Mark J.P. 2006. *Handbook of Alternative Assets*. 2nd ed. Hoboken, NJ: John Wiley & Sons.

Aragon, George O. 2007. "Share Restrictions and Asset Pricing: Evidence from the Hedge Fund Industry." *Journal of Financial Economics*, vol. 83, no. 1 (January):33–58.

Arnott, Robert D., and Peter L. Bernstein. 2002. "What Risk Premium Is 'Normal'?" *Financial Analysts Journal*, vol. 58, no. 2 (March/April):64–85.

Asness, Clifford S. 2000. "Stocks vs. Bonds: Explaining the Equity Risk Premium." *Financial Analysts Journal*, vol. 56, no. 2 (March/April):96–113.

———. 2003. "Fight the Fed Model: The Relationship between Stock Market Yields, Bond Market Yields, and Future Returns." *Journal of Portfolio Management*, vol. 30, no. 1 (Fall):11–24.

———. 2004. "An Alternative Future: An Exploration of the Role of Hedge Funds." *Journal of Portfolio Management*, vol. 30, no. 5 (30th Anniversary Issue):94–103.

Asness, Clifford S., Robert Krail, and John M. Liew. 2001. "Do Hedge Funds Hedge?" *Journal of Portfolio Management*, vol. 28, no. 1 (Fall):6–19.

Avramov, Doron, Robert Kosowski, Narayan Y. Naik, and Melvyn Teo. 2011. "Hedge Funds, Managerial Skill, and Macroeconomic Variables." *Journal of Financial Economics*, vol. 99, no. 3 (March):672–692.

Bacchetta, Philippe, Elmar Mertens, and Eric van Wincoop. 2009. "Predictability in Financial Markets: What Do Survey Expectations Tell Us?" *Journal of International Money and Finance*, vol. 28, no. 3 (April):406–426.

Backus, David, and Jonathan Wright. 2007. "Cracking the Conundrum." *Brookings Papers on Economic Activity*, vol. 1:293–329.

Baker, Malcolm, and Jeffrey Wurgler. 2006. "Investor Sentiment and the Cross-Section of Stock Returns." *Journal of Finance*, vol. 61, no. 4 (August):1645–1680.

Baldacci, Emanuele, and Manmothan S. Kumar. 2010. "Fiscal Deficits, Public Debt, and Sovereign Bond Yields." International Monetary Fund, Working Paper No. 10/184 (1 August).

Bansal, Ravi, and Amir Yaron. 2004. "Risks for the Long Run: A Potential Resolution of Asset Pricing Puzzles." *Journal of Finance*, vol. 59, no. 4 (August):1481–1509.

Barberis, Nicholas, and Ming Huang. 2001. "Mental Accounting, Loss Aversion, and Individual Stock Returns." *Journal of Finance*, vol. 56, no. 4 (August):1247–1292.

Barro, Robert J. 2006. "Rare Disasters and Asset Markets in the Twentieth Century." *Quarterly Journal of Economics*, vol. 121, no. 3 (August):823–866.

Bekaert, Geert, and Eric C. Engstrom. 2010. "Inflation and the Stock Market: Understanding the 'Fed Model'." *Journal of Monetary Economics*, vol. 57, no. 3 (April):278–294.

Benartzi, Shlomo, and Richard Thaler. 1995. "Myopic Loss Aversion and the Equity Premium Puzzle." *Quarterly Journal of Economics*, vol. 110, no. 1 (February):73–92.

Berge, Klaus, Giorgio Consigli, and William T. Ziemba. 2008. "The Predictive Ability of the Bond–Stock Earnings Yield Differential." *Journal of Portfolio Management*, vol. 34, no. 3 (Spring):63–80.

Berger, Adam, David Kabiller, and Brian Crowell. 2010. "Is Alpha Just Beta Waiting to Be Discovered? What the Rise of Hedge Fund Beta Means for Investors." *Journal of Investment Strategy*, vol. 5, no. 1:21–29.

Bernstein, William J., and Robert D. Arnott. 2003. "Earnings Growth: The Two Percent Dilution." *Financial Analysts Journal*, vol. 59, no. 5 (September/October):47–55.

Best, Peter, Alistair Byrne, and Antti Ilmanen. 1998. "What Really Happened to U.S. Bond Yields?" *Financial Analysts Journal*, vol. 54, no. 3 (May/June):41–49.

Bhardwaj, Geetesh, Gary B. Gorton, and K. Geert Rouwenhorst. 2008. "Fooling Some of the People All of the Time: The Inefficient Performance and Persistence of Commodity Trading Advisors." Yale University, ICF Working Paper 08-21.

Black, Fischer, and Myron S. Scholes. 1973. "The Pricing of Options and Corporate Liabilities." *Journal of Political Economy*, vol. 81, no. 3 (May/June):637–654.

Boudoukh, Jacob, Roni Michaely, Matthew Richardson, and Michael R. Roberts. 2007. "On the Importance of Measuring Payout Yield: Implications for Empirical Asset Pricing." *Journal of Finance*, vol. 62, no. 2 (April):877–915.

Brunnermeier, Markus K., and Christian Julliard. 2008. "Money Illusion and Housing Frenzies." *Review of Financial Studies*, vol. 21, no. 1 (January):135–180.

Campbell, John Y., and Robert Shiller. 1988a. "Stock Prices, Earnings and Expected Dividends." *Journal of Finance*, vol. 43, no. 3 (July):661–676.

———. 1988b. "The Dividend–Price Ratio and Expectations of Future Dividends and Discount Factors." *Review of Financial Studies*, vol. 1, no. 3:195–228.

———. 1991. "Yield Spreads and Interest Rate Movements: A Bird's Eye View." *Review of Economic Studies*, vol. 58, no. 3 (May):495–514.

———. 1998. "Valuation Ratios and the Long-Run Stock Market Outlook." *Journal of Portfolio Management*, vol. 24, no. 2 (Winter):11–26.

Campbell, John Y., and Samuel B. Thompson. 2008. "Predicting Excess Stock Returns out of Sample: Can Anything Beat the Historical Average?" *Review of Financial Studies*, vol. 21, no. 4 (July):1509–1531.

Campbell, John Y., Adi Sunderam, and Luis M. Viceira. 2009. "Inflation Bets or Deflation Hedges? The Changing Risks of Nominal Bonds." Harvard Business School Working Paper 09-088 (January).

Campbell, John Y., and Tuomo Vuolteenaho. 2004. "Bad Beta, Good Beta." *American Economic Review*, vol. 94, no. 5:1249–1275.

Campbell, Sean, Morris Davis, Joshua Gallin, and Robert F. Martin. 2009. "What Moves Housing Markets: A Variance Decomposition of the Rent–Price Ratio." *Journal of Urban Economics*, vol. 66, no. 2:90–102.

Chava, Sudheer, Heungju Park, and Michael F. Gallmeyer. 2010. "Credit Conditions and Expected Stock Returns." Working paper (15 May).

Chen, Long. 2009. "On the Reversal of Return and Dividend Growth Predictability: A Tale of Two Periods." *Journal of Financial Economics*, vol. 92, no. 1:128–151.

Chen, Long, Pierre Collin-Dufresne, and Robert S. Goldstein. 2009. "On the Relation between the Credit Spread Puzzle and the Equity Premium Puzzle." *Review of Financial Studies*, vol. 22, no. 9 (September):3367–3409.

Churm, Rohan, and Nikolaos Panigirtzoglou. 2005. "Decomposing Credit Spreads." Bank of England Working Paper No. 253.

Clayton, Jim, S. Michael Giliberto, Jacques N. Gordon, Susan Hudson-Wilson, Frank J. Fabozzi, and Youguo Liang. 2009. "Real Estate's Evolution as an Asset Class." *Journal of Portfolio Management*, vol. 35, no. 5 (Special Real Estate Issue):10–22.

Cochrane, John H. 2005. "The Risk and Return of Venture Capital." *Journal of Financial Economics*, vol. 75, no. 1 (January):3–52.

———. 2008. "The Dog That Did Not Bark: A Defense of Return Predictability." *Review of Financial Studies*, vol. 21, no. 4 (July):1533–1575.

———. 2011. "Presidential Address: Discount Rates." *Journal of Finance*, vol. 66, no. 4 (August):1047–1108.

Cochrane, John H., and Monika Piazzesi. 2005. "Bond Risk Premia." *American Economic Review*, vol. 95, no. 1 (March):138–160.

———. 2008. "Decomposing the Yield Curve." Working paper, University of Chicago (13 March).

Cogley, Timothy, and Thomas J. Sargent. 2008. "The Market Price of Risk and the Equity Premium: A Legacy of the Great Depression?" *Journal of Monetary Economics*, vol. 55, no. 3 (April):454–476.

Conner, Philip, and Youguo Liang. 2005. "Income and Cap Rate Effects on Property Appreciation." *Journal of Portfolio Management*, vol. 31, no. 5 (Special Real Estate Issue):70–79.

Connolly, Robert, Chris Stivers, and Licheng Sun. 2005. "Stock Market Uncertainty and the Stock–Bond Return Relation." *Journal of Financial and Quantitative Analysis*, vol. 40, no. 01:161–194.

Cooper, Ilan, and Richard Priestley. 2009. "Time-Varying Risk Premiums and the Output Gap." *Review of Financial Studies*, vol. 22, no. 7 (July):2801–2833.

Cornell, Bradford. 1999. *The Equity Risk Premium.* New York: John Wiley & Sons.

———. 2010. "Economic Growth and Equity Investing." *Financial Analysts Journal*, vol. 66, no. 1 (January/February):54–64.

Cremers, K.J. Martijn, Joost Driessen, and Pascal Maenhout. 2008. "Explaining the Level of Credit Spreads: Option-Implied Jump Risk Premia in a Firm Value Model." *Review of Financial Studies*, vol. 21, no. 5 (September):2209–2242.

D'Amico, Stefania, and Athanasios Orphanides. 2008. "Uncertainty and Disagreement in Economic Forecasting." Board of Governors of the Federal Reserve, Finance and Economics Discussion Series, No. 2008-56.

Damodaran, Aswath. 2010. "Equity Risk Premiums (ERP): Determinants, Estimation and Implications—The 2010 Edition." Working paper (February).

Davis, Morris A., and Jonathan Heathcote. 2007. "The Price and Quantity of Residential Land in the United States." *Journal of Monetary Economics*, vol. 54, no. 8 (November):2595–2620.

Davis, Morris A., Andreas Lehnert, and Robert F. Martin. 2008. "The Rent–Price Ratio for the Aggregate Stock of Owner-Occupied Housing." *Review of Income and Wealth*, vol. 54, no. 2 (June):279–284.

Davis, Ned. 2003. *The Triumph of Contrarian Investing*. New York: McGraw Hill.

Dichev, Ilia D., and Gwen Yu. 2011. "Higher Risk, Lower Returns: What Hedge Fund Investors Really Earn." *Journal of Financial Economics*, vol. 100, no. 2 (May):248–263.

Diermeier, Jeffrey J., Roger G. Ibbotson, and Laurence B. Siegel. 1984. "The Supply of Capital Market Returns." *Financial Analysts Journal*, vol. 40, no. 2 (March/April):74–80.

Dimson, Elroy, Paul Marsh, and Mike Staunton. 2002. *Triumph of the Optimists: 101 Years of Global Investment Returns,* Princeton, NJ: Princeton University Press.

———. 2005. *Global Investment Returns Yearbook 2005*, ABN.

———. 2010. *Credit Suisse Global Investment Returns Yearbook 2010*. Credit Suisse (February).

Edelen, Roger M., Alan J. Marcus, and Hassan Tehranian. 2010. "Relative Sentiments and Stock Returns." *Financial Analysts Journal*, vol. 66, no. 4 (July/August):20–32.

Elton, Edwin J., Martin J. Gruber, Deepak Agrawal, and Christopher Mann. 2001. "Explaining the Rate Spread on Corporate Bonds." *Journal of Finance*, vol. 56, no. 1 (February):247–277.

Erb, Claude B., and Campbell R. Harvey. 2006. "The Tactical and Strategic Value of Commodity Futures." *Financial Analysts Journal*, vol. 62, no. 2 (March/April):69–97.

Estrella, Arturo. 2005. "The Yield Curve as a Leading Indicator: Frequently Asked Questions." Working paper (October).

Falkenstein, Eric. 2009. *Finding Alpha: The Search for Alpha When Risk and Return Break Down*. Hoboken, NJ: John Wiley & Sons.

Fama, Eugene F., and Robert R. Bliss. 1987. "The Information in Long-Maturity Forward Rates." *American Economic Review*, vol. 77, no. 4 (September):680–692.

Fama, Eugene F., and Kenneth R. French. 1989. "Business Conditions and Expected Returns on Stocks and Bonds." *Journal of Financial Economics*, vol. 25, no. 1 (November): 23–49.

———. 2001. "Disappearing Dividends: Changing Firm Characteristics or Lower Propensity to Pay." *Journal of Financial Economics*, vol. 60, no. 1 (April):3–43.

———. 2002. "The Equity Premium." *Journal of Finance*, vol. 57, no. 2 (April):637–659.

———. 2004. "The Capital Asset Pricing Model: Theory and Evidence." *Journal of Economic Perspectives*, vol. 18, no. 3 (Summer):25–46.

———. 2006. "The Value Premium and the CAPM." *Journal of Finance*, vol. 61, no. 5 (October):2163–2185.

Favero, Carlo A., Arie Eskenazi Gozluku, and Andrea Tamoni. 2010. "Demographic Trends, the Dividend–Price Ratio and the Predictability of Long-Run Stock Market Returns." CEPR Discussion Paper No. DP7734.

Fernandez, Pablo. 2009. "Market Risk Premium Used in 2008 by Professors: A Survey with 1,400 Answers." Working paper, IESE Business School (16 April).

Fernandez, Pablo, Javier Aguirremalloa, and Heinrich Liechtenstein. 2008. "The Equity Premium Puzzle: High Required Premium, Undervaluation and Self Fulfilling Prophecy." Working paper, IESE Business School (26 December).

Francis, Jack Clark, and Roger G. Ibbotson. 2009. "Contrasting Real Estate with Comparable Investments, 1978 to 2008." *Journal of Portfolio Management*, vol. 36, no. 1 (Fall):141–155.

Franzoni, Francesco A., Eric Nowak, and Ludovic Phalippou. 2010. "Private Equity Performance and Liquidity Risk." Netspar Discussion Papers, DP 06/2010-024 (May): http://arno.uvt.nl/show.cgi?fid=115474.

Frazzini, Andrea, and Lasse H. Pedersen. 2010. "Betting Against Beta." Working paper, AQR Capital Management.

Froot, Kenneth A. 1989. "New Hope for the Expectations Hypothesis of the Term Structure of Interest Rates." *Journal of Finance*, vol. 44, no. 2 (June):283–305.

Fung, William, and David A. Hsieh. 1997. "Empirical Characteristics of Dynamic Trading Strategies: The Case of Hedge Funds." *Review of Financial Studies*, vol. 10, no. 2 (Summer):275–302.

———. 2002. "Hedge-Fund Benchmarks: Information Content and Biases." *Financial Analysts Journal*, vol. 58, no. 1 (January/February):22–34.

———. 2004. "Hedge Fund Benchmarks: A Risk-Based Approach." *Financial Analysts Journal*, vol. 60, no. 5 (September/October):65–80.

———. 2009. "Measurement Biases in Hedge Fund Performance Data: An Update." *Financial Analysts Journal*, vol. 65, no. 3 (May/June):36–38.

Gabaix, Xavier. 2008. "Variable Rare Disasters: An Exactly Solved Framework for Ten Puzzles in Macro-Finance." NBER Working Paper 13724 (January).

Gagnon, Joseph E., Matthew Raskin, Julie Remache, and Brian P. Sack. 2010. "Large-Scale Asset Purchases by the Federal Reserve: Did They Work?" Federal Reserve Bank of New York Staff Report 441.

Getmansky, Mila, Andrew W. Lo, and Igor Makarov. 2004. "An Econometric Model of Serial Correlation and Illiquidity in Hedge-Fund Returns." *Journal of Financial Economics*, vol. 74, no. 3 (December):529–609.

Gibson, Rajna, and Songtao Wang. 2010. "Hedge Fund Alphas: Do They Reflect Managerial Skills or Mere Compensation for Liquidity Risk Bearing?" Swiss Finance Institute Research Paper 08-37.

Giesecke, Kay, Francis A. Longstaff, Stephen Schaefer, and Ilya Strebulaev. 2010. "Corporate Bond Default Risk: A 150-Year Perspective." NBER Working Paper 15848 (March).

Goetzmann, William N., and Roger G. Ibbotson. 2006. *The Equity Premium: Essays and Explorations*. New York: Oxford University Press.

Gordon, Myron J. 1962. *The Investment, Financing, and Valuation of the Corporation*. Homewood, IL: Irwin.

Gorton, Gary B., and K. Geert Rouwenhorst. 2006. "Facts and Fantasies about Commodity Futures." *Financial Analysts Journal*, vol. 62, no. 2 (March/April):47–68.

Gorton, Gary B., Fumio Hayashi, and K. Geert Rouwenhorst. 2007. "The Fundamentals of Commodity Futures Returns." Working paper, University of Pennsylvania.

Goyal, Amit. 2004. "Demographics, Stock Market Flows, and Stock Returns." *Journal of Financial and Quantitative Analysis*, vol. 39, no. 01:115–142.

Graham, John R., and Campbell R. Harvey. 2010. "The Equity Risk Premium in 2010." Working paper (9 August).

Greenwood, Robin M., and Dimitri Vayanos. 2010. "Bond Supply and Excess Bond Returns." Working paper (8 January).

Grinold, Richard C., and Ronald N. Kahn. 2000. *Active Portfolio Management*. 2nd ed. New York: McGraw-Hill.

Hallerbach, Winfried G., and Patrick Houweling. 2011. "Ibbotson's Default Premium: Risky Data." Working paper (26 July).

Hammond, P. Brett, Martin L. Leibowitz, and Laurence B. Siegel, eds. 2011. *Rethinking the Equity Risk Premium*. Charlottesville, VA: Research Foundation of CFA Institute.

Harvey, Campbell R. 1989. "Forecasts of Economic Growth from the Bond and Stock Markets." *Financial Analysts Journal*, vol. 45, no. 5 (September/October):38–45.

Hoesli, Martin, and Colin Lizieri. 2007. "Real Estate in the Investment Portfolio." Investment Strategy Council, Norway's Royal Ministry of Finance report (March).

Homer, Sidney, and Richard Sylla. 1991. *A History of Interest Rates.* 3rd ed. Piscataway, NJ: Rutgers University Press.

Hong, Harrison G., and Motohiro Yogo. 2010. "Commodity Market Interest and Asset Return Predictability." Working paper.

Ibbotson, Roger, and Peng Chen. 2003. "Long-Run Stock Returns: Participating in the Real Economy." *Financial Analysts Journal*, vol. 59, no. 1 (January/February):88–98.

Ibbotson, Roger G., and Rex A. Sinquefield. 1976a. "Stocks, Bonds, Bills and Inflation: Year-by-Year Historical Returns (1926–1974)." *Journal of Business*, vol. 49, no. 1 (January):11–47.

———. 1976b. "Stocks, Bonds, Bills, and Inflation: Simulations of the Future (1976–2000)." *Journal of Business*, vol. 49, no. 3 (July):313–338.

Ibbotson, Roger G., Peng Chen, and Kevin X. Zhu. 2011. "The ABCs of Hedge Funds: Alphas, Betas, and Costs." *Financial Analysts Journal*, vol. 67, no. 1 (January/February):15–25.

Ilmanen, Antti. 1994. "Time-Varying Expected Returns in International Bond Markets." Unpublished PhD dissertation, Graduate School of Business, University of Chicago.

———. 1995. "Time-Varying Expected Bond Returns in International Bond Markets." *Journal of Finance*, vol. 50, no. 2 (June):481–506.

———. 1997. "Forecasting U.S. Bond Returns." *Journal of Fixed Income*, vol. 7, no. 1 (June):22–37.

———. 2003a. "Expected Returns on Stocks and Bonds." *Journal of Portfolio Management*, vol. 29, no. 2 (Winter):7–27.

———. 2003b. "Stock–Bond Correlations." *Journal of Fixed Income*, vol. 13, no. 2 (September):55–66.

———. 2011a. *Expected Returns: An Investor's Guide to Harvesting Market Rewards.* Chichester, U.K.: John Wiley & Sons.

————. 2011b. "Time Variation in the Equity Risk Premium." In *Rethinking the Equity Risk Premium*. Edited by P. Brett Hammond, Martin L. Leibowitz, and Laurence B. Siegel. Charlottesville, VA: Research Foundation of CFA Institute (December).

Ilmanen, Antti, and Roberto Fumagalli. 2003. "Consistency of Carry Strategies in Europe." In *Professional Perspectives on Fixed Income Portfolio Management, Volume 4*. Edited by Frank J. Fabozzi. Hoboken, NJ: John Wiley & Sons.

Ilmanen, Antti, Rory Byrne, Heinz Gunasekera, and Robert Minikin. 2004. "Which Risks Have Been Best Rewarded?" *Journal of Portfolio Management*, vol. 30, no. 2 (Winter):53–57.

Ineichen, Alexander M. 2002. *Absolute Returns: The Risk and Opportunities of Hedge Fund Investing*. Hoboken, NJ: John Wiley & Sons.

————. 2008. "AIMA's Roadmap to Hedge Funds." Alternative Investment Management Association report.

Jaeger, Lars. 2008. *Alternative Beta Strategies and Hedge Fund Replication*. Chichester, U.K.: John Wiley & Sons.

Kao, Duen-Li. 2000. "Estimating and Pricing Credit Risk: An Overview." *Financial Analysts Journal*, vol. 56, no. 4 (July/August):50–66.

Kaplan, Steven N., and Antoinette Schoar. 2005. "Private Equity Performance: Returns, Persistence, and Capital Flows." *Journal of Finance*, vol. 60, no. 4 (August):1791–1823.

Kaplan, Steven N., and Per Stromberg. 2009. "Leveraged Buyouts and Private Equity." *Journal of Economic Perspectives*, vol. 23, no. 1 (Winter):121–146.

Kealhofer, Stephen. 2003. "Quantifying Credit Risk I: Default Prediction." *Financial Analysts Journal*, vol. 59, no. 1 (January/February):30–44.

Khandani, Amir E., and Andrew W. Lo. 2009. "Illiquidity Premia in Asset Returns: An Empirical Analysis of Hedge Funds, Mutual Funds, and U.S. Equity Portfolios." Working paper (25 June).

Kim, Don H. 2008. "Challenges in Macro-Finance Modeling." BIS Working Paper No. 240.

Kim, Don H., and Athanasios Orphanides. 2005. "Term Structure Estimation with Survey Data on Interest Rate Forecasts." Board of Governors of the Federal Reserve System Working Paper 2005-48.

———. 2007. "The Bond Market Term Premium: What Is It, and How Can We Measure It?" *BIS Quarterly Review* (June).

Kim, Don H., and Jonathan H. Wright. 2005. "An Arbitrage-Free Three-Factor Term Structure Model and the Recent Behavior of Long-Term Yields and Distant-Horizon Forward Rates." Board of Governors of the Federal Reserve System Working Paper 2005-33.

Kosowski, Robert, Narayan Y. Naik, and Melvin Teo. 2007. "Do Hedge Funds Deliver Alpha? A Bayesian and Bootstrap Analysis." *Journal of Financial Economics*, vol. 84, no. 1 (April):229–264.

Kozhemiakin, Alexander V. 2007. "The Risk Premium of Corporate Bonds." *Journal of Portfolio Management*, vol. 33, no. 2 (Winter):101–109.

Kozicki, Sharon, and Peter A. Tinsley. 2006. "Survey-Based Estimates of the Term Structure of Expected U.S. Inflation." Bank of Canada Working Paper 06-46.

Krishnamurthy, Arvind, and Annette Vissing-Jorgensen. 2010. "The Aggregate Demand for Treasury Debt." Working paper, Northwestern University.

Laubach, Thomas. 2007. "New Evidence on the Interest Rate Effects of Budget Deficits and Debt." Board of Governors of the Federal Reserve System Working Paper 2003-12.

Lei, Qin. 2006. "Cash Distributions and Returns." Working paper (20 April).

Leitner, Chuck, Asieh Mansour, and Sandy Naylor. 2007. "Alternative Investments in Perspective." RREEF Research paper.

Lerner, Josh, Antoinette Schoar, and Wan Wongsunwai. 2007. "Smart Institutions, Foolish Choices? The Limited Partner Performance Puzzle." *Journal of Finance*, vol. 62, no. 2 (April):731–764.

Lettau, Martin, and Sydney Ludvigson. 2001. "Consumption, Aggregate Wealth and Expected Stock Returns." *Journal of Finance*, vol. 56, no. 3 (June):815–849.

Lhabitant, Francois-Serge. 2007. *Handbook of Hedge Funds.* Hoboken, NJ: John Wiley & Sons.

Li, Lingfeng. 2002. "Macroeconomic Factors and the Correlation of Stock and Bond Returns." Yale ICF Working Paper No. 02-46 (November).

Ljungqvist, Alexander, and Matthew P. Richardson. 2003. "The Investment Behavior of Private Equity Fund Managers." New York University Stern School of Business Working Paper 03-29.

Ljungqvist, Alexander, Matthew P. Richardson, and Daniel Wolfenzon. 2007. "The Investment Behavior of Buyout Funds: Theory and Evidence." Working paper, European Corporate Governance Institute.

Lo, Andrew W. 2008. *Hedge Funds: An Analytic Perspective*. Princeton, NJ: Princeton University Press.

Longstaff, Francis A., Sanjay Mithal, and Eric Neis. 2005. "Corporate Yield Spreads: Default Risk or Liquidity? New Evidence from the Credit-Default Swap Market." *Journal of Finance*, vol. 60, no. 5 (October):2213–2253.

Longstaff, Francis A., and Jiang Wang. 2008. "Asset Pricing and the Credit Market." Working paper, University of California, Los Angeles.

Lopez, Florencio de Silanes, Ludovic Phalippou, and Oliver Gottschalg. 2009. "Giants at the Gate: Diseconomies of Scale in Private Equity." Working paper (18 March).

Malkiel, Burton G., and Atanu Saha. 2005. "Hedge Funds: Risks and Return." *Financial Analysts Journal*, vol. 61, no. 6 (November/December):80–88.

Mallaby, Sebastian. 2010. *More Money Than God: Hedge Funds and the Making of a New Elite*. New York: Penguin Press.

Malmendier, Ulrike, and Stefan Nagel. 2011. "Depression Babies: Do Macroeconomic Experiences Affect Risk Taking?" *Quarterly Journal of Economics*, vol. 126, no. 1 (February):373–416.

McKinsey Global Institute. 2009. *Global Capital Markets: Entering a New Era*. Annual Report.

Mehra, Rajnish, and Edward C. Prescott. 1985. "The Equity Premium: A Puzzle." *Journal of Monetary Economics*, vol. 15, no. 2 (March):145–161.

Mehra, Rajnish, ed. 2008. *Handbook of the Equity Risk Premium*. Amsterdam, Netherlands: Elsevier Science.

Merton, Robert C. 1974. "On the Pricing of Corporate Debt: The Risk Structure of Interest Rates." *Journal of Finance*, vol. 29, no. 2 (May):449–470.

Modigliani, Franco, and Richard Cohn. 1979. "Inflation, Rational Valuation and the Market." *Financial Analysts Journal*, vol. 35, no. 2 (March/April):24–44.

Moody's Investors Service. 2010. "Corporate Default and Recovery Rates, 1920–2009." Annual default study.

MSCI Barra. 2010. "What Drives Long-Term Equity Returns." MSCI Barra Research Paper 2010-04.

Naik, Vasant, and Mukundan Devarajan. 2009. "Nomura Quantitative Credit Scorecard: A Framework for Macro Positioning in Global Credit Markets." Nomura International Quantitative Strategies report.

Naik, Vasant, Srivatha Balakrishnan, and Mukundan Devarajan. 2009. "Nomura Quantitative Duration Scorecard: A Simple Framework for Global Duration Positioning." Nomura International Quantitative Strategies report.

Ng, Kwok Yuen, and Bruce Phelps. 2011. "Capturing Credit Spread Premium." *Financial Analysts Journal*, vol. 67, no. 3 (May/June):63–75.

Phalippou, Ludovic. 2007. "Investing in Private Equity Funds: A Survey." *Research Foundation Literature Reviews: Private Equity*, vol. 2, no. 2 (April):1–21.

———. 2009. "Beware When Venturing into Private Equity." *Journal of Economic Perspectives*, vol. 23, no. 1 (Winter):147–166.

Phalippou, Ludovic, and Olivier Gottschalg. 2009. "The Performance of Private Equity Funds." *Review of Financial Studies*, vol. 22, no. 4 (April):1747–1776.

Piazzesi, Monika, and Martin Schneider. 2007. "Inflation Illusion, Credit, and Asset Pricing." NBER Working Paper 12957 (March).

Piazzesi, Monika, and Martin Schneider. 2008. "Bond Positions, Expectations, and the Yield Curve." Federal Reserve Bank of Atlanta Working Paper 2008-02.

Plazzi, Alberto, Walter Torous, and Rossen Valkanov. 2010. "Expected Returns and the Expected Growth in Rents of Commercial Real Estate." *Review of Financial Studies*, vol. 23, no. 9 (September):3469–3519.

Polk, Christopher, Samuel Thompson, and Tuomo Vuolteenaho. 2006. "Cross-Sectional Forecasts of the Equity Premium." *Journal of Financial Economics*, vol. 81, no. 1 (July):101–141.

Pollet, Joshua, and Mungo Wilson. 2010. "Average Correlation and Stock Market Returns." *Journal of Financial Economics*, vol. 96, no. 3 (June):364–380.

Rajan, Raghuram G. 2010. *Fault Lines: How Hidden Fractures Still Threaten the World Economy*. Princeton, NJ: Princeton University Press.

163

Rallis, Georgios, Joelle Miffre, and Ana-Maria Fuertes. 2011. "The Strategic and Tactical Roles of Enhanced-Commodity Indices." Working paper (August).

Rapach, David, Jack Strauss, and Guofu Zhou. 2009. "Out-of-Sample Equity Premium Prediction: Combination Forecasts and Links to the Real Economy." Working paper (8 April).

Reid, Jim, and Nick Burns. 2010. "Long-Term Asset Return Study: From the Golden to the Grey Age." Deutsche Bank Global Markets Research report.

Reid, Jim, Mahesh Bhimalingam, and Nick Burns. 2010. "Default Study 2010." Deutsche Bank Global Markets Research report.

Rietz, Thomas A. 1988. "The Equity Risk Premium—A Solution." *Journal of Monetary Economics*, vol. 22, no. 1 (July):117–131.

Ritter, Jay R., and Richard S. Warr. 2002. "The Decline of Inflation and the Bull Market of 1982–1999." *Journal of Financial and Quantitative Analysis*, vol. 37, no. 1 (March):29–61.

Robertson, Donald, and Stephen Wright. 2006. "Dividends, Total Cash Flow to Shareholders, and Predictive Return Regressions." *Review of Economics and Statistics*, vol. 88, no. 1 (February):91–99.

Rosenberg, Joshua V., and Samuel Maurer. 2008. "Signal or Noise? Implications of the Term Premium for Recession Forecasting." *Federal Reserve Bank of New York, Economic Policy Review*, vol. 14, no. 1 (July).

Rudebusch, Glenn D. 2010. "Macro-Finance Models of Interest Rates and the Economy." *Manchester School*, vol. 78, no. 1:25–52.

Ruff, Jon. 2007. "Commercial Real Estate: New Paradigm or Old Story?" *Journal of Portfolio Management*, vol. 33, no. 5 (Special Real Estate Issue):27–36.

Schoar, Antoinette. 2008. "Capital Flows and the Returns to Private Equity." Presentation to the Institute for Quantitative Research in Finance.

Sharpe, William F. 1991. "The Arithmetic of Active Management." *Financial Analysts Journal*, vol. 47, no. 1 (January/February):7–9.

Shiller, Robert J. 2000. *Irrational Exuberance*. 1st ed. Princeton, NJ: Princeton University Press.

———. 2005. *Irrational Exuberance*. 2nd ed. Princeton, NJ: Princeton University Press.

Siegel, Jeremy J. 2002. *Stocks for the Long Run*, 3rd ed. New York: McGraw-Hill.

164

Siegel, Laurence B. 2008. "Alternatives and Liquidity." *Journal of Portfolio Management*, vol. 35, no. 1:103–114.

Smith, Richard L., Roberto Pedace, and Vijay Sathe. 2010. "Venture Capital Fund Performance: The Effects of Exits, Abandonment, Persistence, Experience, and Reputation." Working paper (23 November).

Stulz, Rene M. 2007. "Hedge Funds: Past, Present and Future." *Journal of Economic Perspectives*, vol. 21, no. 2 (Spring):175–194.

Sun, Zheng, Ashley Wang, and Lu Zheng. 2009. "The Road Less Traveled: Strategy Distinctiveness and Hedge Fund Performance." Working paper (4 February).

Swensen, David F. 2009. *Pioneering Portfolio Management: An Unconventional Approach to Institutional Investment*. Revised ed. New York: Free Press.

Takats, Elod. 2010. "Ageing and Asset Prices." BIS Working Paper 318.

Teo, Melvyn. 2009. "Does Size Matter in the Hedge Fund Industry?" Working paper (22 January).

———. 2010. "How Liquid Are Liquid Hedge Funds?" Working paper (15 March).

Ter Horst, Jenke, and Marno Verbeek. 2007. "Fund Liquidation, Self-Selection, and Look-Ahead Bias in the Hedge Fund Industry." *Review of Finance*, vol. 11, no. 4 (October):605–632.

Till, Hilary, and Joseph Eagleeye, eds. 2007. *Intelligent Commodity Investing: New Strategies and Practical Insights for Informed Decision Making*. London, U.K.: Risk Books.

Trim Tabs. 2010. "Using Equity ETF Flows as a Contrary Leading Indicator." Trim Tabs Research Note.

Ulrich, Maxim. 2010. "Inflation Ambiguity and the Term Structure of Arbitrage-Free U.S. Government Bonds." Working paper (16 December).

Vissing-Jorgensen, Annette. 2003. "Perspectives on Behavioral Finance: Does 'Irrationality' Disappear with Wealth? Evidence from Expectations and Actions." *NBER Macroeconomics Annual*, vol. 18, no. July:139–207.

Wallison, Peter J. 2009. "Not a Failure of Capitalism, a Failure of Government." In *Insights into the Global Financial Crisis*. Edited by Laurence B. Siegel. Charlottesville, VA: Research Foundation of CFA Institute.

Warnock, Francis E., and Veronica Cacdac Warnock. 2009. "International Capital Flows and U.S. Interest Rates." *Journal of International Money and Finance*, vol. 28, no. 6 (October):903–919.

Weitzman, Martin L. 2007. "Subjective Expectations and Asset-Return Puzzles." *American Economic Review*, vol. 97, no. 4 (September):1102–1130.

Welch, Ivo. 2000. "Views of Financial Economists on the Equity Risk Premium and on Financial Controversies." *Journal of Business*, vol. 73, no. 4 (October):501–537.

———. 2009. "The Results of the Equity Premium January 2009 Survey." Working paper (1 January).

Welch, Ivo, and Amit Goyal. 2008. "A Comprehensive Look at the Empirical Performance of Equity Premium Prediction." *Review of Financial Studies*, vol. 21, no. 4 (July):1455–1508.

Wilcox, Stephen E. 2007. "The Adjusted Earnings Yield." *Financial Analysts Journal*, vol. 63, no. 5 (September/October):54–68.

Wright, Jonathan H. 2008. "Term Premiums and Inflation Uncertainty: Empirical Evidence from an International Panel Dataset." Board of Governors of the Federal Reserve System, Finance and Economics Discussion Series Paper 2008-25.

CONTRIBUTION FORM

☑ **Yes,** I want the Research Foundation to continue to fund innovative research that advances the investment management profession. Please accept my tax-deductible contribution at the following level:

Contributing Research Fellow . . . .$25,000 to $49,999
Research Fellow . . . .$10,000 to $24,999
Contributing Donor . . . .$1,000 to $9,999
Donor . . . . Up to $999

I would like to donate $ _____ .

☐ My check is enclosed (payable to the Research Foundation of CFA Institute).
☐ I would like to donate appreciated securities (send me information).
☐ Please charge my donation to my credit card.

   ☐ VISA   ☐ MC   ☐ Amex   ☐ Diners   ☐ Corporate   ☐ Personal

Card Number

____ / _____   _____
Expiration Date   Name on card   PLEASE PRINT
☐ Corporate Card
☐ Personal Card   _____
                                 Signature

☐ This is a pledge. Please bill me for my donation of $ _____ .

☐ I would like recognition of my donation to be:

   ☐ Individual donation   ☐ Corporate donation   ☐ Different individual

_____
       PLEASE PRINT NAME OR COMPANY NAME AS YOU WOULD LIKE IT TO APPEAR

PLEASE PRINT ☐ Mr.   ☐ Mrs.   ☐ Ms.   MEMBER NUMBER _____

_____
Last Name (Family Name)   First   Middle Initial

_____
Title

_____
Address

_____
City   State/Province   Country ZIP/Postal Code

                                                          12ILM

Please mail this completed form with your contribution to:
The Research Foundation of CFA Institute • P.O. Box 2082
Charlottesville, VA 22902-2082 USA

Named Endowments

The Research Foundation of CFA Institute acknowledges with sincere gratitude the generous contributions of the Named Endowment participants listed below.

Gifts of at least US$100,000 qualify donors for membership in the Named Endowment category, which recognizes in perpetuity the commitment toward unbiased, practitioner-oriented, relevant research that these firms and individuals have expressed through their generous support of the Research Foundation of CFA Institute.

Ameritech
Anonymous
Robert D. Arnott
Theodore R. Aronson, CFA
Asahi Mutual Life
Batterymarch Financial Management
Boston Company
Boston Partners Asset Management, L.P.
Gary P. Brinson, CFA
Brinson Partners, Inc.
Capital Group International, Inc.
Concord Capital Management
Dai-Ichi Life Company
Daiwa Securities
Mr. and Mrs. Jeffrey J. Diermeier
Gifford Fong Associates
John A. Gunn, CFA
Jon L. Hagler Foundation
Investment Counsel Association
    of America, Inc.
Jacobs Levy Equity Management
Long-Term Credit Bank of Japan, Ltd.
Lynch, Jones & Ryan

Meiji Mutual Life Insurance Company
Miller Anderson & Sherrerd, LLP
John B. Neff, CFA
Nikko Securities Co., Ltd.
Nippon Life Insurance Company of Japan
Nomura Securities Co., Ltd.
Payden & Rygel
Provident National Bank
Frank K. Reilly, CFA
Salomon Brothers
Sassoon Holdings Pte. Ltd.
Scudder Stevens & Clark
Security Analysts Association of Japan
Shaw Data Securities, Inc.
Sit Investment Associates, Inc.
Standish, Ayer & Wood, Inc.
State Farm Insurance Companies
Sumitomo Life America, Inc.
T. Rowe Price Associates, Inc.
Templeton Investment Counsel Inc.
Travelers Insurance Co.
USF&G Companies
Yamaichi Securities Co., Ltd.

Senior Research Fellows

Financial Services Analyst Association

For more on upcoming Research Foundation
publications and webcasts, please visit
www.cfainstitute.org/about/foundation/.

Research Foundation monographs
are online at www.cfapubs.org.

22371605R00104

Made in the USA
Middletown, DE
28 July 2015